The Economic Status of Australian Aborigines

Publication of this book has
been assisted by a grant
from the Committee on
Research and Graduate Studies
of the University of
Melbourne.

The Economic Status of
Australian Aborigines

JON C. ALTMAN

JOHN NIEUWENHUYSEN

Department of Economics, University of Melbourne

CAMBRIDGE UNIVERSITY PRESS
CAMBRIDGE
LONDON · NEW YORK · MELBOURNE

Published by the Syndics of the Cambridge University Press
The Pitt Building, Trumpington Street, Cambridge CB2 1RP
Bentley House, 200 Euston Road, London NW1 2DB
32 East 57th Street, New York, NY 10022, USA
296 Beaconsfield Parade, Middle Park, Melbourne 3206, Australia

First published 1979

Phototypeset in V.I.P. Palatino by
Western Printing Services Ltd, Bristol
Printed in Great Britain by
The Pitman Press, Bath

Library of Congress Cataloguing in Publication Data

Altman, Jon C   1954–
The economic status of Australian aborigines.

Bibliography: p.
Includes index.
1. Australian aborigines – Economic conditions.
I. Nieuwenhuysen, J. P., joint author. II. Title.
GN666.A25   330.9'94   78–14917
ISBN 0 521 22421 7 hard covers
ISBN 0 521 29490 8 paperback

CONTENTS

TABLES

MAPS

ACKNOWLEDGEMENTS

We record our thanks to the Department of Aboriginal Affairs (DAA), Canberra, for the funds which it provided for the employment, at the Graduate Research Assistant level, of one of the authors (JCA) for 1977. In particular, we owe a very special debt of gratitude to the DAA Research Director in Canberra, David Penny, for his constant interest, initiative, encouragement and assistance in the project. The University of Melbourne also kindly provided an emergency research grant for the month of January 1978, to enable finishing touches to be put to the work, while the research fund of the University's Economics Department was generous enough to provide travel assistance for one of the authors (JCA).

Although none is to be associated with any views or deficiencies in our material, we thank the following for comments on early drafts or parts thereof: David Penny, Peter Williams, Bryan Griffin and Allan Gray, all of the DAA, Canberra; John Hicks of the University of Melbourne; Fred Fisk of the Australian National University; Frank Stevens of the University of New South Wales; and Peter Drake of the University of New England.

Joyce Wood, of the University of Melbourne, graciously agreed to do the cartography, and executed her task with characteristic meticulousness, while Thea Toyne, Colleen Thomas and Lois Payne cheerfully and efficiently undertook the typing.

Finally, we thank the Australian National University Press and Charles Rowley, and the DAA, for permission to use Maps 1 and 4, respectively, for this work.

University of Melbourne   J.C.A.
January 1978.   J.P.N.

PREFACE

The purpose of this book is to provide a survey of the available information on the economic status of Aborigines in Australia. It is true that a few economists (and in particular H. C. Coombs) have studied facets of the economic life of Aborigines in different parts of the country. And it is also true that historians and political scientists (such as G. Blainey and C. D. Rowley, to mention only two names) have vividly described the prehistory, history and contemporary history of the Aboriginal people, and in doing so have touched upon past and present economic issues. But in general there is a lack in the literature of an overall economic view of Australia's Aboriginal population. The closest attempt to a survey is a work which is now more than ten years old (*Aborigines in the Economy* (1966) eds. I. G. Sharp and C. M. Tatz) but in which only one of the twenty-four chapters (comprising conference papers) appears to have been written by a person described as a practising professional economist.

Economists in general have indeed seemed to shun the study of Aborigines in the Australian economy. For example, a widely-used text book in Australia (P. A. Samuelson, K. Hancock and R. Wallace (1970), *Economics*, 2nd Australian edn) dismisses the issue with these words (pp. 124–5): 'The position of the Aboriginals is undoubtedly worse that that of the American Negroes, but their numbers are smaller and the problem of Aboriginal poverty has to date been regarded as a problem more of social welfare than of economic policy'. It is no doubt very largely true that any economic problem connected with Aborigines has been eschewed from 'economic policy discussions'. But whether this is wise or justified is another matter, and it is the intention of the chapters which follow to focus attention, first, on the economic status of Aborigines in different parts of the economy (such as it can be gauged from secondary information) and, second, on the issues for economic policy which seem to arise from these conditions.

It appears that there is in fact a great array of economic policy issues arising from the presence in Australia of a 'mixed or 'dualistic' economy, in the sense of the coexistence of a highly developed monetised economy alongside a spectrum of other forms up to nearly complete subsistence. In many respects these issues resemble those in 'developing' and more heavily dualistic economies elsewhere, especially in the context of self-determination, that is, of Aboriginal communities deciding the pace and nature of their own future development as important components of a diverse Australia. For example, in this setting, should the improvement of economic levels among Aborigines (especially in remote Australia) be left largely to the processes of time and the market mechanism, or is it desirable for Aboriginal communities to plan and regulate economic activity so as to achieve higher living standards? Alternatively, is it necessary for communities to devise methods for their *protection* from the economic impact of 'white' Australia? Should wage rates or industries (and their surrounding infrastructure) employing Aboriginal labour in remote regions be subsidised or should emigration to regions of greater economic opportunities be encouraged? Should land settlement schemes be fostered and, if so, what are the most efficient institutional backdrops for these projects? What should be the educational policy in Aboriginal community schools? The range of questions that could be asked is very substantial. In writing this book, the main intention is to offer a description of the economic status of Aborigines in the various areas in which they live in Australia; and to highlight some of the questions of economic importance which occur. If further enquiry and thought on the issues raised ensues, a major objective of this study will have been achieved.

In attempting this survey, important qualifications have to be entered. There is, firstly, the problem of 'bias' or 'ethnocentrism'. By this is meant a fear lest value judgements may be implied in a study which examines 'standards of living' and 'socio-economic status' from the viewpoint of one set of cultural assumptions. While seeking to document different economic conditions among various communities of people, it is not implied that economic change, especially socially disruptive change, is necessarily desirable. Secondly, there is the problem of encapsulating in the divisions made in this study the great variety of peoples across a number of State and other boundaries. The divisions have been made for purposes of elucidation of available information. But it is important to remember that these demarcations are not rigid. Nor are the people within them homogeneous.

The plan of the chapters is as follows. Chapter 1 summarises the available information on the general demographic and economic welfare indicators of the Aboriginal population. Chapter 2 discusses Aborigines on government settlements and missions, while Chapter 3 is concerned with those on pastoral stations. Chapter 4 reviews the information on the 'decentralised' communities, that is, those Aborigines who have moved from white-controlled communities to found more independent ones of their own, especially in association with traditional land areas. In Chapters 5 and 6 the economic conditions among Aborigines in the towns and cities of Australia are considered. Finally, in Chapter 7 some of the economic questions which the previous chapters suggest are briefly catalogued. In making this chapter division, a general separation between 'remote' and 'settled' Australia – as depicted in Map 1 – needs to be remembered: Chapters 2, 3 and 4 are concerned with 'remote' Australia, and Chapters 5 and 6 with 'settled' Australia. This division is rough (since it hides, for example, some 'settled' portions in 'remote' Australia) but necessary to demarcate a difference of major importance between the influences weighing upon the two basic geographic groupings of Australian Aborigines. Moreover, these groupings are also economic and cultural divisions. In the treatment of the material on 'remote' and 'settled' Australia, therefore, slightly different approaches are required, since in remote Australia special attention needs to be given to 'non-economic' and traditional cultural aspects of Aboriginal life which bear upon the standard of living.

In the discussion, attention is paid to the present, and a stark picture it is, with relatively very poor conditions applying to Aborigines in every economic comparison made with the general Australian society. But the current situation is, of course, the product of the past, and it seems necessary to include in the introduction a brief reference to the historical background of the Aboriginal 'economy'. This is done despite the obvious risks of very severe compression, and merely to supply a framework for the analysis which follows. (In Appendix I, dimensions of Aboriginal economic development (in remote Australia) in terms of subdivisions of the historical phases – pre-contact and

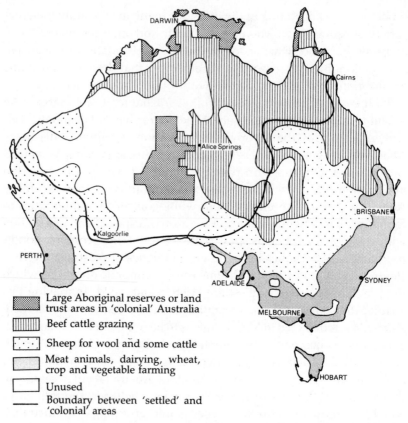

Large Aboriginal reserves or land
trust areas in 'colonial' Australia

Beef cattle grazing

Sheep for wool and some cattle

Meat animals, dairying, wheat,
crop and vegetable farming

Unused

Boundary between 'settled' and
'colonial' areas

Map 1. Rural land use showing 'colonial' and 'settled' Australia
(Source: Adapted from C. K. Rowley *The Remote Aborigines*, A.N.U.
Press 1971, p. 2.)

post-contact – and resource endowment, social systems and external
contact, are itemised as supplementary material.)

In what may be termed the pre-contact era to 1778 (that is, before
contact with European colonists) it is generally agreed that the traditional economy of Australian Aborigines was basically organised for
the needs and with the resources of self-contained subsistence rural
economies. These subsistence units could be characterised by a
number of features: (1) there was a lack of much labour specialisation
and the division of labour was predominantly by sex and age; (2) there
was an absence of regular production of a surplus with a view to sale.
Trade was not the primary object of economic activity. External contact
was limited to trade relations between some far north Australian
Aborigines and Macassans, but this was irregular; (3) the state of

technology was relatively stationary, and had not undergone substantial change over many generations; and (4) although very long established in Australia, Australian Aboriginal society was semi-nomadic and land extensive, without organised agriculture (although as G. Blainey has speculated in *The Triumph of the Nomads* (Macmillan 1975) it was very adaptable within the context of its own amazingly skilful if 'fixed' technology).

A combination of these four features composed a pattern of a largely static economy which all Aboriginal communities exemplified at the turn of the nineteenth century, with relatively inconsequential differences between them (except perhaps that, in the far North, Aborigines had some external contacts). The Aboriginal economic system prior to the incursion of white settlement was basically tribal, land extensive, non-specialising, non-competitive, non-exchange and non-monetised, whereas the alien economic system brought by whites was in the midst of an industrial revolution.

Following initial contact, some haphazard exchange occurred, with Aborigines generally trading foodstuffs and traditional goods for new foods (sugar, flour and tea) and for tobacco. But traditional subsistence economic activity still predominated. From the 1830s, however, spheres of European rural influence were more permanently established. In the geographically remote areas this was generally through Christian missions and government depots, and in the less remote areas in the form of government settlements and pastoral stations. During this phase (that is from the 1830s right up until at least 1960) most Aboriginal land was alienated and there was pressure upon Aboriginal people to exchange their labour services for alien goods. With the encroachment of areas of European settlement, there was some limited assimilation. Because of land alienation, the traditional subsistence economy declined in importance during this phase, and there was a growing dependence on government support.

As contact with whites in rural areas continued, traditional Aboriginal economic norms were drastically undermined and goods from the new economy began to be viewed by Aborigines as essential to their living conditions. And, especially since the 1930s, this phase may be linked with the government policy of assimilation (especially for part-Aborigines) and the abolition of most aspects of the discriminatory laws against Aborigines which had been established down the years. Aborigines became firmly entrenched in the pastoral industry (especially in the Northern Territory) receiving relatively very low wages. Missions and government settlements became 'institutional-ised'. While traditional economic activity had, however, been under-mined, the opportunities to replace it were few and a high level of dependence on church and government sources grew.

Since the start of the 1960s, up until the present (1977), there has been a notable reactivation of Aboriginal traditions and values (espe-cially in remote Australia and partly associated with government-sponsored encouragement of 'self-determination'). Some areas of se-cure land tenure have been established, funds for investment (from the Aborigines Benefit Trust Fund, for example) have been made avail-able, and aspects of discriminatory laws against Aborigines have been reformed, even if informal prejudice and discrimination continues. New economic opportunities in some remote regions, through mining expansion (albeit in largely unskilled labour categories) have arisen, while a 'decentralisation' movement gained momentum (as Abor-igines disenchanted with life on government settlements and missions migrated back to traditional areas to protect sacred sites and take part once more in traditional subsistence economic activity but in a broader mixed framework).

The diversity of Aboriginal–white contact experiences is exemplified by observing that any 'phases' distinguishable in the history of this contact seem to overlap for different communities, in concert with their continuingly changing nature over time. Communities in New South Wales and Victoria which were once remote are now enclaves of a predominantly European society and economy; many missions and settlements have become part of settled areas (on the fringes of towns), while some large cities have engulfed Aboriginal communities.

In the chapters which follow, attention is directed mostly to the last decade, that is since the 1967 referendum when the Commonwealth government assumed new responsibility by receiving authority to subsume the powers hitherto exercised over Aborigines by the several States.

Not only have new policies been in the air, however. There has also been some change in the resource endowment of Aboriginal economic life through recent government initiatives, and there are now at least four possible avenues of response by Aborigines to the changing economic climate: (1) the agricultural–entrepreneurial economic behaviour of whites might be imitated; (2) more Aboriginal people might enter the wage-earning sector; (3) Aborigines might decide that costs of obtaining Western-style goods (through foregone traditional values, and so on) outweigh the benefits and that (with only minor modifications) a traditional hunter-gatherer life-style is to be pre-ferred; (4) complete dependency upon government or mission support could be accepted. Indeed, historically, there is evidence, in different parts of Australia at different times, of each of these responses (which have on many occasions been Hobson's choices). However, in the future economic life of Australia's Aboriginal people, it remains to be seen whether their rising political voice will influence their status in a direction different from the recent past, following Australia's colonisa-tion by whites.

University of Melbourne,   J.C.A.
January 1978.   J.P.N.

ABBREVIATIONS

ABS   Australian Bureau of Statistics
ABSEG Aboriginal Secondary Grants
AICHS Aboriginal and Islander Community Health Service
ASGS   Aboriginal Study Grants Scheme
CDEP   Community Development Employment Project
CES   Commonwealth Employment Service
CSIRO Commonwealth Scientific and Industrial Research Organisation
DAA   Department of Aboriginal Affairs
DAIA   Department of Aboriginal and Islander Advancement
DLI   Department of Labour and Immigration
ETSA   Employment Training Scheme for Aborigines
GEMCo Groote Eylandt Mining Company
NAWU North Australia Workers Union
NEAT   National Employment and Training
NPI   National Population Inquiry
PCM   Protein–calorie malnutrition
PS–SWP Private Sector Special Work Project
QIMR   Queensland Institute of Medical Research
RED   Regional Employment Development
SWP   Special Work Project
TAFE   Technical and Further Education
TMPU   Town Management and Public Utility
TSI   Torres Strait Islander
UCNA   United Church of North Australia

1

Inequality: an overview

> The absence of reliable demographic data on the Aboriginal
> population of Australia reflects their unequal status in
> contemporary Australian society . . . Under the criteria applied
> until recently by Australian immigration authorities to screen
> potential settlers, most Aborigines would have been denied the
> right to settle in their own country: they are non-European, have
> few technologically useful skills, are often unemployed, suffer
> from malnutrition and sickness to such a degree that by age 40
> many are unemployable, figure predominantly in crime statistics,
> and have a low reputation in the large society.
> F. L. Jones, *Racial and Ethnic Minorities: The Case of Aboriginal
> Australians*

What socio-economic differences are there between the Aboriginal
population as a group and the remainder of Australian society? While
most people in Australia could probably give some suggestion as to
these differences, it is unlikely that there is any simple source to which
someone interested in the question could turn to find a reasonable
summary of the information necessary to make a useful comment. In
this chapter, therefore, a synthesis is given of the available material on
various aggregate socio-economic indicators. These assist a comparison of the standard of living of Aborigines as a group with that of the
rest of the Australian population.

For this synthesis, it is not 'primary' material that has been collected:
only the available 'secondary' information has been drawn together;
and Aborigines as a general, internally undifferentiated group are
discussed. In this grouping, the analysis is based upon an examination
of the aggregate 'Aboriginal population' of Australia as at present
'officially' defined. (By 'officially' is meant the definition – self-

1

identification – favoured by the Commonwealth Department of Aboriginal Affairs (DAA). The statistics on Aborigines thus refer to the grouping of people who identify themselves as Aboriginal.) The analysis excludes the Torres Strait Islanders (who were the subject of a recent six-volume study by the Australian National University) except in those instances where the aggregative nature of the data preclude this. Of course, this attempt to describe the socio-economic conditions of the Aboriginal population as a whole is by no means intended to imply homogeneity in this group of people, and the differences within the population will be examined in later chapters. It must also be emphasised that the general material contained in this chapter is somewhat bare and thin. In subsequent parts of the book greater detail is given on particular areas and regions.

Sources and availability of data

In the 1966 Population Census, a question on race asked for distinction by proportion, i.e. people were requested to identify their proportionate 'racial' categorisation (for example, $\frac{3}{4}$ Aboriginal/$\frac{1}{4}$ European, or $\frac{1}{2}$ Aboriginal/$\frac{1}{2}$ European, or 'full-blood' Aboriginal). Because only those with half or more than half 'Aboriginality' were enumerated as Aborigines, the results of the 1966 census are generally regarded as an underestimate of the Aboriginal population. It is only since the 1967 referendum, which abolished section 127 of the Constitution and allowed people to identify themselves as they wished in subsequent censuses, that data on the Aboriginal population have become more reliable. Even so, the paucity of population statistics specifically on Aborigines has frequently been noted – the prefacing quote by Jones (1973) is but one illustration. It is therefore particularly regrettable that the results of the 1976 Census of Population and Housing are not available at the time of writing. (Shortage of staff has restricted the capacity of the Australian Bureau of Statistics (ABS) to publish all but the most aggregative and 'vital' of 1976 census findings.) Most of the statistical material in this chapter is, therefore, perforce based upon the results of the 1971 Census of Population and Housing (although some reference is made to the 1966 census where it is considered that intercensal comparisons are not unduly unreliable. However, comparisons are in general difficult in this regard in view of the different definitions of an Aboriginal person which, as mentioned, were used in the 1966 and 1971 censuses).

Social indicators used

While a great variety of 'social indicators' might be imagined, the statistical material available permits only two to be studied here: (1) demographic indicators, which measure the demographic characteristics of a population and (2) welfare indicators, which seek to measure the degree of 'satisfaction' of human needs. Clearly, of the two, welfare indicators present special problems of measurement: welfare is not directly measurable, and there are inherent imperfections in the indirect methods which must be employed. For instance, indicators cannot cover all components of welfare. On the other hand, even an indirect measurement of welfare is better than none at all or than broad aggregates such as per capita income (which is in any event not available for Aborigines). Secondly, there is a number of ways in which welfare can be measured, i.e. as progress or regression over time, or as the 'quality of life' at one moment in time. It is the simpler of the two – welfare at one point in time – that is discussed below. Thirdly, and most important, a concept of human welfare is not an 'objective' one – it cannot be divorced from value judgements. In this chapter, the broad areas of human well-being examined will be education, employment and occupation, and housing and health. The very selection of indicators to contrast the Aboriginal population with the general Australian population is not neutral in value. For the system of needs considered is, of course, culturally determined – a 'European'-derived system of values.

There are two special problems in the use of the available material which should be mentioned as a further caveat to the analysis. Firstly, many of the census results used are rather aggregative and this may conceal differences within groups, especially as regards employment and education data which measure the quantity rather than the quality of occupations or services delivered. Secondly, as mentioned previously, because censuses before 1971 are not strictly comparable, the analysis is mostly restricted to a cross-sectional one – the comparison between socio-economic factors affecting Aborigines and the Australia-wide population.

The Aboriginal population: demographic indicators

Population
In the 1971 Census of Population and Housing, 106,290 people ident-

ified themselves as Aborigines. In Table 1 the State distribution of the Aboriginal population is indicated. It was also estimated in the 1971 census that there were some 9,663 Torres Strait Islanders (TSIs), making a total of 115,953 together. By contrast, State and Territory estimates suggested that the total Aboriginal and TSI population was apparently 150,945 (according to L. R. Smith, 1975b, p. 368) while the National Population Inquiry (1975, p. 465) estimated the figure as being 153,445.

There is thus an immediate and great discrepancy in the statistics. It arises because the higher estimates are based on whom, in the various parts of Australia, DAA field staff regarded as persons of Aboriginal or Islander descent, whereas the 1971 census employed the test of self-identification. Clearly, because attitudes to group identity shift, this feature can play havoc with attempts to measure population growth rates, and there seems no easy way out of the dilemma.

Table 1. *Enumeration of the Aboriginal population of Australia, by State, 1966 and 1971*

State or Territory	Census year		
	1966[a]	1966[b]	1971
New South Wales	14,219	20,601	23,101
Victoria	1,790	2,707	5,656
Queensland	19,003	23,040	24,414
South Australia	5,505	6,584	7,140
Western Australia	18,439	21,146	21,903
Tasmania	36	79	575
Australian Capital Territory	96	169	248
Northern Territory	21,119	22,306	23,253
AUSTRALIA	80,207	96,632	106,290

[a]Official estimate based on the definition of Aboriginal as someone with $\frac{1}{2}$ or more Aboriginal origin. This is an underestimate.
[b]Jones's (1973) estimate based on definition of Aboriginal as someone with $\frac{1}{4}$ or more Aboriginal origin. This appears to be a slight overestimate.
Source: Jones (1973), Australian Bureau of Statistics (1973).

In the 1966 census, the 'official' estimate of the Aboriginal population (i.e. persons with $\frac{1}{2}$ or more Aboriginal origin) was 80,207 persons. If one includes all persons who identified themselves as having $\frac{1}{4}$ Aboriginal origin, then a more realistic estimate of the 1966 Aboriginal population would be 96,632 (Jones, 1973, p. 56). In the National Population Inquiry it is the latter figure that is taken as the more accurate. In Table 1 this estimate of the 'total' Aboriginal population is also presented by State.

On the basis of the 1971 census population and age profile, and making the assumption of declining fertility and mortality rates, L. R. Smith (1975b, p. 368) estimated that the 1976 Aboriginal and TSI population (self-identifiers) would be 132,789. One can estimate the total Aboriginal population by subtracting from this total Caldwell's (1975, p. 39) estimated projection of the TSI population in 1976, which also utilised the 1971 census and an assumption of declining birth rate, and was 11,254. This method produces an estimate of the 1976 Aboriginal population of 121,535 (self-identifiers).

Recent State and Territory estimates (which are based on a variety of definitions of an Aboriginal person) and communications with L. R. Smith of the Australian National University suggest a 'minimum' 1976 estimate of 'potential identifiers' of 175,600 (Aborigines and TSIs). Subtracting Caldwell's 'high' estimate of TSIs in 1976 (13,732) this gives a total of approximately 162,000 Aborigines (people of Aboriginal descent). This implies that either the 1976 figure based on the 1971 census is an underestimate (which seems a likely possibility and may be confirmed when the 1976 census results are published); or that the number of self-identifiers has reached a saturation point, and a large number of people of Aboriginal descent do not wish to identify as Aboriginal. The second option seems somewhat unlikely on the basis of current trends.

In summary, the most reliable estimates of the Aboriginal population are 96,632 for 1966, 106,290 for 1971 and 121,535 for 1976. This represents 0.83 per cent of the total Australian population in 1966 and 1971 and an estimated 0.87 per cent of the population in 1976. While it is recognised that there may be as many as 40,000 more 'potential identifiers', the numbers of special interest here are those who *have* identified themselves as Aborigines.

Table 1 also shows the State distribution of the Aboriginal population. Most Aborigines live in Queensland, the Northern Territory, New South Wales and Western Australia. Each of these areas had an Aboriginal population of more than 20,000 in the 1966 and 1971 censuses. Victoria and South Australia had smaller but significant Aboriginal populations, whereas only 575 Aborigines were estimated to live in Tasmania and 248 in the Australian Capital Territory in 1971.

The National Population Inquiry (1975, pp. 500–1) noted that the interstate geographic mobility of Aborigines from 1966 to 1971 was extremely limited. The largest inter-State movement was from Western Australia to the Northern Territory, and this involved only 285 people. In general, while as mentioned below the propensity for Aborigines to move from rural to urban areas seemed great, net inter-State movements appeared very limited.

Age Profile of the Aboriginal Population
In Table 2 the age distribution of the Aboriginal population in 1971 is given. The most unusual feature of the Aboriginal population was its

Table 2. *Comparison of percentage age distribution of the Aboriginal population with that of the total Australian population, 1971 census*

Age (years)	Age distribution (per cent)			
	Aboriginal population		Australian population	
0– 4	17.7		9.6	
5– 9	15.4		9.6	
10–14	13.3	46.4	9.6	28.8
15–19	10.1		8.7	
20–24	8.5		8.6	
25–29	6.6		7.3	
30–34	5.5		6.3	
35–39	4.9		5.8	
40–44	4.3		6.2	
45–49	3.5		6.1	
50–54	2.9		5.2	
55–59	2.0		4.7	
60–64	1.8	50.0	3.9	62.9
65–59	1.5˙		3.0	
70–74	1.1		2.3	
75+	1.0	3.6	3.0	8.3

Source: Australian Bureau of Statistics (1976a)

extreme youth, with 46.4 per cent under 15 years of age and 17.7 per cent under 5 years of age, compared with figures of 28.8 per cent and 9.6 per cent, respectively, for the general population. By contrast, only 3.6 per cent of the Aboriginal population was over 65 years of age compared with 8.3 per cent for the general population. As mentioned by the National Population Enquiry (1975, p. 505) 'a population of this kind is the result of high growth in the past and, because of its age structure, carries the potential for high growth in the future, even given relatively modest rates of reproduction per head'. The welfare ramifications of this age distribution are very considerable. The ratio of children aged 0–14 to the population aged 15–64 (the dependent-age ratio) for Aborigines is 0.93, whereas for the general population it is only 0.46. This implies that the burden of bringing up young dependants, which usually falls on the parents, is far greater for Aborigines. Equally, even though the ratio of aged dependants to the population aged 15–64 for Aborigines is 0.07 and for all Australians 0.13, the extended family system among Aborigines implies that the burden of caring for the aged does not fall especially lightly upon them, particularly in view of their relatively low incomes.

Urbanisation and Geographic Distribution

In Table 3, details of the Aboriginal and general population residing in the major urban, other urban and rural areas for the census years 1966

Table 3. *Urbanisation of the Aboriginal and Australian population (percentage distribution)*

	Aboriginal population		Aboriginal population		Australian population	
	1966	1971	1966	1971	1966	1971
Metropolitan[a]	8,310	15,667	8.6	14.7	58.1	64.5
Other urban[b]	22,805	30,594	23.6	28.8	25.1	21.1
Rural[c]	65,420	59,987	67.7	56.4	16.8	14.4
Total	96,632	106,290	100.0	100.0	100.0	100.0

[a] Metropolitan or major urban, defined as population concentrations of 100,000 people or larger.
[b] Other urban, refers to population concentration of 1,000 to 100,000 people.
[c] Rural and migratory.
Sources: Jones (1973); Australian Bureau of Statistics (1973); Australian Bureau of Statistics (1975a).

and 1971 are given, though all reservations of intercensal comparisons mentioned before should be borne in mind. The figures certainly imply that there has been rapid urbanisation of the Aboriginal population.

But this conclusion must be guarded. While there seems little doubt that the number of Aborigines in the rural sector decreased absolutely and as a percentage of the population, the increase of their number in metropolitan areas, by nearly 100 per cent, seems dramatic. However, the extent to which the question of changes in 'racial identification' (racial immigration) entered in to alter the figures, as mentioned above, cannot be judged.

In comparison with the total population, Aborigines were still very much a rural community in 1971. In that year, only 14.4 per cent of the total population lived in rural areas, compared with 56.4 per cent of the Aboriginal population. (In 1971 the Aboriginal population represented 0.19 per cent of Australia's major urban population, 1.13 per cent of the 'other urban' category and 3.28 per cent of the rural population.) There is a welfare implication of the rural concentration of Aborigines, since employment opportunites and educational facilities are likely to be more fully available, on a per capita basis, in urban than in rural areas. As Jones (1973, p.59) has remarked, the 'present geographical distribution (of Aborigines) reflects their marginal status'.

In regard to future Aboriginal population growth rates, estimates in the National Population Inquiry were based on both the possibility of constant fertility and mortality and declining fertility and mortality. Since the age structure of the population is biased towards youth, it was also growth-biased, and the Inquiry concluded (p. 529) that, with either growth rate, the Aboriginal population would double by the year 2000.

Education

Educational status is the first welfare indicator to which attention is turned. The information in Table 4 gives details of school participation rates by Aboriginal and general-population children, according to the 1971 census.

The two features in Table 4 which distinguish Aboriginal children from general-population children are that they tend to start school later (23 per cent more in the 7–11 category as against the 5–6 category) and finish earlier. The marked difference in the 15–18 age group is perhaps the worst, for it is usually during this age that School-Leaving and Matriculation examinations (generally the prerequisites for tertiary education) are taken. This table is purely a quantity indicator – quality considerations are not evidenced. There is every indication, as

later described, that schooling for Aborigines in rural and remote areas
and in small country towns tends to be of a lower quality.

Table 5, which depicts the highest level of formal schooling attended
by Aborigines and others, reinforces the features of Table 4. The most

Table 4. *Aboriginal and general-population children – school
participation rates by age, 1971 census*

| | Percentage of age group attending school | | | |
| | Aboriginal children | | Australian children | |
	Males	Females	Males	Females
5– 6	73.0	73.5	90.9	91.9
7–11	96.5	96.5	99.4	99.4
12–14	97.0	97.2	99.8	99.7
15–18	23.9	26.9	41.5	36.7

Source: Australian Bureau of Statistics (1976a).

notable statistic here is that 24.7 per cent of Aborigines had (in 1971)
never attended school (excluding those of pre-school age) as against
0.8 per cent for the general Australian population. Whereas only 26.1
per cent of the Aboriginal population had attended school past level 5
in 1971, 69.3 per cent of the Australian population had done so. Table 5
refers of course to attendance level and *not* the completion of level.
While the figures in Table 5 are not strictly comparable (since total
general population refers to those over 20 years of age) the indication is
that Aborigines are receiving less schooling than Australians as a
whole. This has two important consequences (apart from the obvious
handicap of illiteracy). Firstly, it acts as a constraint on the type of
occupations for which Aborigines are eligible (on the basis of educational attainment) and, secondly, it makes many Aborigines ineligible
(and insufficiently experienced) for most tertiary courses. The second
of these assertions is borne out by the evidence presented in Table 6,
which shows the post-school qualifications of the Aboriginal and general population. It will be seen that, in 1971, 96.6 per cent of the
Aboriginal population had no post-school qualifications as compared
with 79.1 per cent for the general population. Overall, the proportion
of Aboriginal people with qualifications was between one-eighth and
one-ninth of the proportion of all Australians with qualifications for
both males and females. The largest proportion of qualified Aborigines

was in the trade level category. Examination of the source material for Table 6 suggests that Aborigines had a particularly low number of qualifications in administrative, commercial, health and medical fields.

Table 5. *Highest level of schooling attended, Aboriginal and general population, 1971 census*

Level	Aborigines[a] (per cent)	Australians[b] (per cent)
Never attended	24.7	0.8
Level 1	7.8	0.7
Level 2	5.3	1.0
Level 3	7.4	2.2
Level 4	7.3	3.8
Level 5	14.9	17.1
Level 6	7.0	6.8
Level 7	8.4	14.6
Level 8	7.3	20.5
Level 9	1.8	9.6
Level 10	1.6	17.8
Not stated	6.6	5.1
Total	100.0	100.0

[a]As a percentage of Aboriginal population omitting those currently attending school and children not yet attending school.
[b]As a percentage of the Australian population over 20 years of age.
Source: Australian Bureau of Statistics (1976a).

It can be concluded that Aborigines participate in education far less than the general population and have a significantly lower adult population holding recognised qualifications. The consequences of this situation are all too clear.

Employment

Labour Force Participation
In Table 7, participation rates for the Aboriginal and general populations are presented for 1971. The picture in this table is bleak. Overall participation for Aborigines is extremely low, with 45.6 per cent of the adult population being defined as part of the labour force. This is in

comparison with 60.7 per cent for the general Australian population. Particularly noticeable is the number of young people (15–19 years old) not participating in the labour force, or in schools (see Table 4). Whereas almost all male Australians in this age group were at school or

Table 6. *The Aboriginal and general populations by highest level of post-school qualification obtained, 1971 census (per cent of total)*

	Aboriginal population		Australian population	
	Male	Female	Male	Female
1. Trade level	2.65	0.19	17.93	1.55
2. Technician level	0.20	0.40	3.42	3.46
3. Non-degree tertiary	0.13	0.11	3.31	3.03
4. Bachelor degree	0.07	0.04	2.46	0.95
5. Higher degree	0.03	0.004	0.41	0.09
6. Not classified by level	0.15	0.69	1.02	3.25
7. Inadequately described	0.01	0.00	0.01	0.007
8. Total with qualification	3.24	1.43	28.57	12.32
9. Total without qualification	96.76	98.57	71.43	87.68
Total	100.0	100.0	100.0	100.0

Note: The male-to-female ratio for the Aboriginal population in 1971 was 102.3 and for the general population 101.1.
Source: Unpublished data from Department of Aboriginal Affairs, Head Office, Canberra.

in the labour force, over 20 per cent of young Aboriginal males were not participating in either. In the 35–44 age bracket, when most people might be considered to be reaching their peak of working efficiency, 76.3 per cent of Aboriginal males of that age cohort participated in the labour force, as against 97.8 per cent for all Australians. Finally, in the 60–4 and 65-plus age brackets, the proportion of Aborigines in the work force was approximately half the proportion for the total population. This is probably not because Aborigines tend naturally to retire earlier, but is more likely to be linked with poor health forcing retirement.

It is of interest to compare these participation rates with those compiled by Broom and Jones (1973, p. 27) based on the 1966 census, who estimated participation rates for Aboriginal males of 70.8 per cent, for all Australian males of 83.9 per cent, for Aboriginal females 24.5 per

cent and for all Australian females of 35.2 per cent. It appears as though
participation by Aboriginal males in the labour force has declined
somewhat since 1966. On the other hand, female participation has
remained constant. (Comparisons between the Broom and Jones and

Table 7. *Labour force participation rates by age and sex, Aboriginal
and general population, 1971 census (per cent in labour force)*

Age	Aboriginal population			Australian population		
(years)	Male	Female	Total	Male	Female	Total
15–19	55.8	34.7	45.2	59.0	56.5	57.8
20–24	77.7	29.1	53.5	91.8	60.6	76.3
25–34	79.9	21.8	51.2	97.5	40.6	69.9
35–44	76.3	22.8	49.7	97.8	47.7	73.5
45–54	72.2	22.1	48.2	95.6	42.2	69.1
55–59	63.1	12.8	39.4	90.6	29.5	59.6
60–64	46.1	5.3	24.8	77.4	16.9	46.7
65 and over	10.3	2.4	6.7	22.3	3.8	11.8
Total	66.9	23.6	45.6	82.7	39.2	60.7

Source: Australian Bureau of Statistics (1976a).

the ABS estimates must, however, be used with circumspection, since
the former were based on 'official' and the latter on 'unofficial' numera-
tions.)

Occupational Status
In Table 8, the occupational status of Aborigines in 1971 is examined.
Aborigines in the employer category numbered only one-tenth of the
proportion for the general population – emphasising the present lack
of entrepreneurial skill of Aborigines and the consequences of inadequate education. This finding is again repeated in the self-employed
category – with only 2.2 per cent of the Aboriginal labour force being
self-employed (as against 7.1 per cent for the general population). An
especially important statistic is the high unemployment rate of
Aborigines compared with the general population – 9.3 per cent as
against 1.7 per cent in 1971. The 1971 findings may be compared with
those based on the 1966 census. In 1966, the Aboriginal unemployment
rate was 6.7 per cent and that for the general population was 1.6 per

cent. It seems that while the unemployment rate from 1966 to 1971 remained relatively constant for Australians in general, it increased almost 3 percentage points for Aborigines. (The 'official' census rate may have given the 1966 rate an upward bias – hence there seems little

Table 8. *Occupational status, Aboriginal and general labour force, 1971 census (per cent of total)*

Occupational status	Aboriginal labour force	Australian labour force
Employer	0.5	5.2
Self-employed	2.2	7.1
Employee	87.6	85.4
Helper	0.5	0.6
Unemployed	9.3	1.7
Total	100.0	100.0

Source: Australian Bureau of Statistics (1976a).

doubt that between 1966 and 1971 Aboriginal unemployment increased.)

On the basis of L. R. Smith's census-based population projection for 1976, the DAA has estimated the Aboriginal (plus TSIs) labour force in mid-1976 to be 34,248 (DAA, 1976a, p. 9). (Since these figures include TSIs, they are not strictly comparable with those for 1971). This estimate is close to that made in 1976 by the Department of Employment and Industrial Relations (DEIR) of 35,000 (i.e. including TSIs). Accepting the DAA's estimate as correct, in July 1976 there were 9,667 registered unemployed Aborigines giving an unemployment rate of 28.2 per cent. (By April 1977 there were 11,822 Aborigines registered for employment (DAA, 1977a, p. 13). However, no 1977 estimate of the Aboriginal labour force exists.) This compares extremely poorly with the Australia-wide unemployment rate at the same time of 4.4 per cent. Yet even this estimate of Aboriginal unemployment is regarded in some quarters as an underestimate. In the Interdepartmental Working Paper on Aboriginal Unemployment (DAA, 1976e, p. 9) it was stated that 'Aboriginal unemployment has historically been a major problem. Currently it is in its worst ever state; the unemployment rate based on registered unemployment is over 30 per cent. As many Aboriginals do not register, it is estimated that in real terms 50 per cent

of the Aboriginal workforce is currently unemployed. This compares
with a national rate of approximately 4.5 per cent.' The major reasons
for this situation are closely related to the features mentioned above:
namely, that many Aborigines are located in areas isolated from
employment opportunities (i.e. in rural and remote areas) and that
they tend to be geographically immobile and lack education and work
skills. Other reasons include lack of social experience and motivation,
as well as employer attitudes, as mentioned later.

In Table 9 details are given of the job classifications of Aborigines in

Table 9. *Occupational distribution of employed Aboriginal
population, 1971 census (per cent of total)*

Occupation	Aboriginal population		Total Australian population	
	Male	Female	Male	Female
Total of professional, technical, related workers	1.59	4.77	8.62	13.74
Total administrative, executive, managerial workers	0.70	0.40	8.56	2.54
Total of clerical workers	1.33	8.03	8.38	32.03
Total of sales workers	1.31	4.44	6.08	12.33
Total farmers, hunters, etc.	32.77	5.76	9.51	3.80
Total of miners, quarrymen, etc.	2.62	6.30	0.94	0.01
Total of workers in transport and communication	5.51	1.47	7.00	2.40
Total of tradesmen, product process workers, labourers	42.65	13.76	40.62	13.53
Total service, sport and recreation workers	3.68	50.50	4.03	14.70
Members of armed services	0.81	0.12	1.75	0.16
Inadequately described or not stated	7.03	10.46	4.51	4.77
Total	100.00	100.00	100.00	100.00

Sources: Unpublished data, Department of Aboriginal Affairs, Canberra.

the labour force. This table exemplifies the consequences in a modern
economy of low formal Western-style educational status and remoteness from urban centres (as well as poor housing and health conditions

mentioned below). The areas of work with especially high ratios of Aboriginal workers compared with the total population, are, for Aboriginal males, farming (not farm owners or farm managers), mining and quarrying, and labouring; and, for Aboriginal women, recreation and service work. Because of its aggregative nature the classification system used in Table 9 needs to be qualified. (Moreover there are some Aborigines who are traditional hunters.) But of the Aborigines in the farmers, hunters, and so on, category, most are farm labourers (as against much lower percentages for all Australia). Similarly, in the tradesmen, production process workers, labourers category, 21.67 per cent of Aboriginal males (as against 5.47 per cent for total males) are labourers. The overall feature displayed by Table 9 is that most Aborigines are involved in unskilled work.

Employment—Income Relationships
There are at present no income estimates for the Aboriginal population as a group. The ABS surveys on income distribution do not treat Aborigines as a separate entity. Those income estimates which are available (such as the studies by the Commission of Inquiry into Poverty (1975), discussed in Chapter 6) refer to the major urban sections of the Aboriginal population but not the total. It is consequently of interest to examine the implications of likely relationships between employment status and income earning potential among Aborigines. Proxy (or substitute) variables for income may give some indication of income size.

The most obvious 'proxy' (if it may so be termed) is the probability that since Aborigines occupy jobs on the lower rungs of the ladder of skills, they are likely to receive the relatively low remuneration which is normally (statistically) associated with those avenues of employment. Another, less obvious proxy may be obtained by examining (and recalculating) the dependent-age ratios referred to under demographic indicators, taking into account participation rates and employment levels. To recap, in 1971 50 per cent of the Aboriginal population (those in the 15–64 age bracket) supported 46.4 per cent of the population, whereas for all Australia, 62.9 per cent supported 28.8 per cent. The young dependent-age ratio for Aborigines was 0.93 and for all Australian 0.46. The dependent-age ratio may now be redefined as the ratio of under 15-year-olds being supported by those in the 15-plus age group (not the 15–64 age bracket) who were actively employed. The participation rate for Aborigines was 45.6 per cent and for all Australia

60.7 per cent. The employment rate for Aborigines was 90.7 per cent. and for all Australians 98.3 per cent. This changes the young dependent-age ratios substantially, for it means that 22.1 per cent of the Aboriginal population supported 46.4 per cent of the population (giving a young dependent-age ratio of 2.10) whereas, for all Australia, 42.5 per cent of the population supported 28.8 per cent of the population (giving a young dependent-age ratio of 0.68). Given the low occupational status of Aborigines, one has an indication of the extreme income differences that must exist between the Aborigines and the rest of the Australian community.

Housing

Housing conditions are related to both income, mentioned above, and health, mentioned below. There seems to be, in housing, the clearest possible indication of the under-privileged socio-economic position of Australia's Aboriginal population.

In Table 10 houses and flats in Australia by nature of occupancy are

Table 10. *Aboriginal and total occupied houses and flats by nature of occupancy, 1971 census (per cent of total)*

	Aboriginal-occupied houses and flats		All houses and flats (Australia)	
	House	Self-contained flat	House	Self-contained flat
Owner	21.2	2.8	75.8	20.2
Tenant	62.0	92.9	19.2	74.7
Other (incl. not stated)	16.8	4.3	5.0	5.1
Total	100.0	100.0	100.0	100.0

Source: Australian Bureau of Statistics (1976a).

detailed. This is a quantity indicator and shows the proportion of houses (Aboriginal and all Australia) which are owner-occupied or rented. The divergence between the Aboriginal population and the rest is extreme. Only 19.9 per cent of Aboriginal private dwellings were owner-occupied in 1971, compared with 67.3 per cent for the total population of Australia. Not only, however, is the issue the bare one of owner-occupation – there are also the other tangible advantages of home ownership, such as a lower tax burden in certain income categories and the benefits of 'silent' capital accumulation through the rapid rise in house prices which has been an excellent hedge against inflation for home owners in Australia. (In the last few years, home ownership has in general become more difficult in Australia, but there seems no reason to suppose that the 1971 figures, depicting relative home ownership as between Aborigines and others, have altered substantially.)

Table 11 details the type of dwellings occupied by the Aboriginal and general population. This table also reinforces the picture of Aboriginal poverty. Only 63.5 per cent of the Aboriginal population live in a private (i.e. privately owned, not necessarily by occupier) house or self-contained flat as against 93.6 per cent for the total population. The most notable statistic here is that nearly 18 per cent of the Aboriginal population in 1971 lived in improvised dwellings, the corresponding figure for the Australia-wide community being 0.4 per cent (0.15 per

Table 11. *Aboriginal and Australian population, by type of dwelling occupied, 1971 census (percent of total population)*

	Aboriginal population	Australian population
House	60.7	85.6
Self-contained flat	2.8	8.0
Improvised dwelling[a]	17.9	0.4
Other	3.8	1.3
Total in private dwellings	85.2	95.3
Non-private dwellings	13.0	4.5
Not in dwellings	1.8	0.2
Total	100.0	100.0

[a]Aboriginal 'improvised dwellings' are usually constructed from corrugated iron and are more commonly known as 'humpies', 'wiltjas' or 'wurlies'.
Source: Australian Bureau of Statistics (1976a).

cent of whom were Aborigines). This figure must however, be viewed in the light of subsequent discussion. The discrepancy between the improvised dwelling figures for Aborigines and the Australia-wide community is largely due to those Aborigines in tribal or remote areas who live in traditional shelters. Similarly, 13 per cent of the Aboriginal population lived in non-private dwellings (i.e. on government settlements) as against 4.5 per cent of all Australians.

Turning to statistics on the quality of dwellings in Table 12, room occupancy rates are given for private dwellings. The two extremes of this table indicate the serious position Aborigines face: approximately 50 per cent of Aboriginal dwellings had more than 1.5 persons per room in 1971, as against 2.4 per cent for the total population; and only 9.1 per cent of Aboriginal dwellings had less than (or equal to) 0.5

Table 12. *Room occupancy rate, Aboriginal and total, 1971 census*

	Number of persons per room (per cent)				
Occupied private dwellings	<0.5	0.51 to 0.75	0.76 to 1.00	1.01 to 1.50	>1.51
Aboriginal	9.1	7.2	17.1	16.7	49.9
All Australia	40.8	21.8	26.9	8.1	2.4

Source: Australian Bureau of Statistics (1976a).

persons per room, as against 40.8 per cent for the general population. By Australian standards, therefore, Aboriginal homes appear to be miserably overcrowded. This is hardly a surprising figure, however, as 26 per cent of Aboriginal homes have only one room as against 1.9 per cent for the total population (ABS, 1976a, p. 89).

In Table 13 aspects of the quality of Aboriginal private dwellings are detailed. The difference in quality between Aboriginal and Australia-wide housing is again extreme. It seems clear that Aborigines live in housing which would be regarded as unbearable by non-Aboriginal Australians. While only private dwellings are examined here, there is no evidence to suggest that non-private dwellings occupied by Aborigines (in government settlements and missions) are of a higher quality. (Housing conditions on reserves are referred to later.)

In general, Aborigines are not house owners, and a high proportion live in improvised dwellings. The private dwellings they occupy are generally overcrowded, by the norms of the general society, and lack facilities that most Australians regard as basic. The linkages between this indicator and the others examined must be powerful. As emphasised later, living in overcrowded and unhygienic conditions must have direct effects on educational possibilities and employment opportunities.

Table 13. *Housing facilities: percentage of Aboriginal and total occupied private dwellings lacking certain facilities, 1971 census*

Facilities	Aboriginal-occupied private dwellings	Australian-occupied private dwellings
Without bathroom	26.7	0.7
Without kitchen	24.5	0.5
Without electricity	30.9	0.6
Without electricity or gas	30.3	0.4
Without flush toilet	51.7	9.5
Without connection to public sewer	72.3	32.3

Source: Australian Bureau of Statistics (1976a).

Health

Although many studies have been made of Aboriginal health conditions, these are of individual communities, not of the total population, and nowhere is the inadequate state of separate statistics more apparent than those on Aboriginal health. Only in Western Australia and the Northern Territory are separate statistics on infant mortality, morbidity and age-specific death rates kept. But something of the overall picture may be gauged from a number of specific studies referred to in the Commission of Inquiry into Poverty (1976) and the Senate Select Committee on Aborigines and Torres Strait Islanders (1976). From these two reports it appears as though Aborigines suffer from a number of diseases rarely seen in non-Aboriginal Australia – for example, leprosy, tuberculosis and gastro-intestinal infections. Other serious health problems such as respiratory diseases and eye diseases (especially trachoma) and alcoholism, poor dental health and malnutrition, appear to predominate in Aboriginal communities to an extent which would be regarded as epidemic and unacceptable for the general community. The Senate Select Committee (1976, p. 137) suggested that the main causes of ill health were poor housing, nutrition and hygiene. The frequency with which children suffer from some illnesses, especially ear and eye diseases and malnutrition and gastrointestinal infections, is particularly notable.

The infant mortality rate for the total Aboriginal population is not known, but if statistics for the whole of the Northern Territory and Western Australia can be taken as illustrative of the overall situation, then Aborigines experience much higher infant mortality rates than the total population. This rate (infant mortality per thousand live births) averaged 97.4 for the five years 1970–4, and by 1976 had declined to 52.8 in the Northern Territory. In 1971, the rate was 76.9 in Western Australia. This compares most unfavourably with the rate for the general Australian population which was 16.1 in 1974. (The rate for the total population in 1971 was 17.3.)

Examination of the age structure of the Aboriginal population (Table 2) shows that Aborigines have a much lower life expectancy than the general population. Only 3.6 per cent of the Aboriginal population in 1971 had a life expectancy greater than 60 years of age, compared with 8.3 per cent for the wider society. The National Population Inquiry (1975, pp. 505–6) commented that 'Sixty seven percent of males in the general population reach pensionable age and on average live to collect their pensions for over 12 years. Eighty six percent of females reach pension age, and they live on average to collect it for almost 20 years. In contrast . . . less than 44 percent of Aboriginal males reach pensionable age and those who do so live on average only another 11 years, while only about 47 percent of Aboriginal females survive to pension age and they live on average less than 15 years more.'

The evidence mentioned on health is brief but broadly illustrates both the poor general health conditions of the Aboriginal people and the paucity of adequate statistics on the issue. (A useful discussion of available health studies is, however, given in The Commission of Inquiry into Poverty (1976), Moodie (1973) and L. R. Smith (1975a).) The economic consequences of poor health conditions are referred to later.

Conclusion

This chapter has examined certain aspects of the socio-economic status of Aborigines. Statistics, predominantly from the 1971 Census of Population and Housing, have been presented as demographic and welfare indicators in order to compare the socio-economic status of the Aboriginal population with that of the general Australian population. The findings may briefly be summarised as follows:

(1) The Aboriginal population (excluding TSIs and including only self-identifiers) was 106,290 in 1971 and represented a very small proportion (about 0.8 per cent) of the total population. The Aboriginal population has an extremely young age structure (the age distribution tree is skewed quite noticeably at the 0–15 age level) and a high proportion of young dependants. The Aboriginal population is still predominantly rural or living in smaller urban areas, and is relatively immobile between States. There is an indication of substantial rural/ urban migration within States, while population growth is rapid. It is estimated that the Aboriginal population will double in size by the year 2000.

(2) The formal educational status of the Aboriginal population is extremely low compared with the general Australian community. According to 1971 census data, almost 25 per cent of Aboriginal adults had never attended school (as compared with 0.8 per cent for the general population). Participation rates at school, and post-school quali- fications obtained, were much lower for the Aboriginal population.

(3) The employment status of Aborigines is also extremely low compared with the general community. Participation rates in the labour force are lower and unemployment rates are far higher for the Aboriginal population. When employed, Aborigines hold jobs with low occupational status: predominantly unskilled jobs. Income estimates for the total Aboriginal population do not exist, but low occupational status, low participation rates, high unemployment rates, and high de- pendency rates imply extremely low incomes by Australian standards.

(4) The quality of Aboriginal housing is extremely low. Whereas on average Australians are home owners, the majority of Aborigines are tenants. A large proportion of the Aboriginal population lives in improvised dwellings. Those private dwellings which Aborigines occupy appear overcrowded and lack basic facilities to an extent that would be deemed unacceptable in the wider society.

(5) While health data on an Australia-wide perspective (for Aborigines) are extremely limited, the general conclusion that can be drawn from community studies is that Aborigines experience rela- tively very poor health. The infant mortality rate for Aborigines is more than three times that for Australians in general, and life expectancy is also much lower.

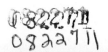

2

Remote Australia I: government settlements and missions

In applying the term 'colonial Australia' to the area . . . which roughly demarcates the desert and sparsely settled pastoral country (of Australia), I have it in mind that in these northern and central regions the social relationships between the indigenous and the settler populations represent an earlier phase of changes brought by European settlement, and that there are many aspects remaining in the relations between the races which are typical of industrial colonialism.
C. D. Rowley, *The Remote Aborigines*

Colonies do not cease to be colonies because they are independent.
B. Disraeli, Speech in the House of Commons (5 February 1873).

The geographic area in which government settlements and church missions for Aborigines are found today has been variously called remote, traditional and 'colonial' Australia. All three adjectives seem appropriate. This vast area of the country is remote, being beyond the fringes of settlement, and isolated from major population centres and economic activity. It is also traditional, since the majority of Aboriginal residents in the region are of full descent and appear less divorced from the social, cultural and kinship systems of their forefathers than those Aborigines in more settled or urban areas. Finally, Rowley's (1971b) expression 'colonial' is apposite as well, alluding as it does to the pluralistic features of society in this part of Australia. But while each adjective is in its own way appropriate, the term used in this chapter is 'remote'.

Geographically, remote Australia comprises half the continent. It encompasses the whole of the Northern Territory, the northern parts of Queensland and South Australia, and the northern and central regions of Western Australia. In Map 2, the heavy line divides Australia into remote and settled parts. The history of missions and government settlements is far from uniform. As the colonies of immigrant settlement expanded over the continent during the nineteenth century, the Aboriginal inhabitants either died out, retreated to remoter areas, or formed population 'pockets'. Only in areas where there were few or no European immigrants did Aborigines survive in large numbers.

Aborigines gathered at missions initially for security and from curiosity and then for the apparently ready availability of both food and water. In many remote areas, there was nothing external to force this centralisation of the nomadic clans, and conglomeration at missions was usually voluntary. As Hamilton (1972, p. 41) states, 'It seems clear that the values and norms of their own society forced them to . . . [congregate at missions]. The twin principles that kept Aboriginal society functioning were the need to find food and the desire to limit effort in doing so – vital elements in a hunting and gathering economy. Put in ecological terms, it was a question of maintaining an energy input/output balance favourable to human survival. When the news came that the whites had abundant, if strange, food, more than they could possibly eat, this was like news of Eden – or the super water-hole, in Aboriginal terms.' The more arid and harsh the environment, the more powerful would have been the attraction of missions. Consequently it seems that in the arid north of South Australia, according to Hamilton (1972, pp. 40–1), centralisation occurred rapidly; whereas (as Long, 1970, p. 141, argues) in the more fertile environment of northern Queensland, missionaries had a more difficult task coaxing Aborigines to mission stations.

While the principal motive for mission establishment was probably the preservation and protection of a threatened people, it had a strong assimilationist bent, based on a pervasive and long-established European ethnocentrism. Many missions made the abandonment of a variety of traditional customs obligatory. In particular missionaries sought to ban polygamy; child marriage and the 'promise' system of betrothal; Aboriginal law and its private retributive justice; sorcery; traditional ceremonies (e.g. initiation rites and so on); and traditional medicine. In a sense the attempts to supplant traditional Aboriginal culture were positive, for the threat of deliberate eradication of Aborigines was still real. The missionaries sought to teach Aborigines the use of European clothing, housing, health, education, law, the economic system and, of course, religion. The success of missionaries in these aims varied considerably.

By the 1930s, it was clear that the Aboriginal population of remote Australia was not disappearing, and policy became an intermingled one of protection and assimilation, although there was little uniformity in the policies of different governments. For example, while the Federal government was establishing settlements in the Northern Territory, the Western Australian State Government was closing down settlements and transferring the control of others to mission bodies.

By 1951, most of the major government settlements and missions had been established, and it was in this year – following the Native Welfare Meeting of Commonwealth and State Ministers – that assimilation became an 'official' policy of governments in some States. However, the concept of assimilation remained a notion rather than a definition, and it was not until 1961 that, as Rowley mentions (1971a, p. 399), its formal meaning was clarified by the Native Welfare Conference: 'The policy of assimilation means that all Aborigines and part-Aborigines are expected eventually to attain the same manner of living as other Australians and to live as members of a single Australian community enjoying the same rights and privileges, accepting the same responsibilities, observing the same customs and influenced by the same beliefs as other Australians.'

It is difficult to see how the policy of assimilation related to the location of most government settlements and missions in isolated regions with scarce natural resources and a harsh climate. It is also difficult to see how the fostering of Aboriginal reliance upon government welfare and transfer payments (and the absence of employment opportunities in European-style jobs, even where training for these was provided) could be reconciled with the assimilation policy. But it is not difficult to understand how, under the economic circumstances engendered by the government settlements and missions, a situation, described by Long (1970, p. 181) as one of 'hostile dependency', developed.

In any event, 'assimilation' was replaced in 1965 by a policy of 'integration' (which seemed little different) and gave way in 1972 to 'self-determination'. The self-determination initiative came five years after the abolition, in 1967, of all discriminatory laws against Aborigines (except those operating in Queensland under the

Aborigines and Torres Strait Islanders' Act of 1965). Self-determination as defined by the Commission of Inquiry into Poverty (1977, p. 185) was 'Aboriginal communities deciding the pace and nature of their future development as significant components within a diverse Australia'. In the wake of this initiative, control of government settlements and missions is shifting to Aboriginal councils.

The material in this chapter must be viewed with these background events (which are extensively described in Rowley (1970, 1971b)) in mind. As usual, the task of describing the economic status of the communities concerned is made difficult by the paucity of the available information. And, again, care must be exercised in assessing economic conditions from a value system not necessarily the same as that held by the people studied. Yet other complications are that (1) the communities concerned are in three different States and the Northern Territory; (2) co-ordination of policies towards them was only begun in 1972, with the formation of the DAA; and (3) the geographic distribution of the communities is so wide (see Map 2) that their resource endowments vary substantially.

Geographic and demographic characteristics

Estimating the number of Aborigines residing on government settlements and missions in the remote regions of South Australia, Queensland and Western Australia, and in the whole of the Northern Territory, is very difficult because the censuses available differ considerably in accuracy and format. However, most of the estimates used are by the DAA and seem reasonably accurate, since the overnumeration which often occurs is generally in State estimates concerning Aborigines of part descent living in more settled areas, rather than of those of full descent residing on government settlements and missions. (While all Aborigines on these settlements would have been enumerated in the 1971 census, this was by electoral district and not by place of residence.) One difficulty that any enumeration must consider, however, is that the communities are sometimes quite mobile, and cross State borders.

In the north of South Australia there are only two government settlements remaining – Amata in the North-West Reserve region (71,540 sq km) and Indulkana adjacent to this reserve. In 1976, their populations were estimated at 400 and 120 persons respectively. There are also three communities: Nepabunna, Pukatja (Ernabella) and

Yalata which used to be mission-sponsored communities but are now formally independent and reside on land leased to them by the South Australian Aboriginal Land Trust. In late 1976, a DAA estimate of their three populations was 900 persons. The total population of govern-

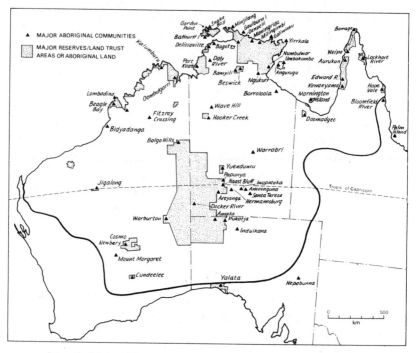

Map 2. Major Aboriginal communities in remote' Australia

ment and government-affiliated settlements in remote South Australia (locations of which are shown on Map 2) is approximately 1,500, or 15–20 per cent of the 1976 estimate of South Australia's Aboriginal population. The population on the government settlements tends to be extremely young, and predominantly of full descent (mainly Pitjantjat-jara speakers).

In Western Australia, there are no purely government settlements in the remote regions. Communities are either missions or mission-affiliated though they are subsidised by the State government. In Table 14, the major missions in remote Western Australia are listed with estimates of their populations, and the size of sites they occupy.

It appears that there are about 2,800 Aborigines living on missions in remote Western Australia. This represents between 10 and 12 per cent of the total estimated Western Australian Aboriginal population. As is evident in Map 2, most of these communities are situated in the north of Western Australia, or on the desert fringe. All land on which they are located today is vested in the Western Australia Aboriginal Land Trust.

Table 14. *Major missions (and ex-missions) in remote Western Australia, 1976*

Mission	Area[a] (sq. km)	Population June 1976[b]
Balgo Hills	20,800	573
Beagle Bay	3,430	267
Bidyadanga (LaGrange)	18	399
Cosmo Newberry	4,520	68
Cundeelee	1,130	240
Jigalong[c]	3,340	369
Kalumburu	1,700	189
Lombadina	140	199
Mount Margaret	1	130
Oombulgarri[c]	13,050	167
Warburton	2,630	273

[a] Land leased from Aboriginal Land Trust, Western Australia.
[b] Estimate of Area Officers of the Aboriginal Affairs Planning Authority, Western Australia.
[c] Jigalong and Oombulgarri communities are ex-mission but still maintain some affiliation with mission authorities.
Source: Department of Aboriginal Affairs, Western Australia (1976) and Aboriginal Affairs Planning Authority, Western Australia (1976).

In the north of Queensland, there are five missions and five Department of Aboriginal and Islanders Advancement (The Queensland State Aboriginal Authority, hereafter DAIA) settlements, on which Aborigines predominantly reside. There are also a number of DAIA Island Reserves which are mainly occupied by Torres Strait Islanders and the Northern Peninsular Reserve which is also predominantly Islander-occupied. The major Aboriginal reserves in remote Queensland are presented in Table 15. It should be noted that while Palm

Island is not geographically in remote Australia, it shares so many characteristics with the remote DAIA settlements that it has been included in the figures. In 1976, there were approximately 6,000 Aborigines on settlements and missions in remote northern Queens-

Table 15. *Missions and DAIA reserve settlements in remote Queensland, 1976*

	Area (sq. km)	Population March 1976[a]
Missions		
Aurukun	7,500	768
Bloomfield	1.16	195
Doomadgee	1,460	805
Hope Vale	1,040	573
Mornington Island	990	681
DAIA settlements		
Edward River[b]	4,660	321
Kowanyama[b]		
(Mitchell River)	2,590	762
Lockhart River[b]	3,130	377
Palm Island[c]	60	1409
Weipa[b]	3,548	654

[a] This Department of Aboriginal and Islanders Advancement estimate includes Torres Strait Islanders, but communities listed here have predominantly Aboriginal populations, hence overnumeration would only be slight.
[b] Ex-missions recently taken over by the Department of Aboriginal and Islanders Advancement.
[c] Not geographically in remote Australia, but sharing many features.
Source: Department of Aboriginal and Islanders Advancement (1976).

land. This represents approximately 20–22 per cent of Queensland's estimated 1976 Aboriginal population. The age structure of this population is not known with certainty. However, the Queensland Institute of Medical Research (QIMR) calculated that in 1972, 42 per cent and 36 per cent of the Kowanyama and Edward River populations respectively were under 15 years of age (QIMR, 1973, p. 22). The DAIA (1976, p. 35) states that 37 per cent of the populations of these communities attended pre-school and primary and high schools. This implies that over 40 per cent of the population was under 15 years of age (including children in the 0–4 age bracket).

Relatively speaking the most satisfactory demographic statistics exist for the Northern Territory, where there are at present thirteen mission communities and twenty government settlements (listed in Table 16). Two of the government settlements, Amoonguna, near Alice Springs, and Bagot, near Darwin, are what could be called 'special-purpose' reserves. They are much smaller than the average mission or government settlement and have more in common with the town reserves of more settled areas (which will be examined in Chapter 5). Most of these communities were until December 1976 on Aboriginal Reserves, but the passing of the Aboriginal Land Rights (Northern Territory) Act has vested the ownership of this land in the hands of Aborigines and is under the jurisdiction of the Northern and Central Land Councils.[1] It is not as yet clear whether groups will receive freehold title to land that was previously reserve land. Land vested in the Land Councils totals 243,615 sq. km at present, but there is a distinct possibility that other tracts of Crown land (for example the Tanami Wild Life Sanctuary) will become Aboriginal lands. Hermannsburg and Santa Teresa missions and Wave Hill government settlement are located on special leases.

In 1973, there were 7,831 Aborigines on mission-sponsored communities, and 8,062 on government settlements in the Northern Territory. These populations were extremely young, with 48 per cent of the mission population and 44 per cent of the settlement population being under 15 years of age. At the end of 1972, the DAA Northern Territory Division (DAA, 1975, p. 42) estimated that 32 per cent of the Northern Territory Aboriginal population lived on government settlements, and 30 per cent on missions. Indications are that this proportion will have decreased since 1972. While there has been some drift to centralised communities from cattle stations (see Chapter 3) this has been more than offset by a migration from missions and settlements to 'homeland' or decentralised centres (see Chapter 4) and in some cases to towns. In general, the somewhat transient nature of settlement communities (with trips to visit kin very

---

[1] By the end of 1977, owing to a flaw in the Aboriginal Land Rights (Northern Territory) Act, no land had been legally transferred to Aboriginal ownership. However it is assumed here that during 1978 amending legislation will be introduced so that land trusts may be set up in accordance with apparent government intentions.

Table 16. *Missions and DAA settlements in the Northern Territory, 1973*

	1973 Population[a]	Population under 15 yrs of age (per cent)[b]
Missions		
Angurugu	604	54.6
Daly River	192	60.9
Galiwinku	1234	49.4
Goulburn Island	222	38.7
Hermannsburg	241	33.1
Milingimbi	970	49.2
Minjilang	232	35.8
Nguiu (Bathurst Island)	902	41.0
Numbulwar	345	45.2
Oenpelli	584	52.6
Port Keats	853	47.2
Santa Teresa	639	44.9
Yirrkala	813	54.7
Government settlements		
Amoonguna[c]	233	60.1
Areyonga	259	42.1
Bagot[c]	539	32.6
Bamyili	494	49.1
Beswick	112	42.9
Borroloola	208	49.5
Delissaville	196	45.9
Docker River	164	38.4
Garden Point	179	46.4
Haasts' Bluff	82	43.9
Hooker Creek	515	38.4
Iwupataka	156	46.2
Maningrida	1289	47.6
Ngukurr (Roper River)	459	46.8
Papunya	548	42.8
Snake Bay	247	43.3
Umbakumba	366	53.8
Warrabri	616	49.2
Wave Hill	139	43.9
Yuendumu	980	38.6

[a] Estimate of Department of Aboriginal Affairs Northern Territory Division DAA (1975).
[b] Proportion of children to 1973 population.
[c] Town or 'special-purpose' reserves.
Source: Department of Aboriginal Affairs, Northern Territory Division (1975).

common) make any accurate estimate of their populations extremely difficult.

In general, therefore, the basic demographic characteristics of Aboriginal communities on government settlements and missions in remote Australia are as follows: the population is predominantly made up of Aborigines of full descent and is extremely young. In the Northern Territory Aborigines living in these communities represent over 60 per cent of the Territory's Aboriginal population. The geographic isolation of the communities has important ramifications, as later parts of this chapter show.

Health

The major aggregative health indicator available is infant mortality rates. It is noted in Chapter 1 that for the five years 1970–4 the infant mortality rate (per thousand live births) for Northern Territory Aborigines averaged 97.4 and by 1976 had declined to 52.8. Despite the decline, this figure compared most unfavourably with the 1974 rate for the total Australian population, which was 16.1. As Aborigines on settlements and missions form over 60 per cent of the Northern Territory Aboriginal population, these figures can be taken as indicative of infant mortality rates on the communities. The Senate Standing Committee on Social Environment (1975, p. 34) presented figures for 1965–7 which can only be described as shocking. The infant (under one year of age) mortality rate (per thousand live births) on missions at that time stood at 161 and on settlements at 144. Mortality rates during the second year of life were 41 for mission children and 63 for settlement children. This means that over 20 per cent of children born on missions and settlements in the Northern Territory from 1965 to 1967 died before reaching the age of two. The corresponding figure for the whole of Australia was less than 2 per cent. Moodie (1973, p. 62) calculated that a Northern Territory Aboriginal child had one chance in two of dying before the age of 25, whereas the average Australian baby had one chance in two of dying before the age of 71. These figures are not meant to suggest that there are no variations in infant mortality rates within the Territory. Middleton and Francis (1976, p. 17) suggest that these rates are higher at Papunya and Yuendumu (Northern Territory) than in the north, owing to greater isolation from medical resources and to climatic factors. They report that, of all babies born alive at Yuendumu from 1953 to 1970, 16 per cent died before the age of one.

Statistics such as these are not, however, confined to the Northern Territory communities. Jose *et al.* (1969) examined infant mortality on nine DAIA settlements and missions in northern Queensland (as well as three communities in settled Queensland) and reported mortality rates six times the Queensland average. A similar observation was made by the 1971 Annual Report of the QIMR. A recent DAA publication (DAA, 1977a, p. 19) gives the figures (presented in Table 17) for infant mortality rates for nine communities in remote Queensland.

Table 17. *Aboriginal infant mortality rates in nine communities in remote Queensland, 1972–4*

	Infant mortality rate (per 1,000 births)		
	1972	1973	1974
Bloomfield River	NA	NA	166.7
Doomadgee	90.9	129.0	64.5
Edward River	200.0	76.9	285.7
Hope Vale	NA	166.7	NA
Kowanyama	90.9	NA	NA
Lockhart River	66.7	300.0	NA
Mornington Island	NA	47.6	120.0
Palm Island	62.5	151.5	81.6
Weipa	NA	NA	100.0

Source: Department of Aboriginal Affairs (1977a).

W. D. Scott and Co. (hereafter Scott) (1971b, p. 6.1) reported that the infant mortality rate for Aborigines residing in the North West Reserve of South Australia was eleven times the South Australian average. The QIMR (1973) conducted a longitudinal study of two remote communities in Queensland. The mean expectation of life at birth at Edward River was 42.8 years for males and 57.9 years for females between 1940 and 1969. At Kowanyama between 1947 and 1972 it was 54.1 years for males and 57.9 years for females. The corresponding figure for Australia for 1962 was 67.9 for males and 74.2 for females. A number of commentators have pointed to the similarity between the patterns of childhood mortality in Aboriginal remote communities and those in very poor developing countries where food is scarce, hygiene poor and disease prevalent. Middleton and Francis (1976, p. 17) note that the infant mortality rate for Yuendumu (to 1970) was higher than that reported for any whole country by the United Nations Statistical Yearbook for 1969.

The major medical causes of death of Aboriginal children appear to be fairly consistent throughout remote Australia. They are respiratory diseases, gastro-enteritis (diarrhoeal diseases) and malnutrition. Middleton and Francis (1976, pp. 17–18) reported that 35.3 per cent of infant deaths in their sample were caused by respiratory disease, 22 per cent by gastro-enteritis and 6.7 per cent by malnutrition. A combination of gastro-enteritis and respiratory diseases accounted for 66 per cent of diagnosed causes of death. Jose *et al.* (1969, p. 83) found that 50 per cent of infant deaths were caused by gastro-enteritis and pneumonia. The proportions vary somewhat, but the causes of infant death appear the same in Queensland (QIMR. 1973), South Australia (Scott 1971b) and Central Australia (Kirke, 1969).

The very high infant mortality rates are, however, only part of the story. Infant morbidity is also severe. This refers to the effects in later life of health problems suffered at an early age, and include physical or sense incapacitation, diminished educability, and susceptibility to disease. The consequences of infant morbidity may be experienced over a lifetime.

Kirke (1969, p. 1005) suggests that subnormal growth results from malnutrition, infection, or both, while normal growth implies the absence of both. Examining a large sample of 870 children under 5 years of age in Central Australia, he found that height and weight indices were significantly below normal trends. Jose and Welch (1970, p. 349) reported similar abnormal growth patterns for Aboriginal children on twelve Queensland communities. They noted growth retardation in up to 50 per cent of their sample of children aged 6 months to 3 years. Sixteen per cent of their sample of 2,250 children experienced severe retardation and exhibited the height and weight measurements of a Caucasian child half their age. Jose *et al.* (1969, pp. 83–6) reported that chronic and recurrent infection of nasal sinuses, throat, middle ear and lower respiratory tract were further causes of morbidity (the ear infections often resulting in deafness). The QIMR (1971), clinically examining a sample of 640 Aboriginal children between the ages of 3 months and 16 years, found a marked retardation of growth. Infections of the upper respiratory tract, ear and skin were common, being diagnosed in 17.9 per cent, 9.7 per cent and 15.5 per cent of the sample respectively. Chest infection (3.8 per cent) was also relatively common.

In 1972, the QIMR (1972, p. 17) estimated that 20 per cent of children on remote communities in Queensland exhibited significant growth retardation. Jose *et al.* (1975, p. 699) examined 235 children at Papunya and found that 35 per cent had clinically active ear disease and 48 per cent had respiratory infections.

The evidence (to which *Medical Journal of Australia* has devoted much space) is overwhelming – infant mortality and morbidity are tragically excessive in Aboriginal communities in remote areas.

Among the complex causes of poor health, malnutrition must surely be counted as one of the most important. In north Queensland (Aurukun and Doomadgee) Jose and Welch have noted (1970, p. 354) that controlled nutrition resulted in normal growth patterns among children. Jose *et al.* (1975, p. 700) suggest that severe protein–calorie malnutrition (PCM) is not common among Aboriginal children, by standards of international comparison, but that moderate PCM affects from 10 to 60 per cent of children under five years of age in remote communities. Certainly, growth retardation appears to be caused more by malnutrition than by infection.

In the light of the statistics mentioned above, it may come as a surprise to add that medical facilities are provided to all the communities concerned. Most Queensland missions and settlements have a hospital (DAIA, 1976, pp. 24–8) and most government settlements and missions in the Northern Territory have both a hospital and an infant clinic. Doctors visit communities at regular three-week intervals, and teams of nurses and dentists pay periodic calls. Urgent medical cases can be evacuated to hospitals in larger urban areas through the Aerial Medical or the Flying Doctor Services. But if medical services seem adequate, this is only nominally and superficially so. Firstly, nurses and aides are generally so fully occupied as to be unable to undertake health education and training. Secondly, there seems to be a high turnover of staff, so that adequate nurse–patient communication rarely develops. Strang (1970, pp. 948–50) has pointed to the difficulty of obtaining patient co-operation in a cross-cultural situation – often patients do not comprehend the purpose of the treatment which they undergo. Interestingly, however, as mentioned in Chapter 4, there seems, with the policy of 'self-determination', to have been a reaffirmation of the role of the traditional Aboriginal doctor.

Another area which is currently the subject of the House of Representatives Standing Committee on Aboriginal Affairs (1977) is that of alcohol and its effect on adult health. While no study has adequately quantified the effect of alcohol on Aboriginal communities in remote Australia, qualitative comments suggest that this is a severe problem. For example, the House of Representatives report on Yirrkala (1975, p. 69) noted that 'A serious social problem facing the people of Yirrkala is the excessive consumption of alcohol.' The House of Representatives interim report (1977) on the alcohol problem of Aborigines noted (p. xi) that 'alcohol is the greatest threat to the Aboriginals of the Northern Territory and unless strong immediate action is taken they could destroy themselves'.

Housing

During the past fifteen or so years State governments have built 'transitional' housing for Aborigines on government settlements and missions. This was intended to serve Aboriginal families until they were able, with the acquisition of greater earning capacity through training in skilled occupations, to graduate to 'conventional' (European) housing. Houses were, it seems, designed, located and built without consultation with those who were to inhabit them; and the Senate Select Committee on Aborigines and Torres Strait Islanders (1976, p. 174) has gone so far as to suggest that the term 'transitional' was only a euphemism for substandard. In any event, 'transitional' housing is semi-permanent but today (1977) represents the bulk of houses occupied by Aboriginal people.

Transitional housing is in three 'stages'. Most of the primary (or stage 1) transitional houses are rudimentary one-room shelters of approximately 12 sq. metres in size. They are made of aluminium and have concrete slab floors with a wide verandah on three sides. These houses have no electrical or water connections, and occupants are expected to use communal toilet, ablution and dining facilities. Standard (or stage 2) transitional houses have two rooms, individual water and electrical connections and elementary facilities (a wood stove) for preparing meals. Stage 3 houses are 'conventional', fully equipped and connected houses similar in design and standard to Housing Commission units.

The shortage of Aboriginal housing accommodation on government settlements and missions has always been severe and in an effort to improve both the standard and number of houses, 'transitional' houses have ceased to be constructed since 1975 while, from 1971, Aboriginal Housing Societies have been formed. Grants have been made to these societies for the construction of housing consistent with features desired by Aboriginal people themselves. By the middle of 1976, 157 of these societies were in operation, funded by the Commonwealth Government Aboriginal Advancement Trust Account. About half of the societies are in the Northern Territory and remote Queensland, Western Australia and South Australia. Despite these efforts, the Senate Select Committee (1976, p. 199) estimated that there was an assessed demand for 6,167 houses in Australia by the societies, of which, perhaps, one-half would be in remote regions. An indication of the backlog involved may be gauged by noting that between 1972 and mid-1976, Housing Societies had sponsored the completed construction of only 501 houses, with 286 more under way, for a total expenditure of $48 million. The Committee also noted an outstanding need for 18,754 houses by Aborigines throughout Australia in 1976.

The proportion of improvised dwellings (humpies) to private dwellings occupied by Aborigines gives an indication of the housing needs of remote communities. In 1971 (according to census data) 65.4 per cent of houses occupied by Aborigines in the Northern Territory were impoverished. In the Kimberley region of Western Australia this figure was 60.4 per cent, in the far north of South Australia 72.7 per cent, and in the north-west of Queensland 22.7 per cent. The corresponding figure for the whole of Australia was less than 1 per cent.

The above statistics reveal an acute shortage of adequate housing for Aborigines in remote Australia. There are, however, rather wide variations in standards between communities. Middleton and Francis (1976. pp. 48–55) describe very poor housing conditions among the people of Yuendumu (Northern Territory), with a high density of inhabitants per house and hopelessly inadequate ablution and washing facilities. These authors commented (p. 55) that 'the people of Yuendumu thus lived in conditions that by the standards of the wider Australian society would be described as even worse than an "extreme slum".' Similarly the QIMR (1972, 1973) reports very poor housing conditions for Edward River and Kowanyama. On the other hand, Long (1970, p. 158) in describing houses at a resettled community at Weipa commented on the good standards and suggested that 'without any doubt the Weipa community was the best-housed Aboriginal community in North Australia'.

But in summary it is clear that both the quality and availability of Aboriginal housing is sorely wanting in the government settlements and missions of remote Australia. This deficiency has been com-

»ounded by a failure to cater for the traditional family and cultural
ıeeds of the Aboriginal people (for example, local customs were often
gnored in locating houses, and this has been known to precipitate
'arious social tensions). As the Senate Standing Committe (1975,p. 62)
ıoted, it seems useless to construct housing if its physical environment
s unsuited for the pattern of Aboriginal ways.

:ducation

\ll government settlements and missions have schools at least at a
ırimary level. But as the Senate Standing Committee (1975, p. 48)
ommented, many school buildings for Aborigines in remote areas
vould be regarded as totally unacceptable to Europeans. The (1977)
Commission of Inquiry into Poverty's figures also suggest poor school
ıttendance rates, as indicated by Table 18.

Table 18. *School enrolment and attendance in
some special schools in the Northern Territory,
June 1974*

Location	Attendance as percentage of enrolment
Croker Island	77
Angurugu	67
Amoonguna	65
Milingimbi	75
Hooker Creek	66
Yirrkala	48
Oenpelli	61
Papunya	42

Source: Commission of Inquiry into Poverty and
Education (1977).

Statistics on educational attendance and attainment are usually
ziven by State. While only the Northern Territory is entirely within
'emote Australia, there is probably little reason to suppose that details
ın the Territory would differ greatly from the remote regions of South
\ustralia, Western Australia and Queensland. According to the
Commission of Inquiry into Poverty (1977, pp. 156–89) only 11.3 per
'ent of the Aboriginal population aged 10–19 years in the Territory was

enrolled for secondary school; and, whereas in 1966 2.9 per cent of
Aboriginal males in the Northern Territory had attended school
beyond level 6 compared with 67.9 per cent of all non-Aboriginal
Australians, this figure had improved by 1971 to 5.9 per cent for
Aborigines (and 73.5 per cent for non-Aboriginal Australians). The
Commission of Inquiry into Poverty (1977, p. 190) also noted that of the
school age (5–14 years) Aboriginal population in the Northern Terri
tory in 1973, only 83 per cent had enrolled for schooling. Of the total
Northern Territory Aboriginal population, only one person had en
rolled for university and seventeen for teachers' colleges. (Moreover in
interpreting these figures, it should be borne in mind that a disparity
may exist – especially at the school level – between the enrolment and
participation rates.)

As discussed by the Commission of Inquiry into Poverty (1977), a
number of aspects seem to act against a good educational performance
by Aborigines (in remote areas and elsewhere). Some of these no
doubt relate to the universal problems of learning in a setting of
poverty where study facilities, especially in the home, are scarcely
encouraging, and where malnutrition and ill health debilitate stu
dents. But others are of a cultural kind. For example, while the great
majority of pupils in settlement and mission schools are Aborigines
the teaching method has encouraged competition, individualism, and
punctuality with little attention to traditional Aboriginal values such a
mutual support and co-operation. This conflict of values often appear
to lead to parental antipathy towards school, making good school
performances by children especially difficult. However, this form of
problem is being addressed by new developments since 1972, includ
ing bilingual programmes and extension of the idea of 'self
determination' to education.

Employment opportunities

There are two main problems in discussing employment opportunities
for Aborigines in remote Australia: (1) many on missions and settle
ments do not appear to register as unemployed (especially those
involved in seasonal employment); and (2) comment on occupational
status is difficult since, as previously mentioned, Aborigines are
involved in a great diversity of occupations including traditional
economic activity, which are hard to fit into concepts of unem
ployment or underemployment.

The Report of the Interdepartmental Working Party on Aboriginal Employment (DAA, 1976c, p. 1) estimated that 50 per cent of the Aboriginal work force is unemployed. Discussions with the DAA suggest that these estimates may be conservative for remote areas. A survey conducted in the Northern Territory in January 1976 by community advisers of the DAA indicated that the number of unemployed Aborigines could be as many as four times the number registered with the Commonwealth Employment Service. The Employment Section of the DAA estimated in mid-1976 that the number of unemployed Aborigines in the States was between 15 and 30 per cent greater than the numbers registered. Certainly the situation in the north of Queensland appears to bear this assertion out. The results of a DAA survey completed late in 1976 are given in Table 19.

Table 19. *Estimated unemployment rates in remote Queensland communities, 1976*

Community	Unemployment rate (per cent)
Aurukun	70
Bloomfield	85
Doomadgee	60
Edward River	70
Hope Vale	65
Kowanyama	70
Lockhart River	80
Palm Island	70–80
Weipa	65

Source: Unpublished data from DAA Survey of Queensland aboriginal Communities, Department of Aboriginal Affairs, Canberra, 1976.

These figures indicate a crude unemployment rate (that is, the percentage of the adult population – not work force – unemployed) averaging about 70 per cent. The estimates do not differ greatly from those made by Scott (1971b, p. 9.9), Anderson (1976, p. 3) or Peterson (1977, pp. 136–45). Data from Scott (1977b, p. 9.9) indicate that the unemployment rate at Amata in 1971 was 39 per cent, at Ernabella (Pukatja) 65 per cent and at Indulkana 58 per cent. Anderson (1976,

p. 3) estimates that only approximately 20 per cent of the potential work force of Yuendumu in 1975 was actively employed. Peterson (1977, pp. 136–45) estimated that at Docker River in 1970 only 50 per cent of the potential male work force was employed. At Warburton mission, this proportion was only 11 per cent, at Amata 32 per cent, and at Ernabella 36 per cent. These figures do not indicate solely unemployment – they also indicate the low participation in employment by Aborigines, and cannot reasonably be compared with the figures for Australia as a whole.

In analysing unemployment among Aborigines in remote regions, it seems useful (a) to exclude initially the role of government and quasi-government organisations and (b) to divide communities into three broad categories according to the predominant private sector employment in which Aborigines partake.

Private sector employment

As mentioned in Chapter 3, missions and settlements have served as a pool of cheap labour for pastoralists. Aboriginal men have found employment as stockmen and general hands, and Aboriginal women have been employed as domestic servants. The labour-exporting missions and settlements are generally located in the 'more settled' regions of remote Australia. In north Queensland, as Long (1970, p. 153) found, this employment tends to be of a contractual seasonal nature, and there is great variation in the type of work and in the mode of travel to undertake it. Long noted that 'Almost all the workers left and returned to Doomadgee by air, though many travelled from Cloncurry onwards to their employment by train, all fares being met by the employers.' The labour-exporting community also exists in Western Australia in the Kimberley region (Scott, 1971a, pp. 10.18 – 10.22) with Aborigines being employed predominantly on pastoral stations, but also finding some irregular employment in towns. Tonkinson (1974, p. 33) reported that residents of Jigalong mission in the centre of Western Australia (on the desert fringe) found seasonal employment on pastoral stations. Scott (1971b, pp. 9.1–9.7) reported similar migrations of Aborigines for employment purposes from the North-West Reserve region of South Australia. The main feature of this type of employment is that Aborigines leave their communities for prolonged periods in search of work, which is usually of an unskilled or semi-skilled nature.

The second category includes missions and settlements that are adjacent to large Australian or multinational mining concerns and where Aborigines are employed as labourers or semi-skilled personnel. A small number of extremely remote missions and settlements have come into sudden prolonged contact with the Western world owing to discoveries of mineral resources on or near Aboriginal reserves. The major discoveries to date have been bauxite at Gove in the Arnhem Land and at Weipa in the far north of Queensland, and manganese at Groote Eylandt off the Arnhem Land coast. Large extractive plants have been established by Nabalco, Comalco and GEMCo (Groote Eylandt Mining Company–a subsidiary of BHP) respectively. The communities that have suddenly found these companies on their doorstep (literally in some cases) are Yirrkala mission at Gove, Weipa and Aurukun in Queensland, and Angurugu mission and Umbakumba on Groote Eylandt. There are two major differences between this type of situation and the previous one. Firstly, employment opportunities have come to Aborigines rather than vice versa. Secondly, the type of employment available is of an industrial rather than agricultural nature.

The final category encompasses communities that have almost no private sector employment opportunities in the European sense of the word. These communities tend to be the more geographically remote, and as a direct function of this, more traditionally orientated. There is no labour market, and they could be called 'closed' or 'semi-closed' communities (in the employment sense) in so far as all economic activity is 'within' the community. The economic activities in which Aborigines in these communities participate are of three types. Firstly, there is the manufacture of Aboriginal artefacts for sale in the market economy – a type of cottage industry that is using traditional Aboriginal skills. Secondly, they partake in what could be termed neo-traditional subsistence activity – the utilisation of European technology (motor vehicles, rifles, and so on) for hunting and gathering. And finally, there is some commercial activity which is usually initially subsidised by the government. Examples of this type of activity are the commercial fishing venture at Maningrida, copper and chrysoprase mining at Yuendumu and Docker River, and the operation of tourist facilities at Iwupataka, and brick-making at Yirrkala. Many missions and settlements operate cattle-raising ventures which provide only a handful of employment opportunities.

These broad categories of employment generalise the major types of employment in which Aborigines participate, and the categories are not mutually exclusive. For example, at Yirrkala, Aborigines work for Nabalco, are engaged in a highly successful artefact industry and operate a small-scale brick-making factory.

Despite the employment mentioned, not one Aboriginal community in remote Australia is self-supporting economically, and in no community is there full employment. The availability of jobs for Aborigines in remote areas is limited because most economic activity there is land-intensive. As will be discussed in Chapter 3, Aborigines have traditionally been employed in the pastoral industry since the nineteenth century, but the number employed has decreased in recent years, due to a variety of factors including no doubt the introduction of award wages for Aborigines and the recession in the industry since 1970.

In the mining industry, opportunities have arisen for the employment of Aborigines, with most but by no means all companies being willing to employ Aborigines and Europeans on the same basis. Turner (1974, p. 169) examined the records of GEMCo from 1964 to 1969 and found that Aborigines averaged longer consecutive periods of employment than whites. These records also revealed that Aborigines tended to hold the manual occupations while whites were concentrated in the skilled and semi-skilled jobs. The only comparative disadvantage of Aborigines, according to the GEMCo employers, was their high rate of absenteeism. The company, however, was happy to employ Aborigines especially from closeby Angurugu mission and from Umbakumba settlement and Numbulwar mission on the mainland.

Rogers (1973) examined the participation of Aborigines in the mining industry and found (p. 133) that in 1968, only 193 Aborigines were employed by 23 major mining companies (throughout Australia). Rogers remarked (p. 133) that 'the bulk of Aborigines had failed to win full acceptance by fellow workers or employers as a permanent part of the workforce. Fundamentally, this was because Aborigines were generally unprepared for the opportunities they were given. They lacked an industrial background, had poor education, were mostly untrained and did not receive adequate training in employment.' Comalco Ltd (1976, p. 18) suggested that it had attempted to provide employment for as many people as possible at Weipa but that difficulties were encountered from the start – especially absenteeism without notice. Many of the mining companies in remote Australia predominantly drew their (non-Aboriginal) labour from other parts of the country rather than use the locally available work force. In general, companies do not often appear willing to modify their work patterns to suit Aborigines, and prefer to import white labour.

In independently generated economic activity, Aborigines appear to be severely constrained. The artefact industry is hampered by depleted resources of raw materials close to missions and settlements and by a lack of effective market linkage and/or demand for produce. Hunting and gathering activity is similarly constrained by resource depletion and in most communities this is seen as a form of leisure rather than a form of employment (even though the food obtained from such activity is popular). Independent commercial activity is constrained by lack of capital and skills, especially of an entrepreneurial nature.

Public sector employment

The bulk of employment available to Aborigines on settlements and missions is in the service sector and is financed by government, either directly or indirectly through mission or settlement authorities. Funds are now often channelled through community Aboriginal Councils. The great majority of employment opportunities are provided through internal services and these are almost entirely financed by subsidies and transfers from the Federal government. It is for this reason that these communities have often been dubbed 'dependent economies'. The inflow of public authority funds is the main generator of economic activity.

Prior to 1969, economic activity for settlement authorities (government agents) or mission authorities (quasi-government) was not paid for by a cash wage. Payment was primarily in kind – free accommodation and rations, with a small supplementary cash allowance ($7.20 per week was the minimum in 1969 on government settlements in the Northern Territory) or 'pocket money' being the only wage received in hand. In February 1969, the Federal government introduced the Training Allowance Scheme in the Northern Territory. The motives for the introduction of this scheme were numerous. Firstly, it was felt that there was a need to rectify the extremely paternalistic nature of the in-kind system of payment. Secondly, it was hoped that the payment of a money wage to individuals would give them experience in the management of resources and a greater sense of responsibility. Finally, it was hoped that the payment of cash wages would provide an incentive for 'advancement' – that is, a conversion to a European–Australian work ethic. An improvement in work skills was supposedly an integral part of this 'advancement' and was to be provided to Aborigines under this scheme.

The Training Allowance Scheme was successful in that many Aborigines sought employment through it. As unemployment benefits were not available to Aborigines who resided on missions and settlements, for many of them training allowances were the only available source of cash income. By the middle of 1973, when the scheme was at its zenith, over 4,000 Aborigines in the Northern Territory were receiving training allowances – there was a drift to missions and settlements from pastoral properties, towns and bush (nomadic) communities. Turner (1974, p. 178) suggested that when, in August 1969, the Training Allowance Scheme was extended to include mission-sponsored communities, mission staff vigorously encouraged Aborigines to take part in it. If the aim of the scheme was to encourage Aborigines to work for wages, then it was certainly more successful than the pre-1969 government employment-training programme. Apart from the Northern Territory, the scheme was also introduced on government settlements in South Australia (Scott, 1971b, p. 9.8) and during this period mission communities in Western Australia and Queensland were also modifying their form of payment of wages – from in-kind to cash.

There were however, also a number of disadvantages associated with the scheme. The Senate Standing Committee on Social Environment (1975, p. 52) went so far as to suggest that 'The scheme was just a disguised form of handout.' The basic problem with the scheme was that vocational training facilities and staff were not available on settlements and missions. The 'Training' Allowance Scheme therefore degenerated into being a euphemism for low pay for low-status work. The level of pay was low because the provisions of the scheme only allowed for the payment of wages well below the award rate. In 1968/69, the minimum award wage rate in the Northern Territory was $40.15 per week, whereas wages under the Training Allowance Scheme at its inception in 1969 started at a base of $25 per week – 62 per cent of the award. There were margins for skill built into the scheme, but the highest training allowance payable was still below the award – $36 per week. In 1972, training allowances increased to a minimum of $28.75 per week and a maximum of $41.50, but by this time the award wage minimum had increased to $53.20 and parity between the two rates had slipped. When in May 1973 the minimum award wage increased to $62.20 per week, parity had slipped further still. According to details on file at the DAA, indications are that the majority of trainees received the lowest allowance, and performed low-status work for this allowance – for example, most Education Department trainees were involved in cleaning classrooms and gardening, and most Health Department trainees were engaged in cleaning hospitals and clinics. Trainees had a definite second-class worker status – they were assistants who had no chance (unless they left settlements) of progressing to the award wage level.[1] Trainees (for example teaching aides) often worked alongside whites for similar hours but without award wages. This appeared to have a negative effect on work effort.

In December 1973, the Labor government decided to terminate this scheme, owing to the inequity of wage rates. In the Northern Territory over 1,000 award wage positions were created for Aborigines by the Public Service Board for the maintenance of settlement communities, including health, education and other services. Approximately 500 positions were created for mission communities. Town Management and Public Utility (TMPU) grants were made to communities to create employment. The Training Allowance Scheme was phased out by October 1974, and Aborigines who were unemployed (over 2,500) and living on settlements or missions were then theoretically able to receive unemployment benefits. The pattern of moving Aborigines off training allowances (discriminatory wages) and on to award rates has been a recent feature of Aboriginal employment at all remote communities except those in northern Queensland.

There is also a tendency for the DAA to withdraw employment opportunities and transfer these to other government departments – such as the Departments of Health, Education, Social Security, and Construction. This tendency is associated with the twin tenets of 'self-determination' and equal treatment of Aborigines.

To conclude this section, some case studies may be mentioned to give an idea of the extent of government subsidisation in the employment field. Scott (1971b) examined the source of employment of males

---

[1] Duncan (1974, p. 55) suggested that wage rates on DAIA and mission-sponsored communities in the Torres Straits Region generally were below the award rates payable on the mainland. On the other hand, the effort of work required was not testing.

and females in the North-West Reserve Region of South Australia. They found (pp. 9.2 – 9.7) that 25 per cent of jobs were provided by the Department of Social Welfare and Aboriginal Affairs (State government), 40 per cent by mission authorities (government subsidised) and 9 per cent by the Education Department. Of the remainder (26 per cent), 14 per cent were self-employed in artefact manufacture and 7 per cent were employed on surrounding stations. The balance were involved in 'other' employment. Coombs and Stanner (1974, p. 15) found that, in 1974, of the 170 employed males and females at Yuendumu, 108 were employed by the DAA, 22 by the Education Department and 9 by the Health Department, that is, 82 per cent of employment originated in these three government departments. At Hooker Creek, of 105 employed persons, 74 were found to be employed by the DAA, 13 by the Education Department and 7 by the Health Department. Ninety per cent of employment was provided by government. Anderson (1976, p. 9) suggested that almost all employment at Yuendumu in 1975 arose from the government sector. (These figures compare rather dramatically with those for the general Australian society. The Employment and Unemployment publication (ABS, 1977b, p. 3) provides data which indicate that, in the 1970s, approximately 30 per cent of all Australians were employed by the public sector, and the majority (70 per cent) were in the private sector.)

By 1975, the method of Aboriginal community subsidisation, but not the extent, had changed somewhat. Government departments still provided employment opportunities directly through the Departments of Health, Education, and so on, but there were also direct lump sum grants to communities for Town Management (municipal services), Aboriginal Enterprises, and Special Work Projects. The extent of these grants is such that substantial unemployment still remains once grants have been disbursed at award rates. A recent DAA initiative which is still only at the pilot programme stage was introduced in mid-1977. This is the Community Development Employment Project (CDEP) Scheme. The basis of this scheme is to pool funds from unemployment benefits paid to Aborigines in remote communities and to provide part-time employment with these funds, sometimes at award rates. The motives for this scheme (DAA, 1977d, p. 1) appear partly to be social – to alleviate problems arising from drunkenness and violence in communities. The scheme basically aims to provide regular part-time work, periodic full-time specified jobs and regular or periodic contractual work. The flexibility inherent in this scheme seems useful.

(In Appendix II, a model is presented which indicates that an economic justification may also exist for this scheme.)

The pilot scheme has been successful at Bamyili in the Northern Territory and in the 1977/78 fiscal year has been (or will be) extended to Ernabella and Fregon communities in South Australia, to Warburton in Western Australia and to certain other remote communities. However, whereas initially it was felt that the opportunity cost of the scheme would be minimal (since once a community decides to join the scheme, the payment of unemployment benefits to residents ceases) this does not appear to be so. More people are seeking work at award rates than was expected. The important difference between this scheme and the Training Allowance Scheme is that the local Aboriginal Council decides whether the community wants to participate or not. While a number of communities in the Northern Territory have indicated a strong interest in the scheme, budget stringency at the federal level has so far curtailed its expansion.

Household income levels

This section has four objects: (1) to examine the available estimates of disposable income per capita for remote communities and compare these with figures for Australia as a whole; (2) to point out some possible shortcomings of these estimates and discuss the conceptual difficulties involved in using National Account type estimates as indicators of economic activity and status in remote Australia; (3) to examine the economic impact of the government sector by estimating the proportion of community incomes arising in this sector; and (4) to examine the proportion of income that is made up of employment, as against non-employment, income.

The only estimates of different community incomes are presented in Table 20. The major features of this table are that annual per capita disposable income in the case studies examined varies from $119 for Warburton in 1970 (Peterson, 1977, p. 140) to $1080 for Papunya in 1974/75 (DAA, 1977b, p. 16). As proportions of the Australia-wide per capita household disposable income, these two figures form a minimum (7 per cent for the former) and a maximum (35 per cent for the latter). Indications are that as a proportion of average national disposable income per head, Aboriginal community incomes are rising but are still only in the vicinity of one-quarter to one-third the size of the national figure.

Table 20. *Estimates of annual disposable income on various
government settlements and missions in 'remote' Australia*

Community	Per capita cash income[a] ($)	Australia-wide disposable income per capita[a] ($)	Aboriginal as percentage of Australian disposable income
Docker River (1970)	375	1739	22
Warburton (1970)	119	1739	7
Amata (1970)	311	1739	18
Ernabella (1970)	220	1739	13
Yuendumu (1970)	305	1739	18
Amata (1970/71)	276	1739	16
Ernabella (1970/71)	198	1739	11
Indulkana (1970/71)	224	1739	13
Kowanyama (1972) (Mitchell River)	295	1880	16
Edward River (1972)	485	1880	26
Kowanyama (1973)	460	2138	22
Amata (1974)	624	2543	25
Yuendumu (1974)	480	2543	19
Hooker Creek (1974)	576	2543	23
Papunya (1974/75)	1080	3099	35
Yuendumu (1974/75)	743	3099	24
Yirrkala (1976)	1054	3506	30

[a] Except for the 1974/75 estimates, these figures are presented with
the utmost reservation for they are based on study periods of only two
to four weeks.
[b] Total household disposable income divided by total population.
Note that these are for the respective fiscal (June) years – 1970/71
and so on.
Sources: Anderson (1976); Australian Bureau of Statistics (1977c);
Brokensha (1974); Coombs and Stanner (1974); Department of
Aboriginal Affairs (1977b, e); Middleton and Francis (1976); Peterson
(1977); Queensland Institute of Medical Research (1972, 1973, 1974);
Scott (1971b); and Data Bank of the Institute of Applied Economic and
Social Research, Melbourne.

To gauge changes in Aborigines' incomes in real terms is difficult, for
the only inflator available is the Consumer Price Index. This index was
designed to calculate changes in the cost of living in urban areas.
Hence it is used here with some reservation. However, in real terms, it

appears that recent estimates (Anderson, 1976; DAA, 1977b, e) represent only slight improvements in real per capita disposable income over the earlier estimate (Middleton and Francis, 1976; Peterson, 1977).

The extremely low level of income of Aborigines who reside on settlements and missions can hardly be regarded with surprise. As has been made abundantly clear, levels of employment are extremely low, and even when work is available it tends to be of a low occupational rank commanding a low wage rate. It must also be recalled that an important demographic feature of the Aboriginal population resident on these communities is that the proportion of the population under 15 years of age is extremely high (say in the 44–8 per cent range) and this results in a high dependency ratio and tends to lower per capita incomes. Certainly, the disposable income estimates of Table 20 appear more akin to those of poor 'developing' countries than those of a rich 'developed' economy.

The reliability of these estimates, particularly the earlier ones, can be questioned, mainly because some were conducted over short observation periods ranging from two to four weeks (which are periods too short to be very reliable), and others (for example, Middleton and Francis, 1976) used only 'target' groups within communities. The sampling error that may have resulted could be high especially with seasonal employment and other irregular sources of income, while the possibly poor communication between researcher and subject is also important. Owing to these irregularities, some researchers (for example Middleton and Francis, 1976) did not estimate income earned by households outside the community (on pastoral stations) or personal remittances that may eventuate. Most did not enumerate such sources of income as interest or changes in bank deposits during study periods, although admittedly these must have been small. One can therefore assume that most of the figures presented here are slight underestimates.

There are two further problems inherent in using a Western-type income indicator for these communities. Firstly, subsistence activities have not been included in any of the estimates. Most studies (for example Coombs, 1972; Tonkinson, 1974; and Turner, 1974) of Aboriginal communities in remote regions report some hunting and gathering activity. Tonkinson (1974, pp. 59–60) suggested that traditional meats (kangaroo and emu) are more popular than introduced meats (such as beef and mutton) at Jigalong. He also reported women gathering yams, wild fruit and grass seeds during certain parts of the year. Since every case study of remote communities mentions some traditional or 'neo-traditional' economic activity being pursued, this implies that these should be included in income estimates as imputed income. The extent of these activities is difficult to estimate, but the DAA (1977b, p. 18) suggests that at Papunya 10–15 per cent of food may come from the bush and a similar figure can be estimated for Kowanyama from the Annual Report of the QIMR (1974, p. 23). While there is little doubt that traditional economic activity is of far greater importance for outstation communities, it is possible that for some communities, especially those in more fertile areas (for example, the Arnhem Land) income of this nature may be significant.

There is also a range of goods and services that is provided without charge or at nominal charge to community residents which could be regarded as income in kind. This is a contentious issue. Whether appropriate or not, housing, health and educational services are pro- vided free for Aborigines[1] and do constitute significant proportions of the expenditure of non-Aboriginal Australia.[2] Furthermore, as Coombs and Stanner (1974, p. 19) have suggested, the needs of Aborigines who have only received a cash income since 1969 are far more limited than those of white Australians – given the low standard of living of the former. Indications are that subsistence needs can be easily met by the above levels of income and a surplus in fact remains to be spent on 'luxury' (non-essential) items. But this is all in the context of facilities and services at missions and settlements which are very far below the standard regarded as 'generally acceptable' in Australia. Moreover, prices of most private sector goods and services in remote communities tend to be inflated, compared with elsewhere, because of transportation difficulties. Middleton and Francis (1976, p. 94) found that over a four-week observation period, the cost of foodstuffs for the Yuendumu community was 9 per cent higher than the same basket of goods at Alice Springs. Of 70 items, 48 were more expensive at Yuen-

[1] Other examples of in-kind income would be: subsidised or free beef for Aborigines living on missions or settlements that operate pastoral enterprises; no transportation cost to and from place of work, education and recreation, and so on.

[2] The recent Household Expenditure Survey 1974–5 (ABS, 1977a, p. 1) found that Australians on the lowest stratum of household income (less than $80 per week per household) spent 21 per cent of income on current housing costs, 5 per cent on fuel and power, and 12 per cent on education, health expenses and recreation – expenses that Aborigines on missions and settlements would not generally have to meet.

dumu, 12 had the same price and the remainder were more expensive at Alice Springs. An unpublished DAA study in 1973 compared the cost of 24 basic foodstuff items at Darwin, with prices at a number of Aboriginal communities in Arnhem Land. It found that, on average, in March 1972 the prices at communities were 5.4 per cent higher and in March 1973 prices were 6.3 per cent higher. Assuming, as seems realistic, that Darwin and Alice Springs prices are no lower than elsewhere in Australia, it appears, therefore, that Aborigines who are on extremely low incomes have to pay more for basic foodstuffs than Australians on average.

It would seem that while the estimates of disposable income above could be underestimates owing to the non-estimation of subsistence economic activity, this shortfall would only be slight, and one could safely estimate Aboriginal disposable income per capita to be no more than 35 per cent of the Australian average. It must be stressed, however, that this indicator, while representing a logical consequence of the demographic and social features of Aborigines residing on missions and settlements and of their low educational, housing and health status, cannot be given too much weight owing to conceptual difficulties in both its formation and comparison with the incomes of the wider society.

The questions about government-derived versus private sector-derived incomes, and non-employment versus employment incomes can be dealt with together. Both are indicators of the economic impact of the government sector on these communities.

The majority of missions and settlements are largely dependent on the government sector for their incomes – for, as discussed above, the only non-government income available to Aborigines is from work as station labourers in the pastoral industry, as workers in the mining industry, in artefact production and as seasonal itinerant labourers – either in small remote towns or as fruit pickers, and so on. The extent of this dependence on the government sector is borne out by all the case study data that are available. For example, Scott (1971b, p. 9.10) in their enumeration of sources of weekly incomes for Aboriginal communities in the North-West Reserve Region found that 2.3 per cent of income came from employment outside communities (in the pastoral industry and so on) and 13.7 per cent came from artefact production. The remaining 84 per cent came from government departments – 27.3 per cent as wages from the DAA for internal (menial) economic activity, 7.7 per cent from the Education Department, and the remaining 39 per

cent as Social Service payments – at that time (1970/71) being predominantly pensions and child endowments.

Peterson (1977, pp. 136–45) divided the incomes of people in Docker
River, Warburton, Amata and Ernabella into employment and non-
employment income. Forty-seven per cent of the incomes of these
communities came from employment (predominantly government-
subsidised), while 53 per cent came from non-employment income.
A very high standard deviation (26 per cent) indicated that large
inter-community differences in the predominance of different income
sources obtained. This variation is a function of the demographic
characteristics of communities, the extent of employment available,
and very often the attitudes of white administrators – if they choose to
help Aborigines (for example those who are illiterate) obtain non-
employment income, community incomes may be boosted considerably. The extent of these differences can be seen when examining the
Coombs and Stanner (1974, p. 32) estimate of monthly income at
Hooker Creek. Here, 12 per cent came from non-employment sources,
whereas 88 per cent came from employment sources – predominantly
in the form of Training Allowances. Interestingly enough, they estimated external sources of income as being nil. Anderson (1976, p. 10)
reported a similar breakdown for Yuendumu in 1975. Approximately
15 per cent of the income of this community came from non-
employment sources (now including unemployment benefits). Of
employment income, only about 1 per cent came from external sources
with the majority being financed by the DAA (directly, and indirectly
through Town Management grants to the municipal council), the
Department of Education and the Department of Health. It is interesting to note that over 10 per cent of incomes were provided by the
Housing Association.

Finally, the data from a recent DAA study (1977b), which has
attempted to derive the expenditure in Papunya in 1974/75 using a
National Accounts format, is relevant. Thirteen per cent of Aborigines'
income on this government settlement came from non-employment
sources, that is from a number of transfer payments which include
child endowment, widows' pensions, single mothers' benefits, old age
benefits, unemployment benefits and student grants (under the Secondary Grants Scheme). The bulk of income came from grants from
the DAA for Special Work Projects, Town Management Projects and
Housing Associations. Salaries and wages paid by the DAA and the
Departments of Education and Health also figured predominantly.

Only about 2 per cent of income came from artefact production. Perhaps the most striking statistic of this study is that, of the total direct income payments made at Papunya, just over 50 per cent went to resident and non-resident Europeans. (Of total transactions, 27 per cent were on material inputs.) The implications of this are twofold. Firstly, much government expenditure on Aboriginal communities may not in fact be received by the intended recipients in a direct form, and secondly, there is a large potential source of income (and employment opportunities) on Aboriginal communities if Aboriginal labour could be substituted for white labour.

Again, a comparison with Australia-wide figures gives some idea of the extreme dependence of Aborigines on the government sector. The Australian National Accounts (ABS, 1976b) indicated that of gross household salaries and wages in 1974/75, 66.39 per cent was paid by private enterprises and 33.61 per cent from the public sector. Social Indicators no. 1 (ABS, 1976a) enumerated household incomes by source for 1974/75. In that year, 79.5 per cent of income was derived from earned income (wages and salaries 68.9 per cent) and only 9.0 per cent was in the form of government transfers (the remaining 11.5 per cent coming from interest and dividends, rent, transfers from overseas, and third-party insurance transfers).

All these figures reinforce those presented in the employment section, and demonstrate the extent of the reliance of Aboriginal communities on the government sector compared with the Australian norm. The enumeration problems discussed above, especially the non-enumeration of imputed and external sources of income as well as interest income, may slightly overstate the extent of this dependence. Similarly, it must not be forgotten that in using a case study approach, large inter-community differences in the composition of household income occur which indicate a far from uniform pattern.

Household expenditure patterns

Given the extremely low levels of income that Aboriginal households on missions and government settlements appear to exhibit, it is of interest to the economist to examine how this income is spent. As Duncan (1974, p. 60) states 'Aggregate cash income in the case of the simple (Torres Strait) island economies comprises only two elements, expenditure and saving. Assessment of household expenditure is therefore not only valuable in its own right, but also because of the light it can throw on household savings.' Unfortunately, the household budget studies of communities that have been conducted are far from adequate. This is because they have been conducted either by social anthropologists who are only indirectly interested in expenditure patterns, or else by health researchers who have been primarily interested in food expenditure patterns only.

It is only since the late 1960s that Aborigines in remote Australia have had cash incomes large enough to say that they actually exhibited expenditure patterns. The anthropologists Brokensha (1974), Peterson (1977), Tonkinson (1974) and Turner (1974) each described community expenditure patterns which appear to have many similarities (although communities were in different States). Cash income appears to be used primarily to purchase basic subsistence foodstuffs – predominantly flour, beef, sugar, tea and rice. These are the European goods for which most Aborigines who resided on centralised settlements have developed tastes, for they are the rations which formed the bulk of in-kind payments (and maintenance payments) prior to 1969. Since the early 1970s it appears as though Aborigines' incomes have been adequate to cover these basic foodstuff needs and provide a surplus for other expenditure. Peterson (1977, p. 143) reported that in Central Australia in 1970, $2.50 per week per capita was adequate to buy these rations. Taylor (QIMR 1973, p. 27, and 1974, p. 22) reported that weekly food expenditure per capita at Edward River in 1970 was $2.13 and in 1972 was $2.67. At Kowanyama food expenditure was $2.30 in 1972 and $3.82 in 1973. Anderson (1976) suggested that $7.90 was spent on food at Yuendumu per capita per week in 1975.

There are two questions of interest here. Firstly, what proportion of total income is spent on foodstuffs, and how does this compare with Australia-wide figures, and secondly, how does the proportion of income spent on foodstuffs change as income increases? As a proportion of total income, the figures vary from nearly 100 per cent of income for Warburton in 1970 (Peterson, 1977, p. 144) to 29 per cent for Edward River in 1972 (QIMR, 1973, p. 27). Examination of the recently published Household Expenditure Survey 1974/75 (ABS, 1977a,) gives some idea of how Aboriginal expenditure patterns compare with all-Australia figures. The average Australian household spent $10.50 per capita per week on food and this represented 15.7 per cent of total income. Even when earlier figures are inflated by the Consumer Price Index, all-Australian 'real' per capita food expenditure was 2.0 to 2.5 times greater than that of Aborigines (in terms of money spent). Only

Anderson's Yuendumu figure ($7.90) approximates to the Australian figure (of which it was 25 per cent less) but at that community 55 per cent of income was spent on food (as against 15.7 per cent for the average Australian household). The quality of the foodstuffs that Aborigines buy will be discussed below.

One would assume that if Aborigines considered their diet inadequate, increases in income would be largely channelled into food expenditure. In fact it seems that Aborigines' expenditure patterns are such that food expenditure tends towards a fairly low saturation point. Turner (1974, p. 178) noted that as incomes at Angurugu mission increased rapidly (in 1969), food expenditure remained fairly static. Taylor (QIMR, 1973, p. 27) reported that incomes at Edward River from 1970 to 1972 almost doubled, yet per capita food expenditure increased only 22 per cent (from $2.18 to $2.67). Similarly at Kowanyama (QIMR, 1974, p. 22) incomes increased by 56 per cent from 1972 to 1973, yet the proportion spent on food remained almost constant. At Yuendumu, incomes rose by 14.7 per cent from the March to September quarters of 1975, and food expenditure increased from 55 per cent to 59 per cent of income. One proviso must be made with these figures. Aboriginal food expenditure may vary significantly depending on two factors – whether relatives (kin) may be visiting or not, and the time of year at which budget studies are conducted, for subsistence activity which provides some proportion of foods varies through the year. Also, it must be remembered that as Aborigines are often seasonally employed, incomes fluctuate, as does food expenditure.

Income that is not spent on foodstuffs will be spent on other goods and services for current consumption or on capital goods or assets. Tonkinson (1974, p. 59) suggested that a narrow range of durable goods are today regarded as necessities. He listed knives, axes, razors, plastic buckets, billy cans, blankets, canvas sheets, tools, matches, flash-lights, waterbags, soap and hair oil as steady sellers at the Jigalong mission store. Tobacco and alcohol are also European goods that are often popular. Taylor (QIMR, 1974, p. 23) noted that the introduction of a 'wet' canteen at Kowanyama in 1973 resulted in 24.2 per cent of total expenditure being on alcohol. Other current expenditure at Kowanyama was on 'other' (non-food) store sales (26.9 per cent), on rent and firewood (3.71 per cent), on court fines (4.7 per cent) and on theatre sales (1.5 per cent). Turner (1974, p. 178) reported that European clothes were popular items at the Angurugu mission store. It can be seen that Aboriginal current expenditure is primarily on foodstuffs, clothing, a limited range of durable goods, alcohol and tobacco. Rent is also a current expenditure item at some communities and petrol is becoming an increasingly important one.

Expenditure on alcohol in some Aboriginal communities is believed to be particularly high in a relative sense. In a recent report (DAA, 1977e) quantitative information on alcohol consumption at Groote Eylandt is presented. It was estimated (Appendix I) that Aboriginal members of Alyangula Club (near Angurugu mission) spent approximately $9.40 (equivalent to sixteen cans of beer) per day per person. Beer consumption at Umbakumba settlement where there is a wet canteen is lower than this as the local Aboriginal council has set a limit of seven cans of beer per person per day. The question of the causes and effects of such alcohol consumption levels is the subject of the House of Representatives Standing Committee on Aboriginal Affairs (1977). They reported (p.4) that in some communities (e.g. Bamyili, Garden Point and Snake Bay) the proportion spent on alcohol could be as high as 50 per cent of total weekly expenditure. These figures must be qualified, however. Firstly, as the Committee noted (p. 3) per capita expenditure on alcohol in the Northern Territory in general greatly exceeds that for the rest of Australia. Secondly, there is very little data on Aboriginal alcohol consumption, and the figures presented here could be atypical.

Any surplus income tends to be pooled and spent on a small range of assets – the most popular being motor vehicles. Traditionally Aborigines were mobile especially in desert regions and cars are today useful for visiting relatives, for ceremonial gatherings and for visiting sacred places. While ownership of a vehicle may be nominally vested in the name of one person, it often (owing to kinship obligations and/or pooled savings) becomes a community asset. Other assets that may be procured include rifles, musical instruments, radios and cassette recorders.

It is interesting that even though Aborigines' incomes are extremely low, positive rates of savings have been recorded. Anderson (1976, p. 11) reported bank savings at Yuendumu being approximately 5 per cent of total income. Taylor's (QIMR, 1974 p. 22) data indicate savings equivalent to 4.8 per cent of income at Kowanyama in 1973 and dissavings of −3.1 per cent of income at the same community in 1972 (QIMR, 1972). It is not possible to say much about savings patterns on the basis of this data.

The lack of budget studies makes generalisations about Aboriginal expenditure patterns on remote communities hazardous. There is however, little doubt that as more cash income has become available, Aborigines have become more interested in European goods. As Coombs and Stanner (1974, p. 32) noted, Aborigines' demands and expectations are rising as they emulate white consumption patterns, and there seems little doubt that even while subsistence needs can be met adequately, a feeling of poverty relative to aspirations is developing. This does not mean that consumption per se has suddenly become associated with status, but rather that Aborigines are recognising and desiring a wider range of useful European goods. That most goods which European Australians regard as basics are still seen as luxuries by many Aborigines in remote Australia, is an exemplification of both their relative and absolute poverty.

Finally, there is evidence that some Aborigines do not fully appreciate differences between foods that tend to be cheap and rich in carbohydrates and calories, and foods that are more expensive and rich in protein and vitamins. In Appendix III patterns of food expenditure on two Aboriginal communities are compared with Australian figures. These figures bear out this assertion. Aboriginal food expenditure tends to be concentrated on cheap poor-quality foods, and their intake of high-quality protein-rich food is indeed low. This explains to some extent the malnutrition referred to in the analysis of health conditions. Aborigines may consume adequate quantities of food, but of a quality not always conducive to good health.

Conclusion

This chapter has highlighted the very poor health, housing and educational conditions which pertain among Aborigines residing on government settlements and missions. These communities were established partly as a defence against their possible extinction. But while abandonment (however fostered) of the nomadic life-style has meant that traditional activities, such as hunting and gathering, have declined, employment opportunities in the 'European' private sector have not been bountiful, while those available in the public sector have been menial. Associated with menial jobs has been low income, and a great array of the problems amounting almost to a vicious cycle of poverty which are generally part of the economically poor nations of the world.

Government settlements and missions may initially have been

regarded as transitional communities where Aborigines could gradually adjust to a 'European' way of life before fuller assimilation. But as government policy has shifted towards self-determination, many communities have displayed a preference for continued but independent existence, rather than absorption in a wider society. This preference poses a dilemma, since economic viability seems difficult given the meagre resource bases of the missions and settlements which are sometimes in semi-desert regions. Heavy government subsidisation occurs both for the provision of social services and for income from transfer payments. Economic independence, even at the low levels of living experienced on settlements and missions today, seems difficult to visualise.

3

Remote Australia II: pastoral stations

(Stockmen) are a funny breed . . . they do not really need a day
off a week. If you have a day off and lay on your back you've got
time to think of your problems. Since I have been here I have had
days off but they don't provide any facilities. You do your
washing and then you lay on your back and think – this is a lousy
place; what am I doing here?
Interview reported in F. S. Stevens, *Aborigines in the Northern
Territory Cattle Industry*

The majority of the Aboriginal population lives in 'remote' Australia,
as defined in Chapter 2. In this region, there are basically four forms of
Aboriginal community: government settlements, church missions,
various Aboriginal-owned or occupied properties, and encampments
of Aborigines on European-owned (pastoral) properties. In this chapter is summarised the available information on those Aborigines who
fall in the last-mentioned group, that is those in pastoral stations.
Again, the somewhat piecemeal components of the outline cannot be
drawn together with ease or comprehensiveness. This is so for three
reasons. Firstly, because Aborigines on pastoral stations are employed
in a scattered private setting, the available information, such as it is,
resides largely in individual studies of certain areas or groups, rather
than in overall surveys. The review relies, therefore, fairly heavily
upon the few available studies: the Gibb Committee (1973); Gruen
(1966); and Stevens (1974), all in the Northern Territory; Scott (1971a)
in the Kimberley region of Western Australia, and Stanley (1976) in
central Australia. Secondly, the pattern of association between Aborigines and the stations has varied considerably. On some stations,
Aborigines today are the descendants of those who have worked and

lived on the station since the last century. But on others, Aborigines may be employed only periodically, without being residents, and may live on government settlements, missions or other stations. Thirdly, there are pastoral stations scattered across various States, and differing government policies under a federal system have influenced the lives and conditions of Aborigines in these heterogeneous jurisdictions.

This chapter therefore concentrates on depicting the economic relationships and standards on a stylised European-owned pastoral station with a resident Aboriginal community or camp, although reference is also made to the recent establishment of some Aboriginal-owned pastoral properties. Attention is focused specifically upon stations in the Northern Territory and in the Kimberley region of Western Australia, since these are the main areas in which Aboriginal communities today reside on pastoral properties, and the chief areas on which studies have been conducted. (In Queensland there are few pastoral properties with permanent Aboriginal camps, and the institutional arrangement there (discussed in Chapter 2) differs from other States with a 'migrant labour' contract system predominating. And in remote South Australia Aboriginal involvement on pastoral stations is minimal: in 1970 Scott (1971b, p. 5.2) reported that only two stations (Everard Park and De Rose Hill) had permanent Aboriginal camps.)

Demographic features

Estimates of the number of Aborigines in the pastoral industry are scarce not only because of the private scattered setting of industry employment mentioned above, but also because Aborigines living on pastoral stations are rather mobile. Traditionally, this mobility was associated with regular annual migrations (usually not exceeding three months' duration) for the purpose of visiting relatives, undertaking traditional ceremonial activities and making marriage arrangements. These trips were generally to other pastoral communities, missions, government settlements or camps on land of traditional tribal significance and their timing was determined by the seasonal demands of the pastoral industry. Since the late 1960s migration off pastoral stations has occurred as a consequence of structural changes in the industry.

The estimates available on the Aboriginal populations of pastoral stations are the following:

(1) The annual report of the DAA Northern Territory Division for 1972–3 (DAA, 1975) estimated (p. 42) that 4,200 Aborigines resided on

Northern Territory stations in December 1972. This represents a steady decline from 4,676 in 1965. As a proportion of the total Aboriginal population in the Northern Territory that residing on stations declined from 31 per cent in 1961 to about 18 per cent by 1973.

(2) In Western Australia (according to Schapper, 1970, p. 37) some 4,000 Aborigines were estimated to be living on stations (sheep and cattle) in 1966. The majority (2,351 Aborigines) was concentrated on 75 Kimberley cattle stations, while the balance (1,484) was spread across another 210 stations in the rest of Western Australia. In 1966 Schapper's estimate represented some 20.8 per cent of the total Western Australian Aboriginal population. Implying a shift away from pastoral stations, Scott's survey (1971a, p. 12.14) enumerated 2,153 Aborigines living on 80 Kimberley stations in 1971.

Because of the low rainfall in the remoter parts of northern and central Australia, most pastoral holdings there are immense. Stevens (1974, p. 30) noted that in the Northern Territory property size ranges from 30,000 hectares to more than 2,400,000 hectares. In the Kimberleys, Scott (1971a, p. 12.1) reported that pastoral holdings averaged 240,000 hectares, with the largest (owned by the Australian Land and Cattle Company) totalling 1,708,000 hectares. Pastoral holdings are not freehold and are leased for 30 to 50 year terms from federal (in the Northern Territory) or State governments.

The size of Aboriginal communities on European-owned pastoral properties appears to vary somewhat. In 1970, the Gibb Committee (1973, p. 22) received reports on 189 (out of 209) pastoral properties in the Northern Territory. Six communities accounted for 20 per cent of the total number of Aborigines on stations; 26 further properties had sizeable groups of 40–100 persons; 41 properties had small but important groups (20–40 persons); and 77 properties had groups of less than 20 persons. Thirty-nine pastoral holdings had no resident Aborigines. The Scott survey (1971a, p. 12.14) in the Kimberley area found that, in 1971, 26 per cent of station Aborigines lived on 5 stations with populations of over 80 Aborigines. A further 52 per cent lived on 29 stations with communities in the 21–80 person bracket, while the remainder lived on 46 other stations.

As to age composition, the Gibb Committee (1973, p. 23) estimated that 37 per cent of the Aboriginal population on stations was under 16 years of age, compared with 49 per cent on missions and government settlements. Using a small sample of 5 stations (which all held sizeable communities) in the Alice Springs area, Stanley (1976, p. 159) found that the proportion of the population under 16 years of age was over 40 per cent in July 1973.

In general, the population structure among Aborigines on stations appears to have a high dependancy ratio and possesses the potential for a high rate of population growth. However, there are no birth and death rate statistics for Aborigines on stations, so the population growth rate cannot be estimated. Moreover, even if these statistics were available, an estimate would be difficult owing to the migratory tendencies which have been noted above.

Standard of living

The first aspect of living standards is health, but unfortunately, there is little systemised information on this. But there is reason to suppose that health conditions on stations are even worse than on government settlements and missions. The reason for this is that stations rarely employ a full-time nurse and aid is usually administered by the manager or his family, who may not always have first-aid skills. Nurses from the Health Department usually visit stations every three weeks and doctors every three months, with emergency cases being evacuated to hospitals in major centres. The only data that exist are the especially high infant mortality rates for the whole of the Northern Territory and Kimberley region mentioned in Chapter 2 and these would imply that general health is poor.

The second aspect of living standards is housing. Many of the 'improvised' dwellings referred to in Chapter 1 are on stations. The available reports of commentators suggest that housing conditions (by European standards) are extremely poor. Most station Aborigines live in camps in and around creek beds, segregated and set at a distance from the European homestead. When housing is provided by station owners it is usually of extremely poor quality and completely unsuited to weather conditions. Stevens (1974, pp. 98–9) noted that this housing is usually constructed from galvanised iron, and is on average 15 sq.metres in size, with a concrete or dirt floor. These 'houses' are generally not used by Aborigines, their more usual accommodation being 'bush wurlies' or humpies constructed from galvanised iron, canvas and tree boughs and resembling Aboriginal shelters. This implies that the housing provided by pastoralists (which is similar to stage 1 housing on government settlements) is so unsuitable for habitation that the Aborigines prefer semi-traditional dwellings. Most camps have few washing or toilet facilities, and little drainage, as a number of surveys have indicated. Scott (1971a, p. 7.14) examined thirty-three stations in the Kimberley area and found that one-third had either no sanitation facilities provided or else facilities that were unusable, while one-quarter of the stations inspected had no washing facilities for employees. Stanley (1976) in his survey of five communities in the Alice Springs area found (p. 164) that half of the population in his sample occupied single-room houses, the remainder occupying 'bush wurlies'. The average housing density was six persons per unit. Stevens (1974, p. 98) found that only three of the thirty stations which he visited in 1965 in the Northern Territory possessed a standard of housing that approached the minimum requirements of the Wards Employment Regulation (applying to all Aborigines of full descent until the end of 1968). Stevens found that only three camps had running water and that only one was linked to the electricity supply of the homestead. Since 1969, the Cattle Station Industry (Northern Territory) Award, which requires employers to provide single accommodation for all employees, has been extended to Aborigines. Yet the Gibb Committee (1973, p. 33) reported that the majority of pastoralists did not comply with Award requirements for Aboriginal employees.

Supplying the educational needs of the remote, geographically scattered Aboriginal population of stations is extremely difficult. According to the DAA's Northern Territory Division (1975, p. 45) twenty-three privately-owned and two government-owned stations (out of a total of about 200) in the Northern Territory have their own government schools. In the Kimberley region, Scott (1971a, p. 12.21) found that three stations (out of a total of 80) had their own school. Stanley (1976, p. 160) found in his sample that these schools were understaffed and ill-equipped. Aboriginal children on stations without schools must either travel to school on other stations or to nearby towns, or else take correspondence courses.

In addition to the problem of the supply of schooling facilities, which is evident for all remote communities, there is also the problem of the type of education which should be provided. Should education be vocational? This is an important question for two reasons. Firstly, it appears (as later discussed) that the station economy will not absorb future Aboriginal population growth and the need arises to find employment outside the pastoral industry. Secondly, the pastoral industry is undergoing certain structural changes and to maintain current employment levels it will be important for Aborigines to learn new vocational skills. While Aborigines are in need of a wide range of education, the task of providing it to the station communities often falls to one or two European teachers who must offer instruction from pre-school to post-primary and even adult education levels.

With the complete absence of school attendance and attainment statistics it is impossible to gauge accurately the educational status of station Aborigines. Stevens (1974, p. 67) did find that a large proportion of the adult population is illiterate. This is not surprising, as most government schools on stations were not opened until the 1960s.

Employment

In the long years before contact with Europeans, Aborigines in what are now pastoral areas, were involved in their traditional economy of nomadic hunting and gathering activities. The environment forced continual movement in search of food. The social organisation was primarily of a small-scale clan type with a complex but cohesive kinship system. With the rapid changes brought on by the incursion into tribal lands of Europeans in the late nineteenth century, Aborigines were encompassed by stations where a more sedentary life-style could be adopted in the presence of a readier supply of food and water. Because it was difficult to attract European labour to the remote regions, station owners were prepared to provide supplies to Aborigines in exchange for the labour services of male adults as station employees and female adults as domestic servants. Rowley (1971b, p. 3) has pointed to the close parallel between the economic structure of the pastoral industry in 'colonial' Australia and the plantation economies of colonised countries elsewhere – capital, control and management was applied by one social class and race, and cheap labour by another.

The first colonial or 'establishment' phase was succeeded only in the post-war era by a period of consolidation and capitalisation, during which there was an almost uninterrupted rise in beef cattle prices. During this phase, some money (cash) wages, in addition to the provision of supplies (payments in kind), were introduced. In Western Australia, for example, a meeting of Kimberley pastoralists in early 1950 agreed to a standard monthly wage for Aboriginal stockmen of $2. And as Scott (1971a, p. 12.16) found, cash wages had by 1968 improved, with stockmen being paid $8–10 per month and female domestics $2–5 per month. (In real terms, this was a substantial rise for stockmen over the eighteen-year period.) Also, in the Northern Territory during this phase, Aboriginal employment conditions were set down in the Wards Employment Ordinance, and allowed a minimum adult weekly wage in the pastoral industry of $5 for males and $2.50 for females. (This was about 20 per cent of the minimum amount payable to whites under the Cattle Station Industry (Northern Territory) Award and diverged even further from actual rates paid to whites. And the standards of food and provisions for accommodation set out in the Wards Employment Regulations were inferior to those in the Award.)

In his 1965 survey of thirty pastoral stations in the Northern Territory, Stevens (1974, p. 44) found 1,647 Aborigines to be residing on these stations, 1,072 of whom were adults at employable ages (that is, total residents minus children and pensioners). Of these, 650 (or 61 per cent) were employed. Most of those employed held jobs with little responsibility, and nearly one-third of their number were females employed as domestic servants. Of the men employed, nearly two-thirds were engaged as stockmen, with gardener (8 per cent) and 'general hand' (7 per cent) as the next most common occupations. The figures given by the Gibb Committee (1973, p. 23) for the Northern Territory show that, of 2,733 adults residing on stations at the end of 1969, some 1,481 (54 per cent) had been employed for at least part of that year.

A third phase in the employment history of Aborigines on pastoral stations may be labelled the 'labour substitution' phase, and began at the end of 1968, when Aborigines were included in the Cattle Station Industry (Northern Territory) Award and the Federal Pastoral Industry Award (applying to all states except Queensland). The inclusion of Aborigines in this Award followed successful application by the North Australia Workers Union (NAWU) which argued that it was necessary, since Aborigines were Australian citizens who performed jobs similar to white employees in the pastoral industry. Pastoralists for their part argued (unsuccessfully) that the consequences of including Aborigines in the Award would drastically reduce the number that they would employ, supposedly because Aboriginal labour was not considered to be 'worth' the Award rate of pay and could not compete with whites in the labour market. This view appeared inconsistent with a survey conducted by Gruen and Stevens, who found (Stevens, 1974, pp. 72–3) that the majority of thirty station managers interviewed regarded Aborigines as more productive workers than whites. None of the managers said that all Aboriginal employees would be replaced were whites available. Most managers did note, however, that Aborigines were not as reliable as, and needed greater supervision than, their white counterparts. (Still the majority was not in favour of award wages for Aborigines.) This 'inconsistency' of view might merely have reflected the desire of pastoralists to maximise profits by maintaining Aboriginal wages at an artificially low level (below the market rate), or else meant that Aboriginal 'productivity' was counter-vailed by their alleged 'unreliability' disadvantages.

In the upshot, can the employment consequences of including Aborigines in the Award be discerned? In Table 21 are set out some of

Table 21. *Aboriginal pastoral workers in the Kimberley region, 1966–71* [a]

	1966	1967	1968	1969	1970	1971
Males	820	969	931	1050	690	611
Females	635	656	628	420	444	329
Total	1455	1625	1566	1470	1134	940
Non-Aboriginal male employees	444	457	852	785	746	NA

[a]At 30 June of each respective year.
Source: Scott (1971a).

the details available, namely those in the Scott survey. It will be seen from the table that, among pastoral workers in the Kimberley region at least, total Aboriginal employees on stations declined substantially in number (from 1,455 in 1966 to 940 in 1971), whereas non-Aboriginal male employees increased in number (from 444 in 1966 to 746 in 1970). The Gibb Committee (1973, pp. 6–7) also noted a decline in the number of Aborigines living on stations in the Northern Territory, while a survey conducted by the Northern Territory Cattle Producers' Council on 17 pastoral properties near Alice Springs found a decline in Abor-iginal employees from 383 to 261 (a decrease of 32 per cent) and an increase of other male employees from 168 to 279 (an increase of 66 per cent) between 1965 and 1971. Again, the employment levels recorded by Stanley (1976, p. 162) on five central Australian stations showed very low crude employment levels in most cases, with an overall employment rate of 26 per cent (i.e. the total employed as a proportion of the adult population). This rate is less than half that reported for 1969 in the same area by the Gibb Committee (1973, p. 23).

While, therefore, the evidence suggests a general decline of Aboriginal populations (and employment) on European-owned pastoral stations both absolutely and as a percentage of total Aboriginal population in the Northern Territory and Kimberley regions, it is not clear what the causes of the decline are. There appear to be four possibilities: (1) that it is due to a decline in the demand for Aboriginal labourers since their inclusion in the Award in 1968; (2) that it is part of a trend that was already under way and was due to structural changes in the pastoral industry; (3) that it is due to demand deficiency resulting from cyclical fluctuations; or (4) that it is the result of a shortage of Aboriginal labour, perhaps because of changes in Aboriginal attitudes to wage employment.

The first possibility is difficult to assess given the inconsistency of viewpoint revealed by the Stevens and Gruen survey mentioned above. The second possibility refers to the widely observed tendency for agriculture to release labour for other purposes as increases in economic efficiency occur. Between 1948 and 1968 (the 'consolidation and capitalisation' phase) there was considerable capital expenditure on trap yards and fencing, leading to better herd control and a smaller labour requirement. Other labour saving devices have included mechanisation (the widespread use of four-wheel-drive vehicles) and helicopter-assisted musters. And as pastoral stations have substituted capital for labour and used technologically more complex equipment, not only has labour been released, but there has also been a new demand for more skilled labour which Aborigines with their low educational and occupational status (in a European context) could not provide. Structural changes in the pastoral industry appear to have resulted in a decline in demand for Aboriginal employees. Whereas in the past three complete musterings of a pastoral property were carried out over ten months of the year, now only one is necessary and this usually takes four months.

In the 1970s beef prices in international markets have slumped, and the third possibility (that there has been a deficiency of demand for Aboriginal labour owing to cyclical, short-term economies enforced by this slump) may be real. Overall, it appears that a decline in the demand for Aboriginal pastoral employees has occurred due to a combination of all three factors.

It seems that a supply constraint has also contributed to the decline in the number of Aborigines employed. With the prospect of award wages in towns and the possibility of training allowances at missions and government settlements, many young Aborigines 'emigrated' in search of employment less arduous and more rewarding than station work. Much of the status and aura which was associated with station work may now have disappeared and the Scott survey (1971a, p. 12.21) suggested that those who were educated at schools in towns or in missions or government settlements, and who boarded away from pastoral stations, have become a young floating work force. There is also some movement of Aboriginal families from stations to broaden the educational opportunities for their children. Finally, as referred to below, a number of Aboriginal groups who resided on stations, particularly in the Victoria River District of the Northern Territory, have walked off European stations in protest against living and working conditions, and refuse to work for some pastoralists.

Income

Because most Aborigines on stations before 1969 received the greater proportion of their income in a payment-in-kind manner, quantification of its size is particularly difficult. However it seems very generally that until the end of the war in 1945, income was at a subsistence level (barely enough to sustain life) and rose only marginally above subsistence in the 'consolidation and capitalisation' period in the industry up to 1969. As many Aboriginal station communities were large (up to 200 persons), and the income of one pastoral station could not support the community, after the war pastoralists received welfare subsidies in the form of maintenance payments from the Federal government to supply Aborigines with provisions. Aborigines on stations have also been eligible for pensions and child endowments, but these, along with welfare allowances, were usually placed in general station funds. Stevens (1974, pp. 90–1) has pointed out that this could easily have resulted in misappropriation since the eventually intended Aboriginal recipients were often illiterate and inarticulate, and stations were only infrequently visited by welfare patrols. Since 1950, cash wages paid to employees have also had two components – a cash-in-hand or 'pocket money' portion, and a credit (the bulk of payment) at the station store. (Again, this arrangement may have encouraged misappropriation, and certainly gave Aborigines little experience in handling cash and adjusting to a money income.)

The only recent estimate of income for Aboriginal communities on European stations is that by Stanley (1976, p. 160), who found an annual per capita income in 1973 of $428 for his sample. More than half of this came from wages and keep, with other major sources of income being age and widows' pensions, maintenance payments, and child endowments. (Maintenance payments are, however, being rapidly phased out in favour of unemployment benefits.) Stanley suggested (p. 161) that the per capita income level estimate of $428 might, however, have been an underestimate for a variety of reasons. For example, occasional mustering contracts undertaken outside the stations examined by Stanley were not included; nor was any monetary value imputed to the hunting and gathering activity which was undertaken. An unpublished study by A. Hamilton (1971, p. 7) estimated that the cash value of game food at Everard Park Station in South Australia in 1971 was approximately $4000 per annum or $50 per capita per annum. (Valuation was on the basis of the total meat weight of game, times a price per pound of 40 cents (approximately 90 cents per kg) that was the common figure charged for beef at adjacent settlements. This valuation did not take into account nutritional value which, Hamilton suggested, was higher for native foods than comparable European foods.) This one case study suggests, therefore, that the contribution of traditional hunting activity to income may have been significant.

The only other recent estimate of Aboriginal income on pastoral stations has been compiled in a DAA report (1977b) on Willowra, which is Aboriginal-owned. In 1974/75 per capita income per annum was $610 (pp. 8–9). Sixty per cent of this was made up of earned income (wages and salaries) and 40 per cent came from transfer payments.

An important question is whether Aboriginal station communities have higher incomes as a result of the 1968 Award? The evidence here appears divided. When the award became applicable, there was scepticism as to whether pastoralists would pay award wages. This was particularly so because, to be eligible for the award, employees had to be members of the Australian Workers Union. Evidence contained in Stanley (1976, p. 162) and Scott (1971a, p. 12.20) suggested that, in general, pastoralists complied with the provisions of the Award. In the Kimberley, the company-owned stations appear to have been pace setters since they have a public image to consider. In a survey conducted by the Department of Labour in 1973 (see Stanley, 1976, p. 162) 28 stations out of 34 in the Alice Springs area complied with award conditions, although not one Aboriginal employee on these stations was a member of the NAWU. However, the Scott survey (1971a, p. 12.20) concluded that 'the Aboriginal stockman has benefitted little in real terms from increased wages. Managers now deduct from their earnings all purchases at the station store for clothing and additional food that they previously had received free. Thus, although they receive more pay, they have not materially benefitted and, in fact, many managers argue that the Aborigines are now worse off than prior to the introduction of the Award . . . whereas before the Aborigines on a station were employed where possible, now only a minimum number are given work.' Similarly Stanley (1976, p. 162) noted that in his case studies most Aboriginal employees were employed only for a part of the year. However, whether the extent of Aboriginal employment is a function of the introduction of the award rate or of other factors remains unclear.

Stanley (1976, p. 169) has suggested that in the short run the total incomes of Aboriginal communities may have increased after the introduction of the Award if the demand for labour was inelastic (i.e. if there was no other labour to substitute for Aboriginal labour). As income filters quickly through traditionally orientated Aboriginal communities via redistribution and reciprocity, an initial improvement in per capita income may have occurred. However, with capital being substituted for labour, the advantages of the introduction of the Award for short-term Aboriginal employment prospects may soon disappear.

Consumption patterns

There are no expenditure studies of Aboriginal communities on stations, but they probably do not diverge greatly from the findings which pertain to those on government settlements and missions described elsewhere. In the past (and in some cases even today) many commodities were not purchased but were provided by the station. This was especially so on larger stations in which the station provided three meals a day for the Aboriginal population. But while pastoral awards and the provision of maintenance payments specify the quality and range of foodstuffs necessary, Stevens (1974, p. 90) noted little correspondence for Aborigines between these specifications and actual provision in the Northern Territory.

Clothing and accommodation have also generally been provided by stations, while cash available to Aborigines has traditionally been spent on consumption goods procured at station stores or, if possible, in nearby towns. In addition, assets may be procured – for example cars (generally of a poor condition) are popular if resources permit their purchase.

A general point about consumption is that, with the transition of Aborigines to a command over some cash transactions, there are problems which arise through lack of experience with money management. The cash income shift has also meant a decline in consumption of traditional foodstuffs and, as mentioned in earlier discussion of government settlements and missions, there is a relative lack of knowledge of the nutritional value of other foodstuffs.

Recent developments

Since 1966 there have been some radical changes in the nature of Aboriginal involvement in the pastoral industry, particularly in the Victoria River District of the Northern Territory. In that year the Gurindji people who were camped and employed on the pastoral lease of Wave Hill, which was owned by the Vestey Group, struck and walked off the property. Doolan (1977, p. 107) noted various causes which precipitated this action including: (1) Aborigines felt that their housing was inadequate, yet saw houses being constructed for European employees; (2) Aborigines believed that they were not receiving their wage and social service entitlements; and (3) they found management unapproachable and felt an antipathy between Europeans and Aborigines. Doolan, who was in the Victoria River region during the early 1970s, noted (p. 112) that Aboriginal pastoral groups aimed to secure some land of their own, preferably tribal land, where they could enjoy rituals and ceremonies, work at their own pace and live as close to the traditional (pre-contact) mode of life as present conditions would permit. (This 'walk-off' European cattle stations parallels the decentralisation movement discussed in Chapter 4.)

Since 1972 a number of pastoral leases have been obtained for Aboriginal groups. In 1972 the DAA purchased Everard Park (Mimili) in remote South Australia and Panter Downs Station in Western Australia, and in 1973 Willowra and Kildurk, two Northern territory cattle stations, were procured for Aboriginal groups. In December 1974, the Aboriginal Land Fund Act established a Commission and Fund to procure properties for Aboriginal groups. Of the properties purchased by the Commission up to mid-1977, ten have been pastoral stations. In the Northern Territory they are Mount Allan, Ti Tree and Utopia stations and a portion of Wave Hill called Wattie Creek (Daguragu); in South Australia Kenmore Park Station; and in Western Australia, Bilanooka, Walgun, Coongan/Warralong, Dunham River and Noonkanbah stations have been procured. Aboriginal groups live at and work all these stations and a new concept, the Aboriginal-owned station, has developed.

To what extent has this development altered the economic status of Aborigines? Doolan (1977, p. 112) suggested that the primary desire of groups that walked off European stations was the acquisition of land and that the idea of running a successful cattle project was only secondary. The Aboriginal Land Trust Fund Commission has recognised this, and social as well as economic considerations have played a large part in the decision to acquire land for Aboriginal groups (for example, the traditional and ritual links of these groups with certain areas are important in the Commission's decision-making processes). The economic fact of land ownership has given some groups of Aborigines land ownership status (rather than a landless, rural dependency status).

To become successful commercial projects, Aboriginal groups need not only land but also capital, and a number of grants have been made to Aboriginal pastoral groups by the Commonwealth Capital Fund for Aboriginal Enterprises and the Aboriginal Benefits Trust Fund (in the Northern Territory). The DAA also funds cattle projects on all properties on an annual basis. By 1976, over $2 million in loan funds had been approved by Aboriginal Loans Commission for use on pastoral enterprises.

These new developments, if continued, hold out the seed of hope for the transformation of the social and economic status of Aborigines on pastoral properties. However, there are a number of inhibiting features among future prospects of progress. Firstly, it seems (Doolan, 1977, p. 110) that some Aborigines do not want to run viable economic enterprises in the European sense of the word. The desire for properties as noted is primarily non-commercial. Doolan has suggested that if Aborigines can provide their own beef and sell enough cattle to provide the necessities of life, their present economic aspirations would be met. Secondly, even if Aborigines do want to operate pastoral enterprises which did not suffer financial loss, this would not be possible for a number of reasons. Since the late 1940s Aboriginal pastoral communities have been subsidised by Federal government maintenance payments. This subsidisation is now continuing in the form of grants for cattle projects. A recent DAA report (1977b, pp. 10–15) questioned whether Aboriginal properties are cattle stations or settlements. Investigating the situation in Willowra, the report suggested (p. 13) that 'if it is viewed from the criteria generally applied to settlements in Central Australia, Willowra is much more "success-ful" because there have long been several positions filled by Aborigi-nals in the cattle operation, whereas there are none such at Papunya'. The report also suggested that the health status of Aborigines is good compared with most settlements and self-sufficiency is greater since a substantial amount of food is obtained by hunting and gathering. On the other hand (on commercial criteria) Willowra is bankrupt. This is basically because the property is overstaffed. As the DAA report (1977b, p. 11) noted, an average sized pastoral property needs (or can provide employment for) 60 man-months of labour per annum. How-ever, the populations of stations increase rapidly when they attain Aboriginal ownership. For example, at Willowra in 1971 when the pastoral lease was bought the Aboriginal population was 130; by mid-1973 it was 167; and by mid-1975, 240. A similar population movement has been noted at Utopia Station (DAA, 1977b, p. 10). It is not surpris-ing that a station which can provide full-time employment for five people cannot support a community of 240. This problem is com-pounded by a number of issues. Firstly, managerial and commercial skills are still scarce among Aborigines. Secondly, depressed overseas beef prices have diminished the prospects of economic viability. Thirdly, variable annual, as distinct from longer-term, financial grants from the Federal government add to uncertainty. And fourthly, many of the properties being purchased by the Commission are the economi-cally especially marginal ones.

Summary and conclusion

The Aboriginal communities on European-owned pastoral stations appear to be of a low income and economically depressed nature. It is probably only those Aborigines who live on government settlements and missions who are economically worse off than the station com-munities. The employment opportunities open to Aborigines on stations have a low occupational ranking. Aborigines on stations are generally concerned with stockwork and seem to be regarded by pastoralists as efficient in this aspect of employment. However, Aborigines are given few opportunities in skilled work, or in the managerial or commercial aspects of the station economy. This means that there is little possibility for upward occupational mobility. In the past, there were few educational opportunities, but today many stations have government schools. The vocational training that Aboriginal youths have received has generally been in stockwork and this limits the horizons of their employment possibilities. Certainly at present the pastoral industry would be the major private sector employer of Aborigines in the Northern Territory and in the Kimberley region. However, with numbers employed on stations decreasing and the Aboriginal population growing at a rapid rate, Aborigines will need to seek employment beyond the stations. Yet the education which Aborigines now receive makes them underqualified even for jobs on stations, let alone beyond. To enable the people to compete outside the station economy, educational and vocational training facilities on stations must be improved.

It is not only the lack of education and training which Aborigines receive on stations that makes adjustment to economic life outside the station economy precarious. The attitudes of pastoralists in most spheres of life are reported as being paternalistic, and Aborigines seem generally to have been viewed as inferior. Many decisions which people make (or learn to make) for themselves in the wider society have been made for Aborigines on the stations. The clearest example of this is the form in which station Aborigines have received income – in kind rather than in cash. Even wages were credited at the station store rather than being given cash-in-hand. This has resulted in a people unfamiliar with the workings of a 'money' economy remaining 'in the dark' about the functions and value of money.

Today there are four apparent avenues of possible economic activity that are open to Aborigines on pastoral stations, each in its own way carrying heavy caveats and restrictions born of the economic plight of the people concerned. Firstly, those on the stations may remain there, enclosed in a generally debilitated economic and social environment. Secondly, those on stations may seek to migrate to employment elsewhere, particularly in towns, if their lack of training does not prevent this. Thirdly, those working on stations may do so on a contract basis and live between an employment situation on the station and a family setting elsewhere, for example on mission or government settlements (as in Queensland). Or fourthly, if government finance is made available, and Aboriginal properties procured, they might be transformed from landless insecure employees to landowners as part of a more socially cohesive group inhabiting tribal land with unpromising economic prospects.

4
Remote Australia III: decentralised communities

There has been an increasing number of instances of small groups
of Aborigines breaking away from missions and settlements and
adopting a more remote satellite role. This tendency to form
smaller and more homogeneous communities can be understood
as one response to the complex problems created by contact with
our society – a move towards a more traditional type of
relationship between societies based upon agreed mutual
obligation without mutual interference.
H. C. Coombs, 'Decentralization Trends Among Aboriginal
Communities', Presidential Address, Anthropology Section, 45th
ANZAAS Congress, Perth, 1973.

It is true that the people who are belonging to a particular area
are really part of that area and if that area is destroyed, they are
also destroyed. In my travels throughout Australia, I have met
many Aborigines from other parts who have lost their culture.
They have always lost their land, and by losing their land they
have lost part of themselves.
S. Roberts, Chairman of Northern Land Council (*Second Report of
the Ranger Uranium Environmental Inquiry*, 1977, p. 47)

In recent years, there has been a growing tendency for groups with a
feeling of traditional Aboriginal kinship to leave white-controlled
settlements and to establish 'decentralised' communities, usually on
lands of ancestral affiliation. This tendency is an intriguing response to
the historical pattern of relationships which has evolved between
whites and Aborigines. It has been pastoralists, missionaries and government representatives (in that order) who have, down the years,
provided the points of contact with an alien society for the Aboriginal

76

people. With white encroachment upon Aboriginal land, the capacity of Aborigines to maintain the scope of their hunting and gathering economy was severely constricted. Moreover, as mentioned before, the desire for security and the apparently ready availability of rations and water on pastoral stations, missions and government settlements, were tempting reasons for a nomadic people to throw in their lot with the newcomers. But there were conditions attached to the supply of goods and services from the new economy. The objective of pastoralists was to acquire a cheap supply of labour; missionaries sought converts among Aborigines; and government settlements hoped first to 'protect and preserve' but later to 'assimilate' Aborigines. As Coombs (1974, p. 136) has observed, 'the benefits they offered Aborigines aimed to produce the social change by which these policies were to be made effective'.

The result of the historical pattern of these Aboriginal–white links has been a diverse number of Aboriginal settlements under white dominion, some numbering more than 1,000 people. But there appear to have been at least two sources of detrimental effect on the small nomadic Aboriginal clans which have been drawn to the newer closely settled, sedentary environments. These sources of dissolution are the removal of Aboriginal people from land to which they held strong spiritual ties; and the impact on their new lives among a conglomeration of clan groups with various geographical origins, differing dialects and other points of dissimilarity. The centralised communities, established for administrative ease and economy, have thus damaged the traditional Aboriginal social structure through the creation of new inter-clan or group tensions. Evidence on this is ready to hand (for example Coombs, 1974, and the Council for Aboriginal Affairs, 1976).

However, while the centralisation of communities has induced friction and dissatisfaction among Aboriginal groups, Coombs (1977, p. 4.11) has noted that clans at centralised communities have united in several instances when faced with a common external threat. Examples are the Jigalong group's resistance to missionary dominance; the struggle of the Yirrkala people for land rights and against the mining venture of the Nabalco Company at Gove; and the (long-standing) tenacious fight for independence by Don MacLeod's 'mob' (the Nomads Group) in the Pilbara. But these examples are the exception rather than the rule, and a growing dependence upon the goods and services provided at the centres must have, over time, encouraged inactivity. Yet a number of developments in recent years have seemed

to strengthen the desire of groups to decentralise to satellite communities and partake in the 'old way of life'. While the reasons for this
preference may vary from place to place, there are a number of recurring themes, which have been noted by the Aboriginal Land Rights
Commission *Second Report (1974)*, Coombs (1974) and Gray (1974).

Motives for decentralisation

The special relationship which Aboriginal people have with the land
seems best described by the word 'spiritual'. Stanner (1968, p. 44) went
so far as to suggest that 'No English words are good enough to give a
sense of the links between an Aboriginal group and its homeland. Our
word "home", warm and suggestive though it may be does not match
the Aboriginal word that may mean "camp", "hearth", "country",
"everlasting home", "totem place", "life source", "spirit centre" and
much else all in one.' But many of the clans moving to settlements were
required to abandon their land, since centralised communities were
established with little thought for Aboriginal affiliation to the areas
concerned. And an increase in mining activity, as well as the desecra-
tion of sites of religious significance, have increased Aboriginal anxiety
about lands regarded as their spiritual and physical own. This anxiety
has been allayed in the first instance by the Whitlam administration,
and by the (Woodward) Land Rights Commission Reports, which have
laid open the way for the ownership by Aborigines of some of their
traditional lands.

Adding to the impetus of decentralisation, it is probable that life for
Aboriginal people on government and mission-sponsored settlements
is deteriorating in quality. The 'comforts' of the material advantages of
more available and European-style goods and services in centralised
communities seem increasingly to be outweighed by the many social
costs for Aboriginal groups of settlement life. Among these costs is
social tension, mentioned before. Gray (1974, p. 6) suggested that part
of this tension arises because settlements are established on land to
which a particular group may claim ownership and on which, therefore, other Aboriginal people must bow in authority to the local descent group. In Arnhem Land, Gray suggested that village councils
reflect the authority of the local land-affiliated group, with the chairman usually being a member of the clan group upon which the settlement is situated. In addition there are the social costs of cross-cultural
(black–white) tensions. Settlements have always been dominated by

European law and authority. Traditional Aboriginal values and laws have been forced to play a subservient part, generally recognised only among the Aboriginal people themselves. Clearly, there are many problems in attempting to live within the constraints imposed by two different sets of laws and social obligations. Furthermore, social problems in settlement life have been compounded by the easing of alcohol restrictions. Witnessing the breakdown of the traditional Aboriginal way of life and the debilitating effect of alcohol, clan elders have seemed to desire a land base where the authority of the individual clan group can be recognised.

Government policies and attitudes during the 1970s have provided the avenues necessary to make some exodus from the settlements economically possible. Whatever the forces of social push to encourage decentralisation, most groups do not wish to abandon completely the access to goods and services to which they have become accustomed on the settlements. And it is only with the advent of social security endowments for Aborigines that finance has been available for the continued purchase of European foodstuffs by those divorced from settlements. A government policy of self-determination, begun in 1972 by the Liberal–Country Party, has been subsequently continued and has supported decentralisation, both financially and in principle. And the apotheosis of self-determination seems to be departure from centralised institutions in order to lead an independent life on ancestral land.

In the paragraphs which follow, an attempt is made to garner, from the very few sources available, some idea of the economic activities and situation among decentralised communities. Understandably, perhaps, but unfortunately nonetheless, there is almost no quantitative information on the communities to which a survey can turn. Most observations are, therefore, reports of 'qualitative' information and are usually generalised. (The only intensive study of a decentralised community is that by B. Meehan, a 1975 doctoral thesis in the Department of Prehistory and Anthropology at the Australian National University.)

Demography and geographical location

Little is known of the demography of decentralised communities, although a study which the DAA hopes to compile early in 1978 should provide some information. In October 1976, there was estimated to be slightly more than 100 decentralised communities with a total population approaching 4,000 people (unpublished community listing, DAA, Canberra). However, for a number of reasons, these figures must be used with much circumspection. Firstly, there is no clear-cut definition of an outstation. In Chapter 2 it was noted that Aborigines have often moved temporarily from centralised settlements and missions and in Chapter 3 a recent movement away from European-owned pastoral stations was also discussed. Neither of these migrations are encompassed in the definition of outstation, which here generally refers to an established semi-permanent camp (which as indicated below may, however, have almost no infrastructure). Secondly, the number of outstations appears to be increasing rapidly. For example, in October 1976 about 50 outstations were enumerated in Arnhem Land. A DAA Report (1977f, p. 7) notes that 'At present (1977) there are 65 outstation communities in Arnhem Land. DAA area staff there anticipate that there will be 80–90 in a few months time.' A consequence of the rapid increase of the numbers on decentralised communities has been a decline in the populations of some government settlements and missions. A DAA Report on Yirrkala (1977e, p. 5) noted that in 1977 the population at that mission was estimated at 650 and the population of outstations associated with it at about 200. According to a verbal report from the DAA, Maningrida, an Arnhem Land settlement, had a population in 1977 of about 250 people, compared with 1,289 in 1973, with the balance living on a number of outstations. A further problem in estimating the size of Aboriginal outstation communities in remote Australia is that the population is extremely mobile and estimates rough, while migration to and from centralised settlements and missions (resource centres) is frequent.

Most decentralised communities are located in the Northern Territory, on land which is now (following the passage of the Aboriginal Land Rights (Northern Territory) Act) Aboriginal land (see qualifying footnote on p. 29). Ownership is currently vested in the Northern and Central Lands Councils, which are in the process of allocating land to 'traditional' owners. Outstation communities are also located in remote South Australia, Queensland and Western Australia on Aboriginal reserves or Land Trust Areas.

Outstations are most firmly established in the Arnhem Land, a region of some 95,830 sq. km at the far north of the Northern Territory. At the end of 1976, there were approximately 55 outstation communities here, ranging in size from small groups of ten people to communities of 75, with an average size (per community) of about 30 people. Each decentralised community appeared to have a strong affiliation with one resource centre, usually the settlement or mission from which community members came, and with whose remaining residents there may be kinship and cultural ties. Three major resource centres in Arnhem Land, Maningrida settlement, Yirrkala mission and Galiwinku mission, each have more than ten associated outstations. The remaining outstations in the Arnhem Land were associated with one of Ramingining/Nangalala and Oenpelli mission settlements.

In the south-west of the Northern Territory (Central Australia) there are the Haasts' Bluff, Lake Mackay and Petermann Ranges reserves totalling 116,030 sq. km. In late 1976, there were approximately 30 outstations in this region ranging in size from 15 to 100 persons. There are three resource centres in this region – Hermannsburg mission, and Papunya and Yuendumu settlements.

While these two regions contain the majority of outstation communities in the Northern Territory, it seems that groups are decentralising from most government settlements and missions. Recently decentralised 'camps' have been established near Bamyili, Goulburn Island, Hooker Creek, Milingimbi, Port Keats and Warrabri.

In the Central Reserve of Western Australia (121,700 sq. km) there are about 7 decentralised communities with an approximate average community size of 80 persons. The major resource centre in this region is the Warburton Ranges mission. And the North-West Reserve of South Australia (71,540 sq. km) has four homeland centres, with an average community size of 50 persons. The resource centre here is Amata settlement.

There are a number of other decentralised communities scattered throughout remote Australia. For example some communities have decentralised from Aurukun mission and, as noted in Chapter 3, groups have also decentralised from pastoral properties.

The variability in the number of these communities in different areas has been the result of a number of causes, as mentioned above. In general, decentralisation seems to have been encouraged and actively supported by settlement staff in the Arnhem Land (particularly at Maningrida and Galiwinku) to a greater extent than in the centre. The tropical environment of the former region is also more conducive to decentralisation than the barren, semi-desert of Central Australia. The size of individual communities may also be influenced by administrative attitudes. In Western Australia, substantial establishment funds

have been provided for only four communities, whereas in the Northern Territory, these funds were initially more readily disbursed. There
is thus a larger number of small decentralised communities in the
Northern Territory (with average community populations of approximately 30 persons) than in the Central Reserve (where there is an
average community size of nearly 80).

Little else can be said of the demography of decentralised communities at present except that the characteristics of their populations
tend to be relatively homogeneous: residents are almost universally of
full descent. It is very probable that, as the people in outstations
originated in government settlements and missions, they exhibit similar population features, that is, a young population, with an extremely
rapid population growth rate.

Standard of living

Any attempt to measure the standard of living of decentralised communities is beset by the major dilemma of whether indicators based on
the needs of the general Australian society, or those based on the
needs of the traditionally-orientated outstation communities, should
be used. The socio-economic evaluation of these communities should,
it seems, incorporate both these needs. Nowhere is this dilemma more
clearly evidenced than with the supply of education services. Most
Aborigines in decentralised communities appear to desire strongly the
provision of educational facilities, particularly for their children (see
for example J. Edwards, 1977, p. 8). But should this education be of a
European or traditional style? Should it be taught in English or in the
predominant local Aboriginal language? Should the teachers be qualified or unqualified (for formal education purposes) tribal elders? These
dilemmas seem impossible to resolve in making an assessment of
needs, or of indicators of the satisfaction of needs. But the issues
should at least be borne in mind.

In gauging the educational provisions for Aborigines in these communities two aspects are relevant – the quantity of education provided,
and its quality. At present (in 1977) the format of the educational
system varies greatly from community to community. In some, children are sent to centralised settlements or beyond for educational
purposes. In most there is some education available at the primary
level. However, there is a number of problems associated with education provision at outstations. Logistically, it is extremely difficult to

provide them with buildings, supplies, and of most importance, suitable teachers. This problem arises basically because of the extreme remoteness of most of the communities. Another, more philosophical problem, arises since most of the communities are only in the 'establishment' phase, and there is uncertainty about the future direction of their growth. This uncertainty means that, on one hand, as a possible hedge against failure, Aboriginal parents on outstations might prefer their children to be educated in the Western style, so that future options are left open for the child. However, on the other hand, the present survival and success of the movement may be considered to depend on factors inconsistent with this goal. For example, camp sites may shift frequently, and there is rarely the possibility for a permanent school building; and in many communities there is no desire for a white presence, even in the form of a school-teacher.

This uncertainty is also evident in government attitudes (in this instance as represented by the Departments of Education and of Aboriginal Affairs). It is often extremely difficult to justify economically a school building and full-time teacher for a community because of the small number of children in many outstations – in some there is only a handful. This problem (which has a parallel in white rural communities) is compounded if the permanency of the community is in question. In the North-West Reserve Region (South Australia) Coombs (1974, p. 137) reported that administrators actively discouraged parents from taking children to outstations.

At present, in 1977, most communities are managing with what resources are available. In the Northern Territory, a member of a community is usually chosen as a teaching assistant and is given support services by a visiting teacher from the resource centre. According to a DAA report (1977f, p. 7) approximately 50 outstation communities are served in this way by government and mission schools. Further training is available to these teaching assistants through the Aboriginal Teacher Education Centre at Batchelor. The position in the Western Australia Central Reserve area in the North-West Reserve of South Australia is similar, with itinerant teachers based at resource centres travelling around outstations, and being assisted at each place by an Aboriginal teaching aide from the group. Often, this type of 'formal' education is supplemented by education in traditional languages, customs, and production techniques by one or more elders. There are usually no school buildings and little equipment. Heppell and Wigley (1977, pp. 30-32) noted that some communities in the eastern desert zone of Western Australia, for example Jameson and Wingelina, have 'bush' schools. By general Australian standards these conditions in communities are comparatively very poor, even though they may be adequate for the form of livelihood pursued at outstations. It is only when these communities have superseded their 'establishment' phase, and definite objectives and philosophies have crystallised, that their educational requirements and conditions can be accurately assessed.[1]

An appraisal of health conditions must be conducted, as with education, in two separate spheres. Firstly, there is the question of the supply of medical services for the treatment of maladies. Here again there is the problem of servicing remote scattered communities with limited resources. At present, the Department of Health is attempting to cope with decentralised communities by providing intensive training courses for chosen members of the communities at resource centres. In the Northern Territory a more formal, but short, course in nursing is available at Darwin. Aborigines trained in this way return to their communities to deliver day-to-day medical help, and are supported by periodic (but not necessarily regular) visits from staff of local government settlement or mission hospitals. Decentralised communities do not have a building which could be called a hospital or a clinic, although in some communities (in Western Australia) clinics do operate from caravans. Emergency evacuation is generally arranged by radio (when it is available) and patients are flown out by the Royal Flying Doctor Service. (One of the first amenities constructed at isolated decentralised sites tends to be an air strip for communication purposes.)

Another aspect is the present health status or condition of the Aboriginal populations of the outstations. This may be further subdivided into physical and mental health aspects, although there is a close connection between these two features of health. Firstly, there

---

[1] An additional problem is caused by what may prove a permanent feature of outstation communities: a great deal of migration between decentralised and centralised settlements for short periods of time. This problem has been noted by the House of Representatives Standing Committee on Aboriginal Affairs (1975, pp. 91–2): 'The movement of children between the outstations and Yirrkala is already making problems for the Yirrkala school as staff cannot keep a check on the progress of those concerned. This disruption and lack of continuity tends to destroy the educational program and the Committee fears that until the facilities and teachers are available in the settlements (i.e outstations) and parallel standards and courses maintained in them, the difficulty will remain.'

are indications that physical health may have improved as a result of decentralisation. This appears due to dietary changes and a decrease in alcohol consumption. As suggested in Chapter 2, Aborigines in centralised communities have become dependent on low quality, store-purchased European foodstuffs – predominantly carbohydrates. As a result of decentralisation and a revival of traditional subsistence economic activity, there seems to have been and increase in protein intake and a resultant improvement in physical health (especially among children). Alcoholism, which has become a chronic problem on many centralised settlements, is linked to the social and cultural tensions described above. Most decentralised communities ban alcohol consumption.

In the absence of infant mortality and morbidity, cause of death, life expectancy, and other data, it is extremely difficult to provide an accurate assessment of physical health status. Edwards (1977, p. 8) does report that among the Pitjantjatjara of Central Australia nasal and chest conditions among children, and trachoma among the elderly, are still common. He relates both of these conditions to dust and outdoor living.

'Psychological' health has been referred to by Morice (1976) in his article on the psychological benefits of the Aboriginal outstation movement. Morice described changes which appear to have brought improvements for mental health through rising general community and individual self-esteem following decentralisation. He noted (p. 941) three causes of improvement. Firstly, decentralised communities are smaller, more homogeneous groups with common kinship ties. Outstation sites are often those providing a strong mythical or spiritual bond between group members, thus breaking down tensions within the community and aggressions felt towards outside groups. For individuals, Morice noted (p. 941) that 'by returning to a more traditional lifestyle . . . the result was an integrated participating member of the community, a better husband and father and a happier individual'. Secondly, Morice (p. 941) observed the re-establishment of traditional social sanctions on outstations, thus obviating the confusion (mentioned above) which often resulted at centralised stations and missions from the conjunction of 'white' and a sub-layer of 'traditional' authority. Finally, Morice identified the recognition of traditional medicine on outstations as one of the causes of improved mental health. This type of medicine was generally actively suppressed on centralised communities, especially missions. He suggested (p. 941) that 'modern medicine is, of course, essential to the health of Aborigines, but the reinforcement of traditional medicine has allowed for the more rapid and complete resolution of states of psychic discomfort and dysfunction'.

As to housing conditions, most abodes at decentralised communities are fairly traditional in style, and could be called semi-traditional houses for introduced (European) materials such as corrugated iron and canvas have often been used. People live in a variety of structures, depending to some extent on the geographic region of the outstation. In the Arnhem Land, Meehan (1975, Appendix 1, p. 42) reported that some families have corrugated iron huts made along European rectangular lines. O'Connell (1977, p. 6) referred to Aboriginal houses as shelters and noted that in Central Australia the most common types of structure are brush or sheet-metal windscreens, sheet-metal lean-tos and fully enclosed box-like huts with stout wooden or metal frames and brush, grass or sheet metal walls. In winter, unroofed shelters are preferred as they provide occupants with maximum warmth from the sun and in summer roofed shelters are essential for shade. Heppell and Wigley (1977, p. 52) noted that further south in the Central Reserve of Western Australia people lived in simple bush shelters, clad in bush materials, galvanised iron and tarpaulin.

The present stock of houses at outstations (or decentralised camps) would have an extremely low status if one were to apply a Western-value scheme of assessment. All houses have no services such as electricity, gas supply, water supply or drainage available and no cooking or toilet facilities. In the Arnhem Land some communities can utilise nearby rivers or streams for washing, but in general, outstation camps have no ablution blocks or shower units. In the arid centre, where communities are dependent on bore water, it is not unusual to see one tap servicing an entire outstation.

However, for two reasons, a Western value system may be of minimal use in this context. Firstly, even if European housing were to be introduced, it would only be used occasionally by its owners – during the wet season in Arnhem Land and during the winter in the centre. For the majority of the year, the community population prefers to sleep outdoors in the climatic conditions concerned, and would only use houses for storage purposes. Secondly, and of equal importance, tribalised Aborigines may for many reasons shift households. (Short-and long-term settlement dynamics are discussed at length in O'Connell (1977)). Factors that precipitate a shift may be of a physical or social nature. The former generally results in a shift of camp site and the latter in a shift of shelter (or people between existing shelters) possibly within a site. Physical factors include the need to shift the camp site owing to an accumulation of refuse; weather conditions (in summer this may induce a shift closer to water supplies); health reasons (especially where no ablution facilities exist); and resource depletion (for example, firewood, water and food supplies) especially where the subsistence economy is vital to the community. Social factors that precipitate a shift include the death of a clan member; conflicting social obligations; domestic strife; and 'the arrival or departure of people whose presence affects the matrix of intra-site social and economic relationships' (O'Connell, 1977, p. 13). For these reasons, it is difficult if not impossible to measure the housing status of decentralised Aborigines using the yardstick of the general society which regards individual freehold home ownership of a permanent nature as the ideal.

Economic activity

There are, once more, difficulties in assessing the economic activities of Aboriginal people in the decentralised communities. But it does seem, to start, that the decision of groups to decentralise has apparently kindled a drive to economic endeavour which was muted by the conditions on settlements. Leaving the centralised settlements has symbolised a break from dependency; and even if the payment of social welfare benefits has expedited the break, it has seemed more necessary for Aborigines in the new decentralised communities to become involved in economic activity.

As mentioned before, the outstation movement is linked to a strong revival of traditional Aboriginal values. Part of the apparent disenchantment with life on the centralised settlements is a rejection of aspects of the white production and economic systems, since acceptance of white values in this sphere results in inroads being made into other (social) spheres of traditional value systems. In decentralised communities, production and division of labour is often organised on traditional rather than European bases. But this does not, of course, imply that the people concerned have rejected European goods and services. The economic activity in decentralised communities is divided between subsistence, or non-market, and market-oriented (or cash income earning) activity. This raises the well worn problem of how the extent of non-market activity can be measured. (As Duncan (1974, p. 86) has said, 'effective valuation of subsistence production is a problem that economists have not yet managed to solve'. The problem arises, of course, because subsistence production is not marketed and its value or price is indeterminate.)

Beginning, therefore, with *non-market economic activity*, it is clear that the decentralisation movement partly involved a return to pre-contact times when Aboriginal communities were purely subsistence units. In this, the hunting and gathering production systems of clans provided them with all their needs. And in discussing the economic activities of this form of production entity, it may be useful to employ some of the terminology and method of economics. (In Appendix IV a simple model is presented of the decentralised community economy.) The clans were what Fisk (1962, p. 463) has called a 'pure subsistence unit'. (That is, a self-sufficient non-monetary production unit.) Each clan's hunting and gathering activities were confined to a fairly fixed area of land. Technology and capital were firmly limited. In this setting, production (that is subsistence output) was determined by (1) fixed technology and capital; (2) a substantial but constant supply or fixed area of land; and (3) the amount of 'labour input'.

This simple relationship implies that output was a function of labour input. Following the work of Fisk (1962) it can be argued that, as in the traditional setting clans were nomadic and subsistence output was either perishable or immobile (for example, housing), there was a clearly defined ceiling to the demand for output. During 'normal' times, it might therefore be possible to expend only a relatively limited labour input, and leave other time available for leisure; while during 'abnormal' years, for example when floods or droughts occurred, the maximum available labour input would be insufficient to generate the 'ceiling' output.[1] On these occasions, there would be a production

---

[1] The question of the amount of labour self-sufficient subsistence units had to expend to reach their demand ceiling has been hotly debated in both the anthropology and economic anthropology literature. Sahlins (1972, pp. 1–39) in a chapter aptly titled 'The Original Affluent Society', examined data on the subsistence activity of an Arnhem Land group (at Fish Creek in 1960) and suggested that adults worked only intermittently for 4–5 hours per day to meet all their needs. The study period was only 14 days and hence any conclusion is highly speculative but Sahlins stated (pp. 36–7), Hunters and gatherers have by force of circumstances an objectively low standard of living. But taken as their objective, and given their adequate means of production, all the people's material wants

shortfall below the ceiling which might mean starvation or a need to forage on territories normally associated with other clans.

Today, however, the situation is quite different from the assumed possible sequence so far mentioned. There is no doubt that, compared with pre-contact times, the nature of subsistence activity, and Aboriginal expectations of its possibilities, have changed quite markedly. This is because of the movement of Aborigines to centralised communities, and their experience with market (European-style) goods. Obviously, there is a preference now for consumption beyond the traditional 'ceiling', and the prospect of turning to the market economy to meet needs.

Another aspect of subsistence activity is that, in pre-contact times, Aboriginal clans were nomadic and mobile. The environment supplying their needs was, in normal times, not overtaxed (and in central Australia has always been fragile). The population appears as well to have been reasonably stable owing to cultural constraints on population growth as well as unplanned controls including warfare and disease. But the outstations developing today will very probably need to be far more permanent in order to maintain communications with resource centres (and in the centre to remain close to water supplies). There is thus the real possibility that the marginal productivity of labour may tend to zero (i.e. that the addition of an extra worker would produce no further net return) owing to a combination of rapid population growth and resource depletion.

It is not possible at present to very rigorously 'test' the above suppositions. But examinations of subsistence activities on outstations conducted by Brokensha (1975), Coombs (1974, 1977), Meehan (1975) and Morice (1976) do give the framework of supposition some empirical backing. Meehan (1975, Appendix I, p. 39) showed that a community at Kopanga in Arnhem Land provided (during 1972–3) all of the flesh protein in its diet from subsistence activity. On average about 1 kg of flesh was consumed per head per day, mainly from fish and shell fish. However, Meehan (p. 38) indicated that traditional sources of carbohydrates and sugars, such as root crops, wild honey and fruit were no longer regularly consumed, since their collection and preparation was considered too arduous for them to be used every day.

Brokensha (1975) who was at Pipalyatjara Camp (a small decentral-

usually can be easily satisfied.' For a fuller exposition of the issues involved here, see Le Clair and Schneider (1968).

ised group of Western Pitjantjatjara people in South Australia) in early 1975, noted (p. 25) that hunting and gathering provided about 80 per cent of this group's meat intake and something less than 5 per cent of the vegetable food. Coombs (1974, p. 140) reported similar hunting and gathering activity among a variety of outstation communities. Morice (1975, p. 939) noted that approximately 50 per cent of food supplies at Kungkayunti (a Papunya outstation) were obtained by traditional and neo-traditional means. Women spent approximately 6 hours a day gathering witchetty grubs (an important source of protein), goannas and a range of native vegetable foods. Whenever a vehicle was available men would travel to hunt kangaroo. A hunt such as this might provide enough meat for a whole community for a week. Finally, Edwards (1977, p. 9) suggested that approximately 25 per cent of the decentralised Pitjantjatjara communities' diet comes from 'bush tucker'.

Traditional exploitation of the land also provides most of the raw material for the construction of shelters (wiltjas or humpies), for traditional weapons, for utensils, for religious objects and for artefact manufacture. Non-traditional subsistence activities are also being undertaken by decentralised communities and include horticulture and cattle-raising. Generally, these ventures are still only at the experimental stage owing to their recent establishment and because Aborigines at present lack expertise in such non-traditional activities. It must be stressed that environmental differences do dictate the type of subsistence activities and the contribution their output makes to total consumption.

The possibility of depletion of raw materials and game from the land has been mentioned by Coombs (1974, p. 141) in reference to the fragile arid environment of Central Australia. Much ecological damage has already been done by animals introduced by Europeans. Coombs gives the examples of grazing cattle, wild foxes, rabbits and cats. And an indication of the depletion of resources by sedentary Aboriginal communities is given by the lack of game and raw materials in areas surrounding centralised settlements. This seems to lend substance to the suppositions about the possible negative marginal productivity of labour mentioned above.

So far, reference has been made to non-market economic activity. The difficulties in assessing 'market' activity in decentralised communities is no less than that encountered in discussing non-market occupations. As mentioned, it is largely through non-economic forces that communities appear to have felt an incentive to migrate to 'decentralised' areas. In doing this, people have removed themselves from contact with a European-style labour market (artificial though this may have been in centralised settlements). But even if the motives for movement may have been primarily social, they are not necessarily economically irrational, since there are alternative sources of cash income from some market-oriented economic activity and from transfer payments.[1]

The only major market-oriented economic activity undertaken in decentralised communities is artefact production. This form of paid activity is far more common in the Arnhem Land than in Central Australia. Morphy (1976,p. 2) has suggested that income derived from artefact production by the Yirrkala community from 1970 to 1974 was in the region of $30,000 per annum. By 1976, he estimated that this would have grown to nearly $100,000. Most artefacts are produced by outstation communities. The dramatic increase in gross revenue from these sources (from $260 in 1954 and $22,217 in 1970) has both demand and supply explanations. There has been a rapidly increased demand for Aboriginal artefacts from southern States since the early 1970s, and at Yirrkala a strong local demand associated with the growth of the Nabalco mining town of Nhulunbuy. Marketing arrangements have also improved dramatically, with the United Church of North Australia (UCNA) organising a central marketing outlet in Darwin from mission communities under its jurisdiction, and attempting to find outlets for this produce in southern States, and an Aboriginal-owned Arts and Crafts Corporation with eight marketing outlets including those at Alice Springs, Darwin and Sydney also being established (with a DAA grant).

The positive supply response of Aborigines has been due to two factors. Firstly, as mentioned above, with a growth in the outstation movement, there has been a need for cash income to procure essential supplies and (sometimes) four-wheel-drive vehicles to maintain communications with resource centres. The desire to decentralise, and the optimism associated with this desire, has provided the incentive so often lacking in the past. Secondly, the return of groups to traditional areas has meant that raw materials necessary for artefact production

---

[1] But, in the language of economics, this behaviour need not be economically irrational, even if there were no alternative sources of cash: if the high cost (disutility) of social disharmony were introduced into the preference function of individuals, the utility of decentralisation (and reliance only on subsistence production) might outweigh any disutility from the loss of European-style goods and services.

(which are very often depleted around settlements and missions), have become available. Artefact production is predominantly in the form of bark paintings, carvings and painted wooden objects. Morphy (1976, p. 3) reported that craft production in the Arnhem Land is the result of co-operative effort. Women over 15 years of age produce most of the output. For example, some 90 per cent of carvings are produced by women. Men generally create the highly valued, high quality bark paintings, some of which reach prices of $1,600 in Melbourne galleries. The need for cash incomes appears to have eroded the traditional division of labour. There tends to be an annual production cycle (related to the availability of raw materials) with carvings produced during the dry seasons and bark work during the wet. Most produce is sold through stores in resource centres which control the quantity and quality of output by apparently unilateral price adjustments. Output is usually aimed at two markets – the souvenir market, catering for the lower quality artefacts, and the collectors' market, for the high quality produce. Stores may mark prices up by 15 per cent or more to cover the cost of making marketing arrangements, but this seems to be an average mark-up, with much variability and some subsidisation of poor quality or unpopular products.

The artefact industry is of particular interest to decentralised communities, for a number of reasons. It capitalises on skills (human capital) already inherent in the community; it requires a very low capital outlay; the raw materials required for the production process are abundantly available (at present); and it allows most members of the community to participate in the production system. Perhaps most importantly, to communities reviving traditional values, it is a production system that utilises unique Aboriginal skills, and can be at least partly controlled by Aboriginal people. On the other hand, it must be mentioned that there are those who regard the industry with distaste, since they feel that it commercialises the externalisation of the people's ethos and spirit.

There are no other regular market-orientated enterprises in which outstation communities are at present (in 1977) involved. Meehan (1975, Appendix I, p. 42) reported the occasional sale of fish and shell fish by the Kopanga community to Maningrida settlement. But, generally, production of perishables is constrained by lack of storage facilities at outstations and ineffective market linkage (communications) with resource centres. At present, market-oriented production of foodstuffs is more a potential than an actual source of income, and would appear more likely in the Arnhem Land Reserve region, than in the drier regions of Central Australia.

The major sources of cash income for decentralised communities are transfer payments from the Federal government. These are made up of benefits such as child endowments, widows' pensions, old age pensions and invalid pensions. However, unemployment benefits are not paid to Aborigines on outstations in the Northern Territory, although according to a DAA report (1977f, p. 3) decentralised groups in the Western Australia Central Reserve region do receive them. Similarly Brokensha (1975, p. 33) noted that South Australian outstation communities receive unemployment benefits.

There is also a variety of other irregular sources of income. Government financial aid has come to many decentralised communities in the form of an establishment grant. In 1974, in a policy statement, the Minister of Aboriginal Affairs, Senator Cavanagh, advised that groups with a 'demonstrated commitment' to decentralisation should be granted $10,000 on initiation and grants up to a further $10,000 in any one year thereafter (DAA, 1977f, p. 5). These grants were intended for the provision of secure water supplies with a flexible system of reticulation; basic communications equipment (a vehicle and/or radio); access to health, stores, legal and educational services; and the construction of reasonable shelter. In reality, the size of these grants has fluctuated somewhat from community to community. In 1973, the Pintubi who established a camp at Yai Yai received a $30,000 grant from the government. More recently established groups in the Arnhem Land have received aid in the $2,000–$3,000 range (DAA, 1977f, p. 2). It seems that government funding (at a per community rate) has decreased with the recent rapid increase in the number of decentralised communities, associated with the Land Rights Act in the Northern Territory.

Some groups, for example the Bardi at One Arm Point (Coombs, 1974, p. 139), are able to obtain irregular employment in road building and projects associated with the establishment of the decentralised settlement. However, most work on community infrastructure is on a voluntary basis. Some groups (for example, Yirrkala outstations) earn occasional income by sending some of their members into nearby centres for work (or if no work is available to collect unemployment benefits). Finally, a recent development has been the inclusion of some Western Australian decentralised communities (in the Central Reserve) in the Community Development Employment Projects Scheme.

Estimates of the per capita incomes of community members are extremely limited, and vary somewhat. Coombs (1974, p. 137) estimated that the per capita cash income of the Pitjantjatjara community at Puta Puta in the North-West Reserve Region of South Australia was $10 per week in 1971. For the Bardi at One Arm Point his estimate was approximately $6 per capita per week in 1973. J. Hunter, who was superintendent at Maningrida settlement, collected unpublished income data for ten outstations in 1973. These data indicate that on average weekly income was about $7 per capita (however on a community-by-community basis, cash income ranged from a low of $3.45 per capita to a high of $12.23). Meehan (1975, Appendix 1, p. 39) estimated a weekly cash income for the community at Kopanga in the Arnhem Land of nearly $10 per capita in 1972–3. Brokensha (1975, p. 33) noted that during January 1975 at Pipalyatjara, the average income of 19 adults was $40 per week – $30 per week coming from social service payments and $10 from artefact sales. At a per capita rate these incomes are approximately $23 per week. Finally, Coombs (1977, p.1.6) estimated that the average weekly income of the Pitjantjatjara communities of Central Australia at the end of 1976 was $15–20 per capita.

These figures tell us little – except that homeland communities have extremely low cash incomes, compared with average Australian incomes, but do not appear to differ significantly from cash incomes on government settlements and missions (see Chapter 2). However, the income levels of communities presented here are not strictly comparable. This is because the value of the subsistence component of income has not been estimated. As noted above, all available evidence indicates that subsistence production provides a significant proportion of these communities' needs and is a form of in-kind income. Meehan (1977, p. 4) noted that if the 1.15 kg (gross weight) of seafood that the average person at Kopanga received per day, was valued at $1.00 per kg (which was cheaper than the current prices at Maningrida) then cash incomes would almost double. It seems that if subsistence production were to be valued in monetary terms, even below the market price, it would inflate cash incomes to a more realistic level.

While one may suspect that the regular payment of widows' pensions, child endowments and old age pensions to women may skew income distribution in their favour, it appears that, owing to traditional redistribution patterns, cash income filters rapidly through the community.

Expenditure patterns

People in decentralised communities divide their expenditure of available cash for goods and services into two types: regular expenditure, and expenditure on larger items for which there may be target saving.

Regular expenditure is on items regarded as essential. Meehan (1977, p. 4) listed these goods as being primarily foodstuffs – flour, tea, and sugar but also including non-foodstuffs such as clothes, blankets, mosquito nets, canvasses, torches, tobacco, matches, beer, and so on. Coombs (1977, p. 1.6) listed essential stores as being carbohydrates (flour, rice and rolled oats) and sugar as well as items such as tea and soap. Data collected by Brokensha (1975, p. 33) indicated that at Pipalyatjara approximately 56 per cent of income is used for the purchase of food and 16 per cent for the purchase of blankets, bullets, and so on – i.e. over 70 per cent of cash income was used for essential provisions. These goods are usually procured at the resource centre store at regular intervals, or are delivered to the outstations by supply truck from these centres. When the latter is the case, all the market transactions of a community may be completed in a short time (one or two hours). Social service checks and marketable goods (artefacts) are exchanged for cash which is spent on essential supplies bought by the mobile store.

European foodstuffs are not constantly available to outstation communities, and there is a great reliance on traditional foods. This may have beneficial dietary consequences – especially as alcohol purchase is not allowed at many communities. As Meehan (1977, p. 4) stated 'The Anbara living on their traditional lands were aware that their diet was superior to that of their countrymen at Maningrida or in Darwin despite the fact that the latter usually earned wages and had access to meals subsidised by the government. A superior diet was often stated to be a major factor in their decision to live where they were.'

Even though Aboriginal decentralised community incomes are extremely low, a surplus remains which is either saved for the occasional purchase of 'luxury' items (though the line between luxury and necessity items is finely drawn), or for remittance to relatives elsewhere. Coombs (1977, p. 1.6) listed luxury goods as motor vehicles and petrol, rifles and ammunition, transistor radios and cassette players, and musical instruments – generally guitars. These expenditure patterns are fairly similar to those of Aborigines in centralised communities. It appears that these material aspirations for European goods developed on settlements and missions, especially during the 1960s and early 1970s when many Aborigines participated in the now defunct Training Allowances Scheme and received substantial cash incomes for the first time. Most of these 'luxury' goods would be regarded as basic in Australian society and reflect the comparatively low income status of Aborigines now in decentralised communities.

The development potential of decentralised communities

The economic development goals of the wider Australian society are basically to achieve a high and growing standard of living (usually depicted by per capita national income), to maintain price stability and a high level of gainful employment, and to strive for an equitable distribution of income. These differ substantially from the apparent development goal of decentralised communities, which is probably (at first) to attain some degree of self-sufficiency. This does not mean a reversion to the purely subsistence activities of pre-contact times, but to an amalgam of traditional and market-oriented economic activities. Both may employ traditional modes of production, but the aim of market-oriented activity will be to earn cash income to procure market (European-style) goods.

The economic viability of these outstations depends on a number of considerations. The major question to be asked is: what productive resources (factors of production) do Aborigines in these communities have at their disposal? At present, the nature of the ownership of the land that the communities occupy varies somewhat. In the Northern Territory, following the Land Right Act at the end of 1976, title is in the process of being vested in individual clans, depending on traditional associations. This allocation process is under the control of the Northern and Central Land Councils, and is proving to be lengthy. In Western Australia, South Australia and Queensland, communities occupy either Land Trust Areas or Crown land and while they are granted usage of its natural (non-mineral) resources, they have no security of tenure. In South Australia there is a possibility that land rights legislation will soon be initiated that will transfer ownership of the North-West Reserve to Aboriginal groups. The quality of the land which communities occupy also varies somewhat: in general the communities in the Arnhem Land and those in the far north of Queensland (Cape York) have relatively fertile, potentially productive land; but those communities in Central Australia occupy land that has little development potential since it is in an arid, fragile environment, and can probably not be used for anything except land extensive pastoral activities (as described in Chapter 3) or possibly intensive horticulture dependent on sophisticated irrigation. The land constraint alone would appear to exclude the Central Australian communities from achieving self-sufficiency.

Turning to labour supply, there is no doubt that a potential labour force exists in these communities, but it tends to possess as its only unique skills the traditional ones which are utilised through hunting and gathering activity and through artefact production.

Capital is at present the scarcest factor of production at decentralised communities. The income levels of the communities are too low to generate enough savings for productive investment purposes. The communities are dependent on government and quasi-government organisations for funds. These organisations include the DAA (grants-in-aid, enterprises and special assistance to significant Aboriginal communities schemes), the Aboriginal Loans Commissions, and the Aboriginal Benefits Trust Fund (available only to Northern Territory Aborigines). One consequence of the recent granting of land rights will be that sources of capital from mining and forestry royalties will greatly augment the resources of the Benefits Trust Fund, and will directly benefit communities adjacent to projects (in terms of cash availability anyhow).

Given the existing resources at the disposal of Aboriginal groups, what income earning activities are possible? A large number of suggestions have been made and include market gardening, cattle projects, and fishing industries such as trepanging (in the Arnhem Land). However all these are dependent on effective market linkage which does not exist at present. Infrastructure investment by government and communities will be necessary to improve communications, and communities will need vehicles such as trucks or four-wheel-drive cars to transport produce to the market. (At present the DAA Northern Territory Division is opposed to the provision of vehicles to groups as in the past they have caused a severe financial drain on the group and have sparked off group dissension.) Decentralised communities are still faced by the basic problem that they are extremely remote.

Another distinct problem that Aboriginal groups interested in pursuing market-oriented economic projects face is that they lack the managerial expertise necessary to operate enterprises which are 'viable' in the European sense of the word. (This problem is similar to that described in the previous chapter in relation to cattle projects on Aboriginal stations.) Groups in Western Australia (and the Northern Territory in certain instances) are at some advantage as they are provided with a community adviser. In general, Aborigines at decentralised communities lack expertise in non-traditional economic activities, such as market gardening, and many groups are in desperate need of extension services, especially in the arid centre.

A final problem facing tribalised decentralised communities is the lack of a clear distinction between economic and non-economic activity among traditionally oriented Aborigines, and this may be a constraint to economic viability (again in the Western sense).

Artefact production appears to be the only current enterprise with a promising future, yet even the growth of this is dependent on improved market linkage, the expansion of markets, domestically and overseas, and protection from cheap imported substitutes. But artefacts are at present only produced in large quantities in the Arnhem Land, and other decentralised communities, particularly in central Northern Territory, appear to lack a viable economic enterprise to earn sufficient cash income. Coombs (1977, p. 6.10) seems to place some hope on the research work of the Commonwealth Scientific and Industrial Research Organisation (CSIRO), which held its second workshop in October 1977 in Alice Springs with the theme 'The Nutrition of Aborigines in Relation to the Ecosystem of Central Australia' and which recommended 'that a program of research and experiment be designed to examine possible activities by which Aborigines could contribute to improved nutritional standards and to greater economic independence, with special emphasis on the possible development of indigenous species'.

It appears, at present (1977), that only the communities in the Arnhem Land may achieve self-sufficiency and become economically viable. This means that many communities, despite a desire for self-sufficiency and independence, may have to remain dependent upon government support. Given this state of affairs it appears desirable that the DAA should formulate some consistent policy towards decentralised communities, to overcome the variability in financial arrangements that exist at present between decentralised communities in different States. Given that Government subsidisation of the communities is necessary in the near future at least, the question arises as to what may be the best method of making transfer payments. The new initiative by the DAA (its Community Development Employment Projects or CDEP) may be the most effective method for transferring cash incomes to the communities. A grant could be made to each outstation 'council' not exceeding the total entitlement of individual members to unemployment benefits (which communities in the Northern Territory are not receiving). In this way, each community will have to make decisions as to how income is distributed and the type of projects to be undertaken. There is reason to believe that the scheme might prove useful in decentralised communities. Other transfer payments, such as child endowments, old age pensions, widows' pensions, and so on, would continue to be paid.

Finally, the response of Aborigines in outstations to income earning opportunities must be mentioned. As noted previously, there is scope for involvement in market-oriented economic activity. This scope was represented by the total amount of labour input available minus that utilised in the production of subsistence output. The question remains as to whether Aborigines will be willing to sustain the work effort required to achieve self-sufficiency. It is possible only to speculate, but it does seem that, if a regular and reasonable return can be made from productive enterprises, such as artefact manufacture, Aborigines may be willing to participate in the cash economy from a position of relative decentralised independence.

Conclusion

Two features – the general lack of socio-economic information and the recent advent of decentralisation as a 'movement' and its variability – have constrained the assessment in this chapter. But, in general, compared with the overall Australian economy (and using a Western value system) conditions are obviously relatively very poor on the outstations. By European standards the expanding decentralised communities have access to few social services such as educational and health facilities. There are few community services or public utilities available, and employment (for cash income) is almost non-existent. The result is (by European standards) a poorly housed, poorly educated population with a low health and income status.

However there is another criteria which could be applied in assessing the status of these Aboriginal communities. One should compare their present standard of living with that of their brethren in centralised settlements (described in Chapter 2) where most decentralised Aborigines lived not five years ago. The rapid social disintegration of centralised groups and the resulting dependency, deliquency and alcoholism evidenced at settlements and missions is markedly less evident at outstations. Residents seem to have recaptured their Aboriginal identity and self-esteem. They are once again taking part in traditional economic activity, in self-initiated community projects and cash-earning activities. Their socio-economic status appears higher than that of Aborigines in central settings, even though many of the facilities (nominally) available at resource centres are inaccessible to them. But if the outstation movement is in general quite viable socially, long-term economic success appears more likely in the well established Arnhem Land communities than in those in Central Australia. However, all of these communities will no doubt remain dependent for some time on government financial support.

5

Settled Australia I: urban and rural communities

> Don't treat us all the same. There's good and bad amongst us, same as with you whites. Comment by part-Aboriginal, reported in F. Gale, *A Study of Assimilation*

> An inherent fact of Aboriginal life. . . is the constant pressure of living among a white majority where low status is always ascribed and acceptance must always be achieved. L. Lippman, *Oceania*, **42**

The preceding three chapters have been concerned with Aborigines in 'remote' Australia. In Chapters 5 and 6 attention is directed to Aborigines in the more closely settled areas which Taylor (1947, p. 4) has called 'economic', in contrast to (on the basis of land use patterns) 'empty' Australia. The Aboriginal inhabitants of 'economic' Australia are predominantly of part-Aboriginal descent, whereas those in 'remote' Australia are mostly of full Aboriginal descent.

In Map 1, the heavy line represents the division between 'remote' and 'settled' Australia; it will be noted that New South Wales, Victoria, Tasmania and the Australian Capital Territory and parts of South Australia, Western Australia and Queensland are within settled Australia. This division between remote and settled regions seems important since there are distinctions between the Aboriginal populations in the two parts. In the northern and inland regions, Aborigines often form the majority of discernible population groups, especially away from urban areas. By contrast, in 'settled' regions, as Monk (1974, p. 158) has noted, Aborigines are usually in small minority groups of one or two hundred people in 'white' towns or increasingly (as discussed in Chapter 6) as migrants to capital cities.

In remote Australia Aborigines have maintained their traditional value systems with varying degrees of modification. But in settled Australia more prolonged and intense contact between whites and Aborigines has resulted in detribalisation and the virtual disappearance of most of the traditional culture. Gale (1964, p. 170) noted that in settled South Australia there are Aborigines of sixth-generation mixed blood. As Gale (1964, p. 129) suggested, these people apparently share a common attribute of many groups which have sprung from miscegenation: an attraction to both cultures with which they have inherited connections, but difficulty in being fully accepted by either.

The economic analysis of the Aboriginal population in settled Australia is more complicated even than that already made of remote Australia, in which the bulk of the people was found to be living on government settlements, missions, pastoral stations and decentralised communities. In settled Australia, there is a far wider range and dispersion of Aboriginal communities – indeed Rowley has aptly entitled part of his trilogy (vol. 2, 1971a, pp. 130–80) a 'Journey Without Compass: In Search of the Aboriginal in Settled Australia'. Aborigines in settled Australia may live in or on the fringes of rural towns or urban centres; they may live on Aboriginal Land Trust Areas or on reserve lands which may be or have been government settlements, missions managed country reserves or independent 'camping' communities; and, finally, they may live outside predominantly Aboriginal communities, either dispersed as single family units in rural areas or assimilated into the wider society.

Because of the enormous dispersal of small groups in settled Australia, it is necessary to confine the material in this chapter to a case study approach. This method is, of course, imperfect since it cannot comprehend the variations that may exist between communities or within groups, and it is also possible that the case studies available may compose a biased sample. As Monk (1974, p. 159) has suggested, there are at least three features serving to explain variations among Aboriginal groups within settled Australia: differing government policies, the proximity or isolation of communities in relation to white society, and the economic activity in an area.

Differing government policies towards Aborigines in the various States are described in an extensive literature, including the work of Lippman (1973), Long (1970), Metherell (1975), Monk (1972), Rowley (1971a) and (1975). These different policies have resulted in various forms of communities in different States today. But in Victoria,

Tasmania, South Australia, Western Australia and New South Wales, a large proportion of the Aboriginal population lives in or close to white communities, either in the city or country. (Only in Queensland do government settlements continue to exist.) But within each State, and between States, there are important regional differences among the various Aboriginal communities in settled Australia. For example, within South Australia alone Gale (1964, p.391) distinguished six regions on the basis of land-use patterns and market-oriented activity, and suggested that further subdivisions could be made in each region. Similarly, Rowley (1971a, p. vii) noted that inter-community differences within States may have arisen from local variations in resource endowment. And a number of studies (for example Gale, 1964; Hill, 1975; Lippman, 1973; and Monk, 1972) have surveyed differences between Aboriginal communities in or on the fringes of rural towns.

Furthermore, the case study approach has difficulty in describing variations within communities. Reay and Sitlington (1948, p. 206) have noted that a hierarchy obtained within the Moree (New South Wales) part-Aboriginal community, in which some members sought to identify themselves with whites. A similar phenomenon was noted by Fink (1957) in north-west New South Wales and by Hitchcock (1974) in south-west Western Australia. This (unsurprising) stratification provides a warning for the material presented in the remaining parts of this chapter, namely that insofar as the data employed relate mainly to part-Aboriginal communities (for example, on a Land Trust area), it is possible that a downward bias might apply in assessing the group's socio-economic status, since the more ambitious and highly paid members 'associated' with it might be partly or fully assimilated and outside the sample.

Two other difficulties in the case study approach are the following. Firstly, because of the great heterogeneity of the Aboriginal communities in 'settled' Australia, it is not surprising that some, especially in the more sparsely populated regions, may resemble the communities of 'remote' Australia. This is especially so with those government settlements having few effective links with the rest of the economy. More importantly, many urban centres and rural townships in remote Australia resemble those of settled Australia. There are some striking examples: Broome, Derby, Wyndham and Port Hedland in northern Western Australia; Alice Springs, Darwin, Katherine and Tennant Creek, in the Northern Territory; and Cooktown and Burketown in 'remote' Queensland. These communities are not discussed in this chapter, but it is important to bear in mind that there is considerable similarity between the economic status of Aborigines in these towns and those in 'settled' rather than 'remote' Australia. Secondly, the division of Australia into 'remote' and 'settled' parts is somewhat arbitrary and ignores statistical enumeration regions. While the broad division is, therefore, useful, it is also in the 'statistical region' context that the following material is presented.

Prejudice

A special introductory point is that, while the wide-ranging and prejudicial laws characterising Aboriginal affairs up to the mid-1960s have virtually disappeared, there still appear to linger vestiges of the segregationist attitudes which would seek to differentiate Aborigines socially, economically and residentially from the general society. The three best-known studies of prejudice against Aborigines in settled Australia are those of Larsen et al. (1977), Lippman (1972a), and Taft et al. (1970).[1] Taft (p. 39) showed that whites interviewed in Western Australia considered Aborigines to be wasteful with money, unambitious, lazy, dirty, and slovenly, drunken, unreliable and superstitious. In general, he found that those whites with the most ethnocentric views in his sample had grown up in country towns. However, it should be added that 63 per cent of Taft's respondents considered that, given equal opportunities, Aborigines would be able to hold their own with whites. In Lippman's survey, conducted in country towns in Victoria and New South Wales, 52 per cent of white respondents – although not invited to do so – offered negative stereotypes of Aborigines. The most frequently mentioned negative attributes were dirty, drunken, irresponsible and inferior (1972, p. 30). A favourability scale (p. 31) showed that 40 per cent of respondents were favourably disposed to Aborigines and 60 per cent were unfavourably disposed. Larsen et al. (1977) examined the extent of discrimination against Aborigines in Townsville (north Queensland) and reported (p. 20) evidence of substantial discrimination in employment, housing and hotel access. Clearly, prejudice and active discrimination have consequences on health, housing, education and employment, which are the features discussed in this chapter (and others).

---

[1] Two books by Aborigines – Gilbert (1973) and Perkins (1975) also describe prejudice against detribalised Aborigines in the settled areas of Australia.

Demographic patterns

The only reliable population estimates on Aborigines in settled Australia are those in the 1971 Census of Population and Housing. As noted in Chapter 1, it is only in this census that Aborigines were asked to self-identify. In the previous census (1966), the extent of Aboriginality was asked for, and only those with $\frac{1}{2}$ or more Aboriginal descent were enumerated. The 1966 figures are, therefore, not comparable with those of 1971, but are presented nonetheless.

The part-Aboriginal population of settled Australia has fluctuated through much 'ethnic migration'. The varying attitudes of State governments to their Aboriginal (especially part-Aboriginal) populations has helped create ethnic 'out-migration' and 'in-migration' at census time as policies have oscillated. The National Population Inquiry (1975, pp. 464–6) noted that ' . . . during the period that the assimilation policy flourished, Aboriginal administrators placed heavy emphasis on the differences between "full-blood" Aborigines and "part-Aborigines"; . . . People had different legal rights and social status depending on the category into which they were classified, even to the extent that children and their parents, or brothers and sisters, were at one time or another compulsorily separated in order to maintain the distinction. In that period, when identifying as an Aborigine brought overwhelming social and political costs and few benefits, most people who could do so tended to identify as something else.'

Since World War II, this racial out-migration appears to have been reversed, and people of Aboriginal descent have tended to reassert their Aboriginal identity. This is illustrated in the National Population Inquiry (p.467) by a comparison of census populations and State estimates in the post-war period. In general, part-Aborigines have preferred to call themselves Aboriginal rather than 'part-Aboriginal'. However, there still remains quite a discrepancy between State estimates of the Aboriginal population and persons who self-identify as Aboriginal. The National Population Inquiry (p. 455) estimated that between 30,000 and 40,000 people with some Aboriginal descent failed to self-identify as Aborigines in the 1971 census. The difference between census and State estimates of the Aborigines in individual States varies somewhat. In Victoria, State and census estimates are similar, implying that racial in-migration of part-Aborigines has helped deplete the reservoir of potential identifiers (ibid., p. 464). The rate of racial in-migration is exemplified by the rapid growth (over 300 per cent) of the Aboriginal population of Victoria between 1966 and 1971 (see Table

22). In Queensland and Western Australia the differences in estimates
are substantial, perhaps because the process of re-identifying as an
Aborigine has not yet become so extensive among part-Aborigines in
these regions, presumably since this still involves a perceived social
disadvantage (ibid., p. 480).

In terms of statistical divisions, settled Australia is composed of the
whole of Victoria, Tasmania, New South Wales and the Australian
Capital Territory. The northern portion of South Australia (the Far
North statistical division) is excluded, being in remote Australia, as
are the Eastern Goldfields, Kimberley, Pilbara and Central statistical
divisions of Western Australia and the Peninsula, North Western and
Far Western divisions of Queensland (see Map 3). In Table 22, the

Table 22. *The Aboriginal population of 'settled' Australia,
1966 and 1971* [a]

State or Territory	Population		Proportion of total Aboriginal population (of that State), (per cent)	
	1966	1971	1966	1971
New South Wales	14,219	23,101	100.0	100.0
Settled Queensland	12,989	16,820	68.4	68.9
Settled Western Australia	7,361	9,809	39.9	44.8
Victoria	1,790	5,656	100.0	100.0
Settled South Australia	3,541	4,684	64.3	65.6
Tasmania	36	575	100.0	100.0
ACT	96	248	100.0	100.0
Total	40,032	60,893	49.9	57.3

[a]As noted in the text (above and in Chapter 1), the 1966 census
population estimate refers to people who were of ½ or more Aboriginal
descent, whereas the 1971 enumeration is based on self-
identification.
Sources: Commonwealth Bureau of Census and Statistics (1969) and
Australian Bureau of Statistics (1973).

Aboriginal population of settled Australia in the 1966 and 1971 censuses is presented. In 1966, this was 40, 032 persons, or 49.9 per cent of
the estimated Aboriginal population, and in 1971, 60,893 or 57.3 per
cent of Australia's self-identifying Aborigines. The population of
interest in this chapter excludes the metropolitan State capitals (Syd-

ney, Melbourne, Hobart, Brisbane, Perth, Adelaide and Canberra) which are the subject of the following chapter. In 1966 this population was 33,946 (or 42.6 per cent of Australia's self-identifying Aborigines). In Map 4, the population distribution (including Torres Strait Islanders) from the 1971 census is presented.

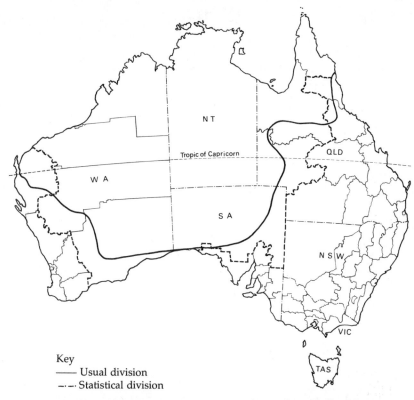

Key
—— Usual division
—·—· Statistical division

Map 3. Australia divided into 'remote' and 'settled' regions

In discussing the age structure of the Aboriginal population in settled Australia, the figures for two complete States, Victoria and New South Wales, may be mentioned first. In the 1971 census, 44.3 per cent of the Aboriginal population of the former, and 48.7 per cent of the latter, was under 15 years of age. These proportions are much the same as those revealed by the 1966 census, and are very similar to the comparable figures for government settlements and missions in remote Australia, as discussed in Chapter 2.

However, it seems useful to concentrate attention on two kinds of case studies – those which have reported the age structure of Aboriginal

108   *Settled Australia I*

populations in country towns or regions in settled Australia, and
those which have examined the structure on government settlements.
The findings of the relevant types of studies are summarised in Table
23.

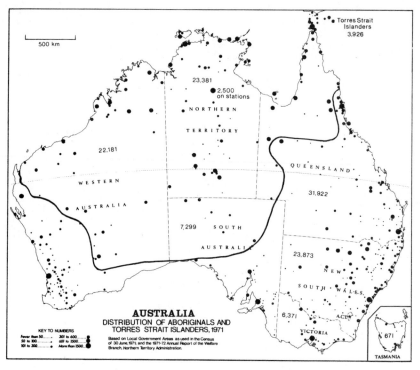

Map 4. Distribution of the Aboriginal and Torres Strait Islander population

The youth of the population recorded in Table 23 is surprising. It
implies that half of the Aboriginal population of rural towns, regions,
and government settlements (generally now open communities) was
under 15 years of age. Two issues are important here. Firstly, it is
possible, as mentioned later, that the infant mortality rate at these
communities may be lower than in remote Australia, resulting in a
younger population, given fertility rates that are fairly similar. Secondly, also as mentioned later, Aboriginal adults often migrate for
seasonal employment, especially from reserves. This migration may
also explain the apparently extremely youthful structure of the Aboriginal population of settled Australia.

As to geographical distribution of the population of settled

Australia, the information is scant. The difficulty in obtaining details is that many communities are stratified in their residential location and type of abode: the people of one town may, for example, be living on a reserve in shanties on 'marginal' land (for instance, a rubbish dump),

Table 23. *The age structure of some Aboriginal communities in 'settled' Australia*

	Year	Percentage of population under 15
Country town		
Eastville[a] (NSW)	1969	49
Westville[a] (NSW)	1969	47
Moree (NSW)	1971	54
Moree (NSW)	1974	58
Norton[a] (WA)	1973	53
Bourke (NSW)	1972	55
Region		
NSW (excluding Sydney)	1965	53
Eyre Peninsula (SA)	1965	53
Government settlements		
NSW govt. settlements (14)	1965–6	54
Lake Tyers (Victoria)	1965	61
Qld govt. settlements (3)	1965	56
SA govt. settlements (5)	1970	50–60

[a]Anonymous towns
Sources: Hill (1975), Kamien (1975b), Lippman (1973), Long (1974), Metherell (1975), Rowley (1971a), Scott (1970).

in caravans, in public (Housing Commission) accommodation, or in privately rented or owned flats or houses. For example, Long (1970, p. 87) in New South Wales enumerated 2,228 Aborigines on government stations (settlements) on what was then Aboriginal reserve land. This represented almost 20 per cent of the State's non-metropolitan Aboriginal population. The remainder was found by Long to be 'camped' either on one of the remaining 77 unadministered reserves in the State, squatted on private or public land, or living in rural towns.

Health

In examining health, housing and educational status in this chapter, it seems necessary to make local comparisons between Aborigines and others (as distinct from the society wide comparisons of Chapter 1). This is because Aborigines in settled Australia are largely a rural or rural/urban population, and share the handicaps of this situation with the rural minority of white Australians and not the metropolitan majority.

A description of the health status of Aborigines in settled Australia is complicated by various features. There is, firstly, a dearth of objective information concerning the health and nutritional conditions among Aborigines living in or near country towns. (Moodie indeed (1973, p. 17) refers to a 'statistical void', and points out that it is often impossible to separate out statistics relating to Aborigines in hospital records.) Secondly, because of the diversity of the Aboriginal population in settled Australia, the notion of an 'average Aboriginal' is evasive. Moreover, as Moodie also suggests (ibid., p. 25), the defined Aboriginal population of a State or region in settled Australia is liable to be a biased sample insofar as there is a tendency to study mainly those in the poorer socio-economic categories. Added to these shortcomings, the examination of the health status of Aborigines is complex because of the diversity of the studies conducted, some of which are now mentioned.

The most aggregative data available are for Western Australia in 1971, and in Table 24 the infant mortality rates for Aboriginal children in that State are presented by statistical division. The average infant mortality rate for settled Western Australia was 52. This can be compared with the total Western Australia rate which was less than 20, and that for remote Western Australia which averaged no less than 163.

In Table 25 the infant mortality rate for 3 Aboriginal settlements in settled Queensland for 1972, 1973, and 1974 is presented. These figures appear similar to those of settled Western Australia (a little higher on average), yet are much lower than those for 9 communities in remote Queensland (as presented in Table 17, Chapter 2).

Two more detailed case studies have also calculated infant mortality rates for Aboriginal communities. Copeman *et al.* (1975, p. 9) reported an average 68.1 deaths per thousand births for the Aboriginal community of Cunnamulla, Queensland for the period 1961–71. This compares most unfavourably with the rate of 17.9 for whites in that town; and put in an international perspective, is higher than the infant mortality rate for the New Zealand Maori or the American Indian. Kamien (1975b, p. 6) calculated that the infant mortality rate for Aborigines in Bourke, New South Wales was 88.2 per thousand births and this too compared unfavourably with the white rate of 9.4 for the same period (1969–71). If the infant mortality rate is an adequate proxy

Table 24. *Infant mortality rates for Aborigines in Western Australia, 1971*[a]

Statistical division	Infant mortality rate (per 1,000 births)
South-west	27.8
Southern Agricultural	53.3
Central Agricultural	49.5
Northern Agricultural	50.5
North-west	78.9
Remoter regions	
Eastern Goldfields	163.0
Central	195.1
Kimberley	130.4

[a] IMR for the Pilbara statistical division is not available.
Source: Department of Aboriginal Affairs (1977a).

of health status, the evidence already points to a low status for Aborigines in settled Australia.

A number of studies have also measured morbidity patterns among

Table 25. *Aboriginal infant mortality rates in three communities in settled Queensland, 1972–4*

Community	Infant mortality rate (per 1,000 births)		
	1972	1973	1974
Cherbourg	24.4	NA	76.9
Woorabinda	NA	52.6	40.0
Yarrabah	80.0	83.3	64.5

Source: Department of Aboriginal Affairs (1977a).

Aborigines. Stuart *et al.* (1972) conducted a survey of a random sample of 100 children at Cherbourg. They reported (p. 857) that a high percentage of this sample was growth retarded; that most of the children had a history of frequent hospital admissions and that morbidity rates were high – for example, they recorded (p. 858) a high incidence of chronic ear disease, with 41 per cent of their sample having hearing impediments. Kamien (1975a, p. 76) noted that, in 1971, approximately 30 per cent of all Aboriginal children in Bourke had a history of recent discomfort from illness and that 72 per cent were in need of medical attention. Dugdale *et al.* (1975) examined a selected sample of children aged 6–10 at Woorabinda settlement, Queensland. They found (p. 5) that only 43 per cent of their sample had normal hearing and that personal hygiene standards were low. (Interestingly enough, they found (p. 5) that despite this handicap, the visual/motor ability of Aboriginal children, tested using the Goodenough Draw-a-Man test, was not very different from that of Caucasians.) Kamien (1975f) conducted a survey of 212 Aboriginal and 382 European schoolchildren in the towns of Bourke and Enngonia in Western New South Wales and noted (pp. 34–5) marked growth retardation among part-Aboriginal pupils and a high degree of partial deafness from recurring ear diseases. (Both ears were abnormal in 51.4 per cent of Aborigines as against 16.7 per cent of Europeans.) Elsewhere (1975a, p. 117), Kamien reported that in a similar sample, perforated eardrums were found in 13.9 per cent of Aboriginal pupils' ears and 0.3 per cent of white childrens' ears. The medical cause of this 'epidemic' level of ear disease is upper respiratory tract infection which Kamien (1975f, p. 37) suggested is associated with overcrowded housing. Malnourishment and lack of medical attention at either a preventative, curative or palliative level, are further reasons for high child morbidity, and are discussed below.

    The infant mortality and child morbidity statistics presented here point to poor physical health conditions. Unfortunately, studies of adult Aboriginal health status are rare. Kamien (1975a, p. 104) reported that in a survey of the health of adult Aborigines in Bourke, he found that almost 70 per cent complained of recent discomfort from medical or dental illness and that 79.1 per cent were in need of medical attention. Severe illness causing chronic bad health was found in 30.2 per cent of men and 39.2 per cent of women. He also noted (1975b, p. 7) that from 1970 to 1973, 14.6 per cent of the Aboriginal population was admitted to hospital for reasons other than childbirth. Similar poor health among adults is described by Moodie (1973, pp. 97–117) in Chapter 6 of his study and by the House of Representatives Standing Committee on Aboriginal Affairs in their report on Aboriginal health in the south-west of Western Australia (1976a).

The causes of the low physical health status of Aborigines in settled Australia are many and complex. Moodie (1973, p. 247) suggested that it was the consequence of a culture of marginality, and that poor health status was the result of low socio-economic status. This contention that poor health status is part of 'the cycle (or culture) of poverty' was supported by the findings of the Commission of Inquiry into Poverty (1976) which reported on the social/medical aspects of poverty among Aborigines (pp. 210–50).

Other causes of poor physical health status have been suggested. Studies by Hitchcock and Gracey (1975), Kamien *et al.* (1975) and Wise *et al.* (1976) all indicated that irregular foodstuff expenditure patterns, and poor nutritional education which resulted in poor dietary practices, were the causes of low health status. Kamien *et al.* (1975, p. 123) noted that the fortification of bread at Bourke, New South Wales resulted in a significant improvement from deficient to acceptable vitamin levels in a large proportion of their sample. Wise *et al.* (1976, p. 192) noted that white wheat flour, processed foods and sucrose figured highly in the diet of Aborigines at Davenport (Port Augusta), Koonibba and Point Pearce communities in settled South Australia. They reported (p. 194) a rate of diabetes ten times that found among Australian whites. Hitchcock and Gracey in their study documented poor dietary practices in the south-west of Western Australia (1975, p. 15). They found different patterns within the Aboriginal community depending on the level of living of the subgroup. Poor dietary habits appear to be the cause of early malnutrition among Aborigines, and also a contributing factor to extremely poor dental health. Moodie (1973, pp. 224–8) noted that poor dental health among Aborigines was the result of early malnutrition, unsuitable foods, poor or absent oral hygiene, and lack of preventative dental care (with a trip to the dentist normally being for extractions only). Kamien (1975a, b) and Moodie (1972) suggested that a cultural chasm separated the white doctor from Aboriginal patients (Kamien, 1975b, p. 9). Kamien (ibid.) stated that in Bourke the 'inverse care law' applies, with those in greatest need receiving the least care. Although ample health services are available, they are only utilised when hospitalisation makes this essential. Cultural factors complicate the doctor–patient interchange. Kamien noted that Aborigines often have a more flexible concept of time and fail to keep regular appointments, and also have differing viewpoints of disease. Financial reasons (ibid., p. 11) were also thought to result in Aborigines refraining from seeking preventative care and even when they see the doctor, they were said to be reticent, with the average consultation time for Aborigines being less than half that for whites.

The Commission of Inquiry into Poverty research report (1974) which examined poverty in northern New South Wales noted (p. 135) that Aborigines were unwilling to complain about the quality of medical services, partly because there had been such a tremendous improvement within living memory. However, discrimination was noted in treatment, and in the quality of facilities available to Aborigines. Kamien (1975b, p. 11) concluded that the high rates of infant mortality, general morbidity and hospitalisation of Aborigines were evidence (among other things) of the lack of effectiveness of preventative, early diagnostic and treatment services.

Apart from poor physical health, a number of studies have suggested that *psychosocial* health among Aborigines in settled Australia is also in a bad state. Gault (1968, p. 132) found that the poor psychosocial health status of part-Aboriginal adolescents in Victoria was related to extreme poverty, low educational aims and achievements, and deprived home backgrounds. Gault suggested that these are also features of whites of low socio-economic status. The Aboriginal adolescent has the added burden of adapting to a part-Aboriginal status in a predominantly white community. As Gault stated (p. 132), the problems which Aborigines in settled Australia encounter (as revealed from her study of 106 Aboriginal adolescents in Victoria) are not those connected with tribal life, but rather those associated with being a 'disinherited' people, living marginally to the white society and feeling discriminated against. Gault *et al.* (1970, p. 31) duplicated these results; while Kamien (1975a, p. 352) found similar poor mental health status among Aborigines in Bourke.

These findings highlight the alienation and what Rowley (1971a, p. 352) has called 'the symptoms of frustration' of Aborigines in settled Australia. One of the major manifestations of this is illustrated by the high rate of alcoholism reported by most studies in this field (for example Lippman, 1973; Long, 1970; Metherell, 1975; and Rowley, 1971a). While there is little objective evidence on the extent of alcoholism among Aborigines, this topic is currently being studied by the House of Representatives Standing Committee on Aboriginal Affairs. It noted in its interim report (1977, p. 121) that alcoholism is not only a real problem for the alcoholic, but also has health implications for the dependants and family whose food expenditure may be diminished by the cost of liquor purchases. The only quantitative study on alcoholism among Aborigines has been done by Kamien (1975a, e). He suggested (1975e, p. 291) that, while people in country areas state that blacks cannot 'hold' liquor, there is no proof that Aborigines are genetically vulnerable to alcohol. (This belief was a main justification for 'special' drinking laws for Aborigines in Australia until 1964 and the view is probably a form of racial discrimination.) Kamien noted (1975a, p. 220) that an examination of the drinking patterns of alcohol in Bourke Aborigines revealed heavy drinking in 53.2 per cent of men and 3.1 per cent of women. The proportion of problem drinkers was 31.4 per cent of men and 3.9 per cent of women. Bourke could be an atypical example, for as Kamien (1975e, p. 296) stated, the prevalence of both heavy and problem drinkers is higher than that evidenced in other surveys. For example, Gault *et al.* (1970, p. 29) reported that alcohol is the main problem in 32.6 per cent of Aboriginal households in Victoria. Kamien also found that a disproportionate number of problem drinkers lived on the Aboriginal reserve at Bourke. Of 57 men on the reserve, 61.4 per cent were problem drinkers (1976e, p. 293). This appears to reinforce the conjecture of Long (1970, p. 90) and Moodie (1973, pp. 23–4) that those who leave settlements are the more economically and socially 'viable' sections of the Aboriginal population; and that the reserves of settled Australia have become places for the socially, psychologically and economically handicapped.

Poor psychosocial health (and the associated problem of alcoholism) appears to have contributed to the number of broken homes among Aborigines in settled Australia. Gault *et al.* (1970, p. 29) found that 41 per cent of families in their sample of Aborigines in Victoria were truncated. Similarly, Rowley (1971a, p. 331) noted that a large proportion of Aboriginal households in New South Wales and the Eyre Penninsula, South Australia, had female heads, and suggested (p.332) that matrifocal households were a part of the Aboriginal 'cycle of poverty'. Long (1970, p. 89) made a similar observation in his survey of 14 government settlements in New South Wales.

Housing

The study of housing conditions among Aborigines in settled Australia is not quite so complicated as that of those in remote Australia. As Scott (1973a, p. 44) noted, 'Generally urbanized or semi-urbanized Aborigines have needs which can be quantified in terms of European

needs or preferred states. . . .' Metherell (1975) noted (p.12) that many Moree Aborigines are now seeking assimilation, and are jealous of the standard of living of their white neighbours. Part of this standard of living is represented by housing status. Hence he reported (ibid, p. 206) the strong desire for conventional housing in a normal 'non-reserve' social setting (a desire so strong that a significant proportion of that town's Aboriginal population would resettle elsewhere to achieve this goal). Not only is there the pull of this desire, but Metherell (ibid., p. 221) also noted that families were anxious to leave the reserves (a push factor) and the tension and outbreaks of violence which occur there.

There not only appears to be a rapid natural rate of population growth among Aborigines which helps contribute to large family sizes, but there is also the feature of 'extended' family groups which readily accept kin folk (though whether this is because of the low socio-economic status of the people or because a vestigial remnant of traditional society continues, cannot be said). Most studies of Aborigines in settled Australia have commented on the extended family relationships apparent. Barwick (1963) dealt particularly with the question, but it is also referred to by Lippman (1973), Long (1970) and Rowley (1971a). While Metherell (1975, p. 165) suggested that a compromise between old and new values was resulting in a change in the character of the 'expression of community', Rowley (1971a, p. 149) observed that kinship coherence is still extremely important to Aborigines in settled Australia, especially in adversity. Similarly, it appears that regional affiliation remains strong. Rowley (1971a, p. 152) pointed out that when in the past Aborigines have been forced to move, either by authorities or the need to find gainful employment, they have maintained contact with kin in 'their' country. There is thus a propensity for Aborigines in settled Australia to be visited by relatives from far away. In general, Aboriginal households display a flexibility in accommodating large numbers. According to Kitaoji (1976, p. vi.1) this is because of the extreme housing shortage among Aborigines. Households expand as 'stable' families seek to cater for less established members within the community.

Because of these features (high population growth rates, shortage of housing, and the extended family relationships which still survive) it is not surprising that average Aboriginal households in settled Australia appear to have more than seven members, which is generally more than twice the number of members per household of adjacent white communities.[1] Moreover, the residential patterns of Aboriginal housing in settled Australia are diverse, including, as the Commission of Inquiry into Poverty research report (1974, pp. 120–4) found, some very undesirable attributes, such as locations on poorly drained, isolated land, with shanty camps based in dishevelled settings, for example on or near rubbish dumps.

What can be said of the adequacy of houses for Aborigines in settled Australia in terms of size and facilities? In Table 26 the figures (from Kamien's study in 1975) suggest that there are variations in household size within communities which the more aggregative statistics may conceal, and that the accommodation pressure is extremely high. The high accommodation pressure (for example reserve housing had 5 persons per bedroom and a mere 3 square metres per person) is not unique to Bourke (where Kamien's study was undertaken.) Metherell (1975, p. 147) noted that Housing Commission reserve homes in Moree

Table 26. *Some estimates of intra-community variations in Aboriginal household density and type, Bourke, 1971*

House type	Number	Persons per house	Persons per bedroom
1. Transitional Housing	8	13.4	4.5
2. Houses for Aborigines	9	9.1	2.8
3. Housing Commission	10	7.1	2.1
4. Privately Owned	12	7.8	3.2
5. Privately Rented	21	7.4	2.8
6. Shanties on Reserves[a]	31	7.4	5.0

[a] Mean size 14.5 sq. m.
Source: Kamien (1975a).

had an average of 9 persons per household, caravans an average of 6.6 occupants each and shanties and shacks possessed an average household size of 4.7. In Metherell's study, accommodation pressure was considered to be about three times as heavy on average for Aboriginal households in Moree compared with non-Aboriginal houses in the town. Kitaoji (1976, p. VI.4) in his survey of the McLeay Valley, New

[1] This estimate is derived from the studies of various communities made by Hill (1975), Kamien (1975a), Kitaoji (1976), Long (1970), Metherell (1975), Monk (1972), Rowley (1971a) and Scott (1972).

South Wales noted that 50 per cent of the Aborigines in this region were members of large households with 9 or more persons, while the Commission of Inquiry into Poverty (1974, p. 119) found in their survey of 286 houses in New South Wales that 37 per cent were overcrowded.

As to the quality of Aboriginal housing in settled Australia, the Commission of Inquiry into Poverty (1974, p. 119) assessed 62 (or 21.7 per cent) of the 286 houses visited in northern New South Wales as shabby and 24 (or 8.4 per cent) as very dilapidated. The balance (about 70 per cent) were regarded as being in good condition. Metherell (1975, p. 173) made a similar estimate in his study of Moree, subjectively assessing 23 per cent of houses to be in a poor condition, 40.2 per cent to be satisfactory, and 36.8 per cent to be good. He noted a marked improvement in recent times through a State Housing Commission renovation programme in Moree, following floods in 1971. Again, in its report the Senate Select Committee (1976, p. 169) commented on the appalling conditions in which Aborigines in urban and settled rural areas lived. It showed that a large proportion of Aboriginal houses in settled Australia are improvised (and, presumably, therefore substandard).

As to the extent of home ownership by Aborigines in settled Australia, a dilemma arises. There are five major types of dwelling: reserve housing; publicly rented housing (that is Housing Commission homes, and so on); privately rented houses and flats; privately owned houses and improvised dwellings (such as shanties, shacks and humpies). Is a caravan or a humpie owner a home owner? Is the responsible occupant of a house located on a reserve a home owner? (Most ownership of reserve land is vested in Aboriginal groups.) The shortest way out of the dilemma is simply to define home ownership as referring to the private ownership of a house.

According to Metherell (1975, p. 191) only 26 per cent of Aboriginal households in Moree were of the owner–purchaser type. From Kamien's study (1975a, p. 246) it can be calculated that 13 per cent of houses inhabited by Aborigines were privately owned. Kitaoji (1976, p. vi.3) noted that of the total Aboriginal population of 683 in the McLeay Valley in New South Wales only 12 per cent lived in either privately built or rented dwellings. Rowley (1971a, pp. 314–15) in his survey of Aboriginal households in New South Wales reported that in general Aborigines were not home owners. The figures for the general Australian society speak for themselves by way of comparison: according to the ABS (1977a, p. 2) nearly 70 per cent of metropolitan dwellers lived in owner-occupied homes in 1974–5.

In conclusion, something may be said about the special problem of prejudice. The Commission of Inquiry into Poverty research report (1974, p. 119) noted that real estate agents in the New South Wales country survey region were reluctant to provide Aborigines with houses for rental in the private sector because of the possible over-crowding and resulting property damage. The report also observed (p. 137) that Aborigines were stereotyped as being more likely than other tenants to induce dangers of disease by a relative lack of hygiene. Again, Larsen *et al.* (1977, p. 8) suggested that discrimination against Aborigines in housing was indicated in their survey by low access to the private renting market, usually as a result of the refusal of land agents to rent to blacks. Higher tariffs – generally in the form of substantial bonds – were also, according to the same survey, required from Aborigines as a hedge against possible property damage. Apart from private rental discrimination, there seems also to be differentiation on the part of the State Housing Commissions in some States, for example New South Wales. This differentiation is implicit (and may at times be explicit) because, as Kamien (1975a, p. 255) noted, the New South Wales Housing Commission is chronically short of funds and needs to balance its income and expenditure. This shortage tends to make the poorer, problematical families less 'rewarding' tenants whom the Commission may prefer, therefore, to avoid. As the Senate Select Committee (1976, p. 186) commented, current administrative practice seems naturally to favour tenants with good (actual or per-ceived potential) rent records, good property maintenance practices, small families, and a breadwinner in regular employment. But Aborigines, especially humpie dwellers or reserve residents, may be unable to meet any of these criteria, and the Commission of Inquiry into Poverty research report (1974, p. 127) has noted 'a stock accep-tance of the status quo' by Aborigines, some of whom have been on waiting lists for seventeen years, while many would wait for five years or more. The extent of excess Aboriginal demand for Housing Com-mission accommodation is illustrated by Table 27, taken from the Senate Select Committee Report.

Poor and overcrowded housing conditions among Aborigines in settled Australia have indirect but important consequences for the economic status of the people, especially their health. Moodie (1973, p. 33) has pointed out that it is not the average number of occupants

per house, but the range that is of special importance in health considerations. For it is at the upper part of the range that the problem of
overloaded household facilities becomes acute and hygiene difficulties
begin to appear. Similarly, Moodie noted (p. 33) that overcrowded

Table 27. *Outstanding applications for public housing,
1976*

State	Housing provided under State grants 1975/76	Outstanding applications 30 June 1976
New South Wales	152	1000
South Australia[a]	143	361
Tasmania	7	55
Victoria	50	160
Western Australia[a]	71	1000

[a] While parts of these States are in 'remote' Australia, the
majority of public housing is in settled areas.
Source: Senate Select Committee on Aborigines and Torres
Strait Islanders (1976).

living conditions added to the risks of contracting communicable diseases, especially respiratory and contact infections. The Commission
of Inquiry into Poverty research report (1974, p. 125) noted that 20 per
cent of Aboriginal houses surveyed had insufficient furniture or floor
covering, and (p. 129) that the poor structural standard of much of
the accommodation resulted in health problems, especially in cold
weather. The report (p. 221) also noted the absence of basic facilities in
many Aboriginal homes and (p. 222) that there was a direct relationship between housing standard and the rate of admission to hospital of
children at Wilcannia in New South Wales.

Education

Education has most important consequences for the economic status of
Aborigines in settled Australia. Whereas in Chapter 2 doubt was
expressed about the validity of applying Western value oriented standards to Aborigines in remote Australia, there is less inhibition here to
do so. In settled Australia the traditional ways as taught by tribal elders
are less in evidence, while Aborigines do not have the same ready

possibility of access to, or opting for, the traditional economic system (compared with those on outstation communities). For employment, Aborigines in settled Australia must for the most part participate in the market economy and compete with white labour. Clearly, educational attainment is an important determinant of occupational status.

Because racially separate statistics are not compiled by educational authorities in most States, it is impossible to obtain comprehensive figures on the educational status of Aborigines in settled Australia. But figures collected by the Commission of Inquiry into Poverty report (1977, p. 187) indicate that the 'formal educational' registrations among Aborigines in Victoria and New South Wales (parts of settled Australia) are greater, proportionately, than those in remote Australia, as discussed in Chapter 2. But the statistics of more interest here are those given in Table 28 which compare the formal educational attainments of Aborigines and those for the general Australian society, at least as reflected by New South Wales and Victoria. From this table it appears that, although there has been a marked improvement for Aborigines between 1966 and 1971, it is obvious that there is a wide discrepancy between their educational attainments in these two States compared with general levels.

Table 28. *Education level of Aboriginal males (over 15 years of age), 1966 and 1971*

	Attended level 10, per cent		Attended level 9, per cent		Attended levels 6–8, per cent		Attended levels 1–5, per cent		Never attended, per cent	
	1966	1971	1966	1971	1966	1971	1966	1971	1966	1971
New South Wales	1.7	3.8	6.5	4.5	33.3	43.7	42.5	37.5	6.9	3.4
Victoria	1.8	10.0	6.4	12.1	26.9	43.0	48.3	26.0	3.5	1.8
Aborigines, all Australia	0.7	1.9	2.6	2.2	14.1	23.5	40.4	42.4	34.5	23.5
Non-Aborigines	16.1	21.5	23.2	12.1	28.5	39.9	28.7	21.3	0.8	0.5

Source: Commission of Inquiry into Poverty (1977).

The results of specific surveys lend support to a picture of comparatively low formal educational attainments for Aborigines in settled Australia, compared with the general society. Metherell (1975, p. 235) quotes the findings of a study by the New South Wales Teachers' Federation which showed that, of the 1,600 Aboriginal students in 172

secondary schools in New South Wales, only 11 per cent had proceeded beyond Form 3, compared with 25 per cent of white pupils. The
survey also reported a high proportion of Aborigines in the 'slow
learner' category, a finding confirmed by Scott's study (1972, p. 9.7) in
certain schools in New South Wales. However, this study also noted
(p. 9.10) a marked improvement between 1969 and 1972. In the former
year, in the schools concerned, no less than 93 per cent of Aboriginal
pupils were in remedial classes.

There is, of course, a variety of difficulties confronting Aborigines
who seek to attain formal educational qualifications in settled
Australia. Health conditions clearly hamper their efforts, especially a
high incidence of ear disease, and absenteeism which must often
spring from sickness. Living in poor quality, overcrowded housing
also has consequences for education. For example, there are often no
proper facilities by way of space or furniture for doing homework; and
commuting long distances to (integrated) schools also presents difficulties. Moreover, there are many other aspects which constrain the
acquisition of educational attainments by Aborigines, a good account
of which is given in Chapter 6 of the Commission of Inquiry into
Poverty report (1977) dealing specifically with Aborigines and education. These constraints include active discrimination by white students
and parents in integrated schools; the home environment of Aboriginal children, in which there may be a lack of parental interest in the
child's performance, especially where families are broken or where
parents experience poor health and have a large family. The themes of
the Commission of Inquiry into Poverty report are similar to those in
the comments of other observers, for example Scott (1972, p. 9.17) and
Kamien (1975, p. 37). In a sense, of course, the basic educational
problem confronting Aborigines in settled Australia is similar to that
faced by other disadvantaged groups: they generally attend schools
where they are in the minority. They are thus subject to a similar
curriculum as are the majority – a curriculum that fails adequately to
take into account different home environments, community experiences and expectations.

The educational opportunities of Aborigines in general, especially
those in settled Australia, have risen rapidly owing to a substantial
government intervention in the education field in recent years. In 1970,
two schemes, the Aboriginal Secondary Grants Scheme (ABSEG) and
the Aboriginal Study Grants Scheme (ASGS) were announced.
ABSEG provided children aged fourteen and over who were still

attending secondary school with a number of benefits: a textbook and uniform allowance, a living allowance (for living at home or away from home), a personal allowance, and all fees and fares to and from school (Watts, 1976, p. 271–2). ASGS offers financial assistance to Aborigines (or Islanders) who wish to continue their education after leaving school. This financial assistance takes the form of a basic living, a dependants' and an establishment allowance. In 1973, the ABSEG scheme became available for Aboriginal secondary students of all ages, and in 1975 the Overseas Study Award was introduced for Aborigines. The criterion for qualifying for these benefits is that one should be of Aboriginal descent. Watts (1976, p. 226) noted that the scheme is generally available to all those qualified *who apply*. In Table 29 the numbers of recipients of both these schemes to 1976

Table 29. *Aboriginal secondary grant and Aboriginal study grant recipients, 1971–6*

Year	ABSEG recipients	ASGS recipients
1971	4,025[a]	499
1972	4,779[a]	689
1973	10,621	1,113
1974	10,669	1,467
1975	11,762	1,875
1976	12,816	2,253

[a] Till 1973 ABSEG was available only to Aboriginal students over the age of 14 years.
Sources: Watts (1976); Department of Aboriginal Affairs (1976).

are shown. Unfortunately, it is not possible to isolate for settled Australia the number of pupils that receive these grants, since the data are too aggregative. However, it is assumed that the majority of recipients is in settled Australia, for most secondary schools are in this region, and as noted above, there appeared to be a greater propensity of Aborigines to attend secondary schools in settled Australia.

The effectiveness of the ABSEG scheme has been the subject of a study by Watts (1976). (This scheme is of greater importance than the ASGS – for example, in 1976, 12,816 Aborigines received ABSEG awards, as against 2,253 who received ASGS awards.) She concluded (p. 228) that although it took time for knowledge of the scheme to spread, it has increased the holding power of schools – in fact, she suggested that ABSEG has been a major factor encouraging students to stay at school after the age of fifteen. However, a 'white backlash' to this scheme, which discriminates in favour of Aborigines, is noted (p. 266). Metherell (1975, p. 239) noted a similar reaction (jealousy and bitterness) among poor whites in Moree – especially as the ABSEG scheme is meant to act as an incentive to Aborigines to attend secondary school and to compensate for the opportunity cost (in terms of wages forgone) of attending school when employable. However, it is probable that many Aborigines are in need of the financial assistance this scheme provides (as described in sections below). Other comments which Metherell noted (p. 238) as being made about the ABSEG scheme were (1) that payment should be subject to adequate attendance and progress, (2) that some proportion of the grant should be paid to the school, and (3) that payments to parents should be spread over the year. (The scheme has now also been extended to whites on a means-tested basis.)

Another scheme, the Employment Training Scheme for Aborigines (ETSA) was established in 1969, predominantly to train adult Aborigines for skilled employment. However, this scheme has had obvious repercussions on Aboriginal educational status. In 1974, the National Employment and Training (NEAT) Scheme was introduced for all Australians. ETSA was integrated with NEAT, with special provisions for Aborigines being incorporated into it. (Aborigines qualify for NEAT generally as a special disadvantaged group.) However, like ETSA, the main purpose of this scheme is specific training for employment, and is discussed below.

It seems, therefore, that government policy has recognised the low educational status of Aborigines, and has introduced special schemes to encourage Aborigines to pursue secondary and further education. However, as noted, low educational status is the consequence of a number of features other than lack of finance.

Employment

Within the confines of available information this section attempts to describe and assess the low employment status of Aborigines in settled Australia; their occupational status in the private sector; and the nature and extent of government intervention in attempting to alleviate the current situation.

As noted in Chapters 1 and 2, the Working Party on Aboriginal Employment (DAA, 1976e) calculated (p.9) that on the basis of Aborigines *registered* for employment, the unemployment rate for Aborigines in Australia was 30 per cent (in mid-1976). However, it estimated that in *real* terms the Aboriginal unemployment rate would be over 50 per cent. The House of Representatives Standing Committee on Aboriginal Affairs (1976b, p. 10) made a similar observation. While it estimated the Aboriginal unemployment rate to be 25 per cent (in September 1975) it noted 'Evidence suggests that the number of Aboriginals registered for unemployment does not reflect the true level of their unemployment . . . figures understate the actual unemployment position of Aborigines.'

To what extent is Aboriginal unemployment in settled Australia similar to the Australia-wide Aboriginal situation? In the same report, the Standing Committee (p. 10) reported a 35 per cent unemployment rate for Aborigines in New South Wales, in contrast to an overall unemployment rate (Aborigines and non-Aborigines) of 4.3 per cent in September 1975. Whether this implies that the situation in New South Wales was worse than elsewhere in Australia, or whether Aborigines in this State, owing to its closer settlement, have a greater propensity to register for unemployment, is difficult to decide. Scott (1972, pp. 4–5) in their survey of unemployment among Aborigines in the south coast region of New South Wales, reported that, on the basis of Aborigines registered with the Commonwealth Employment Service (CES) for employment, the unemployment rate was 12.5 per cent. However, on the basis of a virtual 100 per cent sample survey in the Nowra area, they found 23 per cent of the potential work force unemployed. Other estimates of Aboriginal unemployment for particular regions and towns in settled Australia have been given by Metherell (1975, p. 72) and the DAA (1976d, p. 47), and are presented in Table 30. The implication of these figures is that Aboriginal unemployment in settled Australia is extremely high, by Australia-wide standards. However, the statistics cannot be taken as strictly representative of the whole of settled Australia. The situation in the Casino–Lismore Region (northern New South Wales) gives some indication of how low employment levels can be.

It appears certain (as suggested in Chapter 1) that since 1971, the unemployment situation for Aborigines has deteriorated rapidly, and

that the Aboriginal unemployment rate is many times the overall
Australian rate. This extremely high level of unemployment has reper-
cussions for Aboriginal communities within settled Australia. As
Metherell (1975, p.251) noted, in view of the level of Aboriginal un-

Table 30. *Estimates of Aboriginal unemployment rates in 'settled'*
Australia [a]

	Year	Unemployment rate (per cent)
Region		
Taree (NSW) CES Area	1974	45
Grafton (NSW) CES Area	1974	33
Kempsey (NSW) CES Area	1974	45
Casino–Lismore (NSW) CES Area	1974	84
Taree CES Area	1975	57
Grafton CES Area	1975	36
Kempsey CES Area	1975	46
Casino–Lismore CES Area	1975	99
Town		
Moree (NSW)	1971	4.7
Moree	1974	36.5

[a] Mid-year estimates.
Sources: Metherell (1975); Department of Aboriginal Affairs (1976d).

employment in Moree (36.5 per cent in 1974) it seems to young
Aborigines a token of double standards to hear that a 5 per cent
unemployment rate for whites is regarded as intolerable and unpre-
cedented in the period since World War II. And it is not surprising that
the young are the most disillusioned. For, owing to the age structure of
the Aboriginal population, youth unemployment is particularly high.
The Working Party on Aboriginal Employment (DAA, 1976e, p. 12)
noted that a study undertaken by the DAA in March, 1976, showed
that only 800 (or 40 per cent) of an estimated 2,000 Aboriginal school-
leavers of December 1975 had been placed in employment.

What occupational status do Aborigines hold under such conditions? Unfortunately, there is little data aside from the aggregative
census results. The information implies that Aborigines in settled areas
in general hold unskilled jobs. This observation is reinforced by the
analysis by Metherell of disaggregated census results for Moree, New

South Wales. He reported (1975, pp. 85–7) that in 1971, 0.9 per cent of the Aboriginal work force had white-collar jobs as against 38.2 per cent of the white labour force of that town. Some 73.8 per cent of employed Aboriginal men held labouring jobs. Employed Aboriginal women were mainly in domestic service (70 per cent) and 10 per cent were labourers or operatives. In general, a number of commentators have noted the unskilled nature of the Aboriginal labour force. Monk (1974, p. 166), in her study of six towns in New South Wales, stated that Aborigines have historically occupied a marginal position in the work force. Those employed have been mainly in unskilled positions which bring no status in the white community and little economic security. Rowley (1971a) in his survey in New South Wales noted (p. 337) the casual and seasonal nature of Aboriginal employment. The most common characteristic of the Aboriginal work force (p. 343) appeared to be its 'last on/first off the job' nature. Hill (1975, p. 161) noted that the majority of Aborigines employed in the private sector, in her two case study towns in Western Australia, were engaged in agricultural work. The type of jobs they held were shearing, cropping, crutching, root-picking, and seeding. Similarly the Commission of Inquiry into Poverty (1974, pp. 137–41) noted that the largest occupational category for the 350 households surveyed in northern New South Wales was labourer. Other large categories included truckdriver, stockman/ station hand, mill hand/factory worker, coalminer, and plant operator. The report noted that, while seasonal agricultural work is available (picking tomatoes, digging potatoes and picking peas) it was generally the Aborigines from the poorer western regions of New South Wales that provided this labour. This phenomenon has also been noted by Austin and Murray (1974, p. 2). Seasonal work is available picking fruit in orchards in the Goulburn Valley of Victoria. However, while there is a shortage of labour, local Aborigines do not tend to pick, but leave this work to migratory Aborigines. They also noted (p. 5) that Aborigines took part in seasonal work (grape picking) in the Sunraysia and Coomealla Districts on the Victoria/New South Wales border.

The overall nature of Aboriginal employment in the private sector is extremely difficult to fathom. This is primarily due to the lack of reliable information, partially resulting from the casual nature of many of the employment opportunities open to Aborigines. The variation in labour demand that may occur from one geographic region to another also complicates the analysis, as does the heterogeneity of the location of Aboriginal communities in settled Australia. In rural areas and smaller rural towns, Aborigines appear to represent a primarily unskilled and semi-skilled rural work force. In the larger urban centres in settled Australia, where there may be secondary and tertiary industries, they equally seem to constitute a predominantly unskilled work force. Metherell (1975, p. 252) conducted an employment survey in Moree in 1974, and found that the abattoir was the largest single employer of unskilled Aborigines followed in importance by itinerant rural work. The local flour mill was also an erratic employer of Aborigines, but there were no other employers in the private sector. Similarly, Kamien (1975a, p. 33) reported that Aboriginal men and women employed in the private sector at Bourke obtained seasonal work on sheep stations, at the meat works and in orchards.

There appear to be a number of reasons for the low occupational status of Aborigines employed in the private sector, the hallmark of this status being lack of job security. Firstly, the Aboriginal labour force tends to be poorly educated, and lacks work skills. This is partly evidenced by the low education status of the Aboriginal population of settled Australia mentioned above. Similarly, the poor health conditions among Aborigines constrain their work efficiency; as the Commission of Inquiry into Poverty report (1974, p. 141) noted, the Aboriginal labour force is primarily involved in unskilled labouring which requires physical work from people who are very often in poor health. A combination of these two factors explains the 'last hired/first fired' treatment of Aborigines and their susceptibility to short-term (cyclical) economic fluctuations. Metherell (1975, p. 85) suggested that, until 1971, Aborigines were absorbed into unskilled jobs, but with the onslaught of the recession in the Australian economy in 1974, they have been forced into casual work (with much underemployment) or chronic unemployment. The question arises as to whether the current level of unemployment among Aborigines is mostly of a cyclical or structural nature (the latter perhaps associated with a long-term decline in rural industries). At present, this question is difficult to answer. But some unemployment among Aborigines, especially in the rural sector, appears due to structural changes including especially the substitution of labour by capital. Metherell (1975, pp. 68–9) suggested that, in northern New South Wales, the occupational structure of the work force is changing, with a decrease in numbers employed in primary and secondary industries, and an increase in those employed in the service sector. In Moree, he noted a decline in unskilled occupations (process work, labouring) and non-managerial professions, and an increase in professional and technical occupations. If indeed white-collar, as against blue-collar, occupations are increasing in importance, then unemployment among Aborigines can be attributed more to structural than cyclical forces.

The Working Party on Aboriginal Employment (DAA, 1976e) noted (p. 10) a general lack of social experience among Aborigines (as a result of a chronic isolation from non-Aboriginal society) and as a consequence a difficulty in relating to employment assistance agencies (exemplified by the above-mentioned lack of registration for employment). This also appears to result in a low propensity for Aborigines to become members of trade unions (Austin and Murray, 1974, p. 1). These features imply that a 'cultural chasm' in the employment field may have had great repercussions for Aborigines during the current recession.

While Aborigines may be less attractive than non-Aborigines to many employers (on the basis of educational and other qualifications), an additional disadvantage which Aborigines face is discrimination in employment. As observed in the introduction, the general society appears to have a number of negative stereotypes about Aborigines. The one which seems to have the greatest consequence on the employment status of Aborigines is their alleged 'unreliability'. Moodie (1973, p. 39) noted that employers still hold the stereotype that Aborigines 'go walkabout' as if it were a racially inherited characteristic. He suggested that it is quite rare for Aborigines to leave a locality without a definite reason or objective. A departure is based on a decision not a whim or an 'instinct'. Gale (1964, p. 301) undertook a systematic survey in South Australia to see if Aborigines do 'go walkabout'. She suggested that the attitudes of the general community are inaccurate, and that 66 per cent of Aborigines in her survey in permanent employment had been employed in the same job for over one year. Gale (1964) concluded (p. 302) that Aborigines take seasonal work because it is the only work available and not because they possess, as people, a 'shiftless nature'. (A circular cause/effect argument seems to exist here: are Aboriginal workers itinerant because of a lack of permanent jobs or is there a lack of permanent jobs because they are itinerant?) The 'walkabout' or unreliability reputation attached to Aborigines also appears inconsistent with the strong regional and kinship affiliation described above. The Working Party (DAA, 1976e) also noted this and stated (p. 10) that 'Aboriginal people are generally reluctant to move from their local area for a variety of reasons. A survey at the end of June 1975 indicated that 48 per cent of all Aboriginals in the sample who were registered stated that they were unwilling to move to seek employment. Only 30 per cent of those registered stated that they were willing to seek alternative employment outside of their area, and the intentions of the remaining 22 per cent were unknown.' It seems, therefore, that allegations of unreliability among Aborigines as a justification for failure to employ them in the private sector are in many instances unwarranted. It is more likely that, as with non-Aborigines, some Aborigines are reliable and others are not. Lippman (1973, p. 164) suggested that employment prejudice is sometimes based on a discouraging experience with one or two Aborigines; however, employers do not, it seems, tend to categorise whites in the same manner.

The major way in which discrimination affects Aborigines is that, when they apply for advertised vacancies, they are told that these have been filled (House of Representatives Standing Committee on Aboriginal Affairs, 1976b, p. 11). The only systematic survey of discrimination in employment is that undertaken by Larsen *et al.* (1977) at Townsville in north Queensland. They reported (p. 12) that 50 per cent of Aboriginal applicants for job vacancies were refused an interview, whereas all European applicants for the same jobs were granted interviews. The Committee noted that 'when we add the probably large number who are rejected spuriously after some assessment, we begin to grasp the magnitude of employment discrimination'. This discrimination seems to occur despite the Racial Discrimination Act 1975, which makes it unlawful to decide not to employ someone because of the person's race, colour or national or ethnic origin.

It seems that the low employment status of Aborigines is partly a direct consequence of low socio-economic status – especially low educational qualifications. The low occupational status of Aborigines results in their suffering most owing to cyclical and structural changes in the Australian economy. Even when Aborigines have qualifications *similar* to non-Aborigines they are actively discriminated against in the labour market according to Lippman (1973, p. 92). As Larsen *et al.* (1977, p. 12) noted, Aborigines are well aware of this discrimination, to the extent that they often deliberately inform potential employers of their Aboriginal identity to save themselves possible embarrassment. A Department of Aboriginal Affairs report (1977b, pp. 23–4) noted (p. 24) a similar situation at Port Augusta, South Australia, where no

Aborigines were found to hold jobs with private firms, and resigned themselves to this by stating 'The town is well established and it's hard for Aborigines to get in.'

Given the probable distortion in the private sector labour market resulting from discrimination, and the general low employment status of Aborigines in settled Australia, one would expect government intervention in this field. In fact, since 1969, the Commonwealth government has discriminated positively in favour of Aborigines. In that year, two schemes, the Employment Training Scheme for Aborigines (ETSA) and Special Work Projects (SWPs) were introduced.

ETSA was designed to encourage the employment of Aborigines, and to facilitate their movement to areas where they could obtain regular employment (Department of Labour and Immigration, 1975a, p. 15). Whether this mobility was to escape employment discrimination or to leave depressed areas with a deficient demand for labour, is not clear. The scheme provided for the payment of fares to take up employment (and for junior Aborigines an allowance for living away from home), payment of return air-fares to visit families, payment of the first week's accommodation costs, and assistance with daily fares and clothing grants. In other words, incentives were given to Aborigines to undertake employment, with a training component. Employers were also given an incentive (in the form of a subsidy) to employ Aborigines and to provide on-the-job training for a period of not less than 12 months. The scheme was in full operation from 1969 to 1974 and during this time allocations rose from $24,428 per annum to $615,000. Approximately 4,000 Aborigines were placed in subsidised employment/training. The success or failure of this scheme is not clear. The Department of Labour and Immigration in its submission to the House of Representatives Standing Committee on Aboriginal Affairs (DLI, 1975a, p. 16) suggested that the scheme was important in encouraging Aborigines to enter regular employment to acquire work skills and to move from areas of no employment potential to areas of industrial activity. However, the statistics in the same submission (p. 17) call the success of the scheme to question. Twenty per cent of ETSA participants (male) held unskilled jobs and 38 per cent held semi-skilled jobs. Only 23 per cent of all junior males were apprentices. The rate of success of ETSA can also be judged by its completion rate – 26 per cent of trainees completed their period of subsidised employment/ training, and 49 per cent stayed for four months or longer. Some commentators (e.g. Metherell, 1975, p. 296) suggest that the scheme was not particularly successful because it was not actively promoted among Aborigines.

In October 1974, ETSA was phased out and absorbed into the National Employment and Training (NEAT) Scheme. Under this, nation-wide provisions were made for Aborigines. A major improvement of NEAT over ETSA was the inclusion in the scheme of the possibility of formal training providing the same general benefits as ETSA, but with additional provisions (DLI, 1975a, p. 18), including longer periods of employer subsidy (the full period of apprenticeships is subsidised), the possibility for employers to engage Aboriginal school-leavers, and the possibility of subsidisation of upgrading of on-the-job training. By June 1975, the DAA (1976e, p. 18) noted that 1,470 Aborigines were NEAT trainees (10 per cent of total).

In recent years, there has also been an increase in the availability of pre-vocational and pre-employment training courses which take into account the special needs in education and training of Aborigines (DAA, 1977c, p. 1). These courses have aimed at providing Aborigines with *useful* qualifications (unlike the Training Allowance Scheme, see Chapter 2), which will be recognised by private employers. A particularly successful vocational training scheme mentioned by the Working Party on Aboriginal Employment (DAA, 1976e, p. 14) is that operated by the New South Wales Department of Technical and Further Education (TAFE). This scheme is based on the New Zealand Maori Trade Training Scheme and in 1975 had an 80 per cent success rate.

The distinction between direct employment creating schemes (that is, on-the-job training) and indirect employment creating schemes (such as formal or special vocational training schemes) is indeed fine. As noted above, the ASGS scheme and the ABSEG scheme both aim at encouraging Aborigines to increase their investment in human capital. The NEAT scheme similarly has this intention and while this scheme is primarily employment-oriented, many Aborigines studying in regular or special courses are receiving allowances under it.

The other scheme which discriminated in favour of Aborigines also commenced in 1969, namely the Special Work Projects (SWP) Scheme. Initially, this scheme was conceived as being a temporary unemployment relief measure for Aborigines; no special emphasis was given to on-the-job training, as this was seen as the aim of ETSA. From 1969/70 to 1971/72 funds allocated for this scheme were not large – rising from $35,000 to $352,000 (House of Representatives, 1976b, p. 304). The major share of funds went to local government authorities in settled Australia that had the highest rates of Aboriginal unemployment. This scheme had little opportunity cost, for grants under it were to a large extent offset by the value of social service benefits that would have been paid, and tax paid on wages received by Aborigines on the scheme. The type of work provided for Aborigines was of an unskilled labouring nature.

Since 1972/73, the goals of SWP have expanded to: (1) alleviate unemployment in regions where employment opportunities are lacking and (2) provide on-the-job training for *permanent* employment. (This change of goals can be associated with the formation of the Department of Aboriginal Affairs in 1972 and its involvement with SWP. The allocation of funds for 1972/73 was $3,430,000 and by 1976/77 had grown to $6,500,000.) With the expansion of SWP Aboriginal and other organisations, such as hospitals, became eligible for grants. The proviso was also made that when local (or State) government authorities received SWP grants they should consult with local Aboriginal communities as to how the grants should be spent. (According to the House of Representatives (1976b, p. 6) these authorities still receive the major share of SWP funds.)

In general, it appears that the SWP scheme, while no doubt providing short-term unemployment relief, has been a failure in its twin goals of providing training to Aboriginal participants, and of providing continuing employment. The House of Representatives report (1976b, p. 14), in its examination of 100 SWP positions in the north of New South Wales, found that only 13 clerical positions and 4 technical assistant jobs could provide significant training. The remaining positions (83 per cent) were described as being 'at best of a semi-skilled or labouring nature'. It also noted (p. 14) that few permanent jobs have resulted from SWP positions because many State and local government authorities do not have funds available to permanently employ Aborigines. A Department of Aboriginal Affairs field study of Special Work Projects in the north coast area of New South Wales duplicated these findings (DAA, 1976d, pp. 45–6). Furthermore, it stated (p.45) that 'Aboriginal communities have rarely been consulted about projects and few Aboriginal organisations have partaken in the Scheme.' The House of Representatives report (1976b, pp. 14–15) suggested that benefits of a social nature have resulted from SWP – owing to improved (black–white) community relations, increased Aboriginal morale and improvements to community facilities. The DAA (1976d, p. 45) suggested that 'any changes in attitudes or behaviour of whites towards Aboriginals have been gradual and cannot really be attributed to SWPs'.

The apparent lack of success of the SWP scheme in the public sector resulted in a pilot scheme, initiated in 1976, in the private sector. A condition of Private Sector Special Work Project (PS-SWP) grants, was that the employer guarantee job permanency. A DAA report (1976f) which analysed PS-SWPs when they were at the pilot scheme stage, suggested (p. 1) that the permanency rate (per position) was much higher (with a ratio of 4 permanent positions out of every 5 as against a ratio of 1:15 in the public sector) and that the average period of the grant (employer subsidy) was shorter, and hence the cost per permanent position much lower ($5,000 compared with $175,500). However, the 58 pilot project employers were carefully selected and this may have biased the results. The DAA report noted (p. 5) that even if employers did not honour the permanency guarantee, the training received was generally marketable, whereas the training received in unskilled jobs with local government authorities is rarely so. This is because two-thirds of the positions created under the PS-SWP Scheme were in skilled trades or clerical positions (DAA, 1976e, p. 16). Another difference between the PS-SWPs and the local government SWPs is that (up to 1977) women have been employed in the former but not in the latter.

Aborigines have also been employed in Australia-wide employment schemes. The major scheme of this nature was the Regional Employment Development (RED) Scheme which was introduced in September 1974 to improve employment opportunities in areas of excessively high unemployment (DLI, 1975a, p. 22), by funding labour intensive programmes of a 'socially useful or economically viable nature'. Aborigines had no special advantage in this scheme – employment was provided to people who had been unemployed the longest and who had dependants. It is some indication of the low employment status of Aborigines that they were recruited for RED to a greater extent (proportionally) then non-Aborigines. The House of Representatives report (1976b, p. 17) enumerated 1,800 Aborigines taking part in RED in July 1975 (5.6 per cent of the total number under this scheme). At the end of 1975, RED was abolished by the Liberal–Country Party coalition government, and many of these people were once again unemployed.

The DAA also funds a number of Aboriginal organisations which provide employment opportunities for Aborigines (*not* only in settled

Australia). The major organisations are Aboriginal Hostels Pty Ltd, Aboriginal Arts and Crafts Pty Ltd, and various legal aid offices, housing associations and medical centres (House of Representatives, 1976b, p. 19). It also makes grants to Aboriginal communities (often in remote Australia) and individuals to establish long-term economic projects (DAA, 1976e, p. 20). The Aboriginal Loans Commission also makes loans to Aboriginal communities or individuals to establish economically viable enterprises that have employment potential.

Another employment creating scheme is the 'relocation scheme', initiated in New South Wales in 1972, and which has assisted 42 Aboriginal families (by 1976) from depressed areas in western New South Wales to resettle in towns of good economic potential (DAA, 1976d, p. 23). However, the extent to which such a relocation programme will be a success is dependent on the willingness of Aborigines to move. Evidence above suggests that many Aborigines are reluctant to leave areas with which they have some affiliation.

Finally, the Commonwealth government has adopted the policy that its departments and instrumentalities employ a percentage of Aborigines corresponding to their proportion of the total Australian population (approximately 1 per cent). In Table 31 Aboriginal em-

Table 31. *Aboriginal employment in the Australian Public Service, 1973–5*

	Aboriginal staff				Ratio of Aboriginal to total staff (per cent)			
	1973	1974	1975	1976	1973	1974	1975	1976
NSW	29	77	107	94	0.10	0.25	0.33	0.28
Vict.	4	20	33	26	0.01	0.06	0.09	0.07
Qld.	34	57	70	72	0.27	0.43	0.47	0.51
SA	7	13	28	33	0.07	0.12	0.21	0.27
WA	14	30	29	40	0.19	0.38	0.35	0.50
Tas.	2	1	1	1	0.09	0.04	0.04	0.04
NT	435	1,470[a]	1,233	1,274	4.91	14.17	12.34	13.09
ACT	59	89	90	85	0.22	0.29	0.26	0.25
Aust.	584	1,757	1,591	1,625	0.42	1.19	1.01	1.04

[a] This significant increase is due to the abolition of the Training Allowance Scheme (see Chapter 2).
Source: Department of Aboriginal Affairs (1977g).

ployment in the Australian Public Service, by State, is presented. If one excludes the Northern Territory (where most Public Service positions resulted from the abolition of the Training Allowance Scheme), only 0.23 per cent of the Public Service (358 Aborigines) was Aboriginal in 1976. It also appears that Aborigines are generally recruited to the lower echelons of the Public Service. As the House of Representatives report (1976b, p. 32) noted, 94 per cent of Aborigines (in 1975) were recruited to the 4th Division as against 71 per cent for public servants generally, and only 3 per cent went to the 2nd or 3rd Divisions compared with 29 per cent for all public servants.

In conclusion, therefore, it appears that Aborigines in settled Australia experience an extremely low employment status, owing predominantly to their lack of qualifications and vocational training in comparison with non-Aborigines with whom they must compete in the labour market. Discrimination by employers appears to present a further employment barrier to Aborigines. Since 1971 the relative employment status of Aborigines appears to have worsened substantially, due to the recession of the Australian economy. Government intervention has not been substantial enough to alleviate extremely high levels of Aboriginal unemployment. However, this intervention has resulted in some upward occupational mobility with most Aborigines in professional occupations being employed by the Commonwealth government, its agencies, or schemes which it funds directly. (Many of these positions are, however, in the lower echelons of the occupational hierarchy.)

Income status and expenditure patterns

As a result of the low employment status of the Aboriginal population of settled Australia, combined with the young age structure of the population and high dependency rates, one would expect consequently low incomes. Unfortunately, data shortcomings once again curtail analysis. Only four studies have estimated the income levels of Aboriginal communities in non-metropolitan Australia and only two of these are in depth. Moreover, all these estimates have been made in New South Wales, giving the analysis a regional bias. The income estimates for six towns in New South Wales made by Monk (1972, p. 265) are presented in Table 32.

The mean per capita disposable income for these six towns was $349 per annum in 1965. An interesting feature of Table 32 is the high variation in per capita income between towns (the standard deviation was $132.25) with Aboriginal residents of Fingal Point enjoying an income 2½ times that of those at Coraki. This emphasises the inter-regional differences in the economic status of Aborigines in settled Australia. The average income estimate derived by Monk represents approximately 29 per cent of the average per capita disposable income of all Australians for that year.

Table 32. *Disposable income estimates of Aborigines in six towns in New South Wales, 1965*

Town	Mean annual household income ($)	Average number of members	Per capita income ($)
Fingal Point	3,426	6.3	544
Deniliquin	3,377	7.4	456
Griffith	2,452	6.7	366
Coff's Harbour	1,853	8.1	229
Cowra	2,058	7.2	286
Coraki	1,638	7.8	210

Source: Monk (1972).

Kamien (1975a, p. 34) estimated that in mid-1971 'a time of almost full employment for Aborigines in Bourke, per capita income from all sources was just over $8 per week or at most $416 per annum'. This figure represents about 23 per cent of the average Australia-wide disposable income for that year.

Kitaoji (1976, p. VI.8) conducted a survey of 77 Aboriginal households in the MacLeay Valley, northern New South Wales. He estimated average weekly household income to be $58.25 or $8.56 per capita. This figure is similar to Kamien's estimate, and on an annual basis is approximately $445, or 25 per cent of Australian disposable household income per capita.

Metherell (1975) also conducted a survey of 174 Aboriginal households in Moree, New South Wales in 1974, the results of which are presented in Table 33. He found (p. 91) average weekly household income to be $102.97 with a per capita income of $14.50 per week, (average household size being 7.1 persons). At an annual rate this was $754 per capita or 29 per cent of Australian-wide per capita disposable income in 1974. (It should be noted that child endowment payments were not included in Metherell's estimates, hence this figure would be a slight underestimate.)

Table 33. *Average income per household, per capita, by household type, in Moree, New South Wales, 1974*

Housing type	Net weekly household income ($)	Average household size (persons)	Per capita income ($)
Housing Commission reserve houses	113.82	9.0	12.65
Housing Commission town houses	98.3	6.7	14.67
Owner/purchaser	103.58	5.9	17.56
Private rental	123.64	7.0	17.66
Self-contained flats	86.67	3.0	28.89
Non self-contained flats	90.00	5.1	17.65
Converted garages	70.00	2.0	35.00
Caravans	92.75	6.6	14.05
Shanties/shacks	61.75	4.7	13.14
Total Moree Aborigines (average)	102.97	7.1	14.50

Source: Metherell (1975).

It is quite surprising that per capita incomes of Aborigines in settled Australia appear to be of a similar magnitude to those of Aborigines in remote Australia (see Chapter 2). One would expect per capita incomes of the former to be higher, owing to their proximity to and greater involvement in the market economy. In Chapter 2, it was noted that Aborigines may have in-kind sources of income which non-Aborigines do not enjoy. In general it seems as though Aborigines in settled Australia do not have these sources of income to the same extent as Aborigines in remote Australia. However, subsidised education and subsidised housing are two exceptions. Subsidised education comes in the form of ABSEG and ASGS grants that have been described above; the only condition one must fulfil to qualify for these is to prove one's 'Aboriginality'. It also seems that while Aborigines may not be adequately accommodated from a 'quality of housing' or 'size of house' point of view, they are securely accommodated from an income point of view. Metherell (1975, p. 202) found that, in Moree, 86.8 per cent of households paid less than 20 per cent of weekly household income for rent or repayments; (24.1 per cent paid 5–10 per cent and 32.8 per cent paid less than 5 per cent). In his household survey (p. 197) he found that on average in 1974, households paid $8.43 per week for housing, which represented 8.19 per cent of household weekly income. This compares extremely favourably with figures presented in the recently completed Household Expenditure Survey 1974–5 (Australian Bureau of Statistics, 1977a) which found that Australians on the lowest stratum of household income paid 21 per cent of income on current housing costs. (Metherell (p. 202) noted some resentment among poor Moree whites owing to subsidised Aboriginal housing.) Hitchcock (1974, p. 59) noted a similar subsidisation of Aboriginal housing in settled Western Australia in 1973. Again, quality considerations aside, rent on reserve housing was $1 per week; on transitional housing, $4 per week; and on State Housing Commission units $12.50 per week.

Evidence presented by Kitaoji and Metherell supported the intuitive contention that poorly paid jobs and high dependency rates are major causes of low income. Kitaoji (1976, p. VI.9) examined inter-household differences in incomes. He found that households with employed heads had the highest average weekly income ($64.42) followed by households headed by pensioners ($60.00), those headed by unemployed persons ($58.57) and finally by those headed by women in domestic employment ($48.81). On the more relevant per capita basis, households headed by an employed person had the highest weekly income ($10.43 per member) while those headed by unemployed persons had the lowest ($6.95 per member). This implies that employment and income status are closely related. While Kitaoji did not examine the number of dependants per household, he did note that household income was directly related to the age of the household head; and that as the age of the household head grew, per capita household income increased (p. VI.8). This is supposedly a consequence of changes in structure of the family – with the number of dependants per earning adult decreasing over time. As mentioned above, in settled Australia a high proportion of Aboriginal households are matrifocal, and most commentators (for example Rowley, 1971a, p. 332) assume that this is a further disadvantage which Aborigines face in a male-dominated society. Kitaoji observed that while households headed by males had higher average weekly incomes ($62.09 versus $48.63), households with female heads had higher per capita weekly income ($8.99 versus

$8.16). Kitaoji concluded (p. vi.9) that the age and employment status of household heads are important differentiators of household income. But owing to a high rate of welfare dependency and unemployment, households headed by females and widowed or separated persons do not on this account experience any income disadvantages.

Metherell (1975, pp. 252–5) in his survey found that over half (52 per cent) of the Aboriginal households in Moree were *totally* dependent on social service benefits for their income while only 48 per cent had at least one permanent income earner. He also found that 24 per cent of those unemployed did not receive unemployment benefits. It seems that the high propensity of Aborigines not to register for employment may have severe income status consequences. He also noted the high dependency rate among Moree Aborigines, as a consequence of the youth of the population – with Aboriginal wage earners in 1971 supporting on average more than three times the number of dependants that white wage earners support (p. 63). The ratio of actual dependants to actual work force was 8.3 to 1 for Aborigines and 2.5 to 1 for whites (p. 81). Metherell's breakdown of household income by housing type (Table 33) reinforces the suggestion that people who live on reserves or in shanties are especially disadvantaged subgroups in the Aboriginal population. They appear to experience lower health, housing, educational and income status than other Aborigines.

It seems that, on a per capita basis, the income of Aborigines in settled Australia is less than 30 per cent of that for non-Aborigines. This appears a direct consequence of low employment status (and its multiple causes) and a high young dependants ratio. There is no evidence that employed Aborigines receive below award wages (see for example Austin and Murray, 1974, p. 10; Gale, 1964, p. 294) except in Queensland where discriminatory (below award) wages are still legally condoned on Department of Aboriginal and Islander Advancement (DAIA) settlements. Doobov and Doobov (1972, p. 162) show that Aborigines in Queensland were paid weekly wages well below that which it was legal to pay non-Aborigines. For example at Yarrabah, they found wage rates varied from 15 per cent of the European rate for Aboriginal police constables to 32 per cent for motor mechanics.

There are no studies which examine the expenditure patterns of Aborigines in settled Australia. Rowley (1971a) in his household survey in New South Wales and the Eyre Peninsula noted (pp. 326–7) that the Aboriginal householder 'is only a marginal consumer of commodities catering for comfort or prestige'. He also noted the lack of furnishing, discussed above under housing status. This state of affairs is not surprising given the abject poverty in which many Aborigines must live. It was also noted in the section on health above that studies by Hitchcock (1974), Hitchcock and Gracey (1975), Kamien (1975a), Kamien *et al.* (1975) and Wise *et al.* (1976), showed that the food expenditure patterns of Aborigines in settled Australia, indicated a predominance of inferior foodstuffs. Hitchcock and Gracey (1975, p. 14) found a direct correlation between the standard of living of Aborigines and their nutritional and dietary standards. Some of their results are presented on Table 34.

Table 34. *Breakdown of calorie sources, by housing type, in a Western Australia town (percentages)*

Source	Housing type		
	Reserve	Transitional	Town
Carbohydrates	74.9	58.9	50.1
Meat and eggs	10.2	15.0	19.0
Milk products	3.7	7.5	11.6
Fruit and vegetables	2.9	5.2	5.8
Fats	8.3	13.4	13.5

Source: Hitchcock and Gracey (1975).

The indication of this study is that as the socio-economic status of Aborigines improves, their calorie intake shifts from poor sources to those comparable with the recommended dietary intake of most Australians (p. 15). It seems that the food expenditure patterns of Aborigines may perpetuate their poor health status. However, it is difficult to report anything conclusive on the expenditure patterns of Aborigines in settled Australia on the basis of such scant data.

Conclusion

In this chapter, the economic status of Aborigines living in non-metropolitan settled Australia has been examined. These people, owing to prolonged contact with Europeans and to miscegenation, are today almost entirely detribalised; and their traditional economy (of pre-contact times) has completely disappeared. Hence, like most Australians they are predominantly dependent on the 'market' economy for their livelihood. The conditions examined were of an extremely heterogeneous nature, owing to government policies that have varied from State to State ; to variations in the density of the European settlement pattern; to differing regional resource bases; and finally to the varying extents that Aboriginal communities have wished or have been permitted to assimilate.

Examination of a variety of social indicators revealed that the Aboriginal population of settled Australia is extremely young, and experiences a health, housing, and education status which, using Western value-oriented indices, is far below the Australian norm. (The only disadvantaged group in Australia that appears to have lower status is the Aborigines of remote Australia (see Chapters 2–4).) Moreover. there seems to be a great deal of interlinkage between social and economic aspects, and there is the appearance of a cycle of poverty: most piecemeal policies which have aimed to improve Aboriginal standards (for example, in education or employment) have been hampered in their impact by other features such as poor health and housing conditions. And a negative stereotyping and prejudice against Aborigines by many whites seems to influence aspects of economic life, especially the ability to secure private sector employment. But if Aborigines in settled areas have not been fully accepted into the socio-economic pattern of the wider society, they are also less easily able than those in remote Australia to fall back on their traditional culture, social system, land or economy for support.

6

Settled Australia II: the major urban areas

For them Aboriginality is a fact primarily of being racially different from the white community – rather than deriving from cultural and historical tradition.
H. C. Coombs, *The Future of the Australian Aboriginal* (The George Judah Cohen Memorial Lecture, 1972)

The dominant class asserts a set of values that prizes thrift and the accumulation of wealth and property, stresses the possibility of upward mobility and explains low economic status as the result of individual personal inadequacy and inferiority.
O. Lewis, 'The Culture of Poverty' (*Scientific American*, 1966)

Australia ranks as one of the three most urbanised societies in the world, and in 1971 some three-fifths of the country's population lived in metropolitan centres. Economic developments in the post-war period have increased the pace of urbanisation and, in relative terms, the rural population of Australia has been declining rapidly. Although, as noted in Chapter 1, the Aboriginal population is predominantly rural, in 1971 some 15 per cent of Aborigines (compared with 60 per cent of the total population) resided in major urban areas, defined as centres with populations in excess of 100,000 (1971 census; ABS, 1973, p. xiv). Because of the marginal economic status of Aborigines in rural areas, especially in settled Australia, it might have been expected that the 'push' to migrate to cities would have been stronger than for other Australians as a group. However, as Rowley (1971a, p. 362) has noted, certain influences act to discourage the migration of Aborigines to the cities: kinship ties and community loyalties attach Aborigines to rural areas, while greater difficulties (such as the sheer economic cost of migration) deter many poor potential migrants. Rowley (p. 363) also

143

suggested that initial accommodation difficulties (especially in large cities such as Melbourne and Sydney) inhibit migration. But, despite these constraints, there is no doubt that Aborigines are migrating in increasing numbers to the cities.

The evidence gathered in this chapter lends support to the suggestion made in a case study of Brisbane by Smith and Biddle (1975, p. xi) that Aborigines living in large cities possess a higher socio-economic status than those who continue to live in small country towns, rural areas and in remote Australia. This does not imply that the transition from rural and small town to larger city living is a simple process. On the contrary, as Gale (1972, p. 1) has noted, there are inevitable social and individual stresses involved in transition from one environment to another, especially where the differences are as marked as in Aboriginal migration to a large Australian city. As in many 'dualistic' economies and societies, there are those Aborigines in the cities who continue to seek to identify themselves with the Aboriginal community, and to hold themselves apart from white society, while there are others who become more integrated in the white world. As Scott (1973a, p. 4.2) suggests, even in an urban setting the Aboriginal community retains a distinct subculture based on the Aboriginal aspects of its past.

But while increased urbanisation may have produced a differentiated urban Aboriginal community, there are other forces moving in the direction of greater economic and cultural integration, relative to other regions of the country. Firstly, as Gale (1972, p. 261) noted, Aborigines do not present the same 'threat' to the rest of the urban community as they are sometimes perceived to do in the smaller towns and rural areas, where they form a significant if mostly segregated segment of the population. This is especially so since the larger Australian cities have acquired a more cosmopolitan population in the wake of Australia's post-war immigration programme. It thus appears – as the survey by Taft *et al.* (1970) in Perth suggested – that overt prejudice against Aborigines is less evident in the cities than in rural areas. While Taft *et al.* (p. 22) found that Perth residents were equally prejudiced against Aborigines and other 'out-groups', yet they appeared less discriminatory against Aborigines than were the country town residents in the survey. Secondly, the only study which has sought to compare the attitudes of a sample of urban and rural Aborigines (that by Dawson (1970) in New South Wales) found that Sydney Aborigines in the sample were more favourably disposed to integration, placed less emphasis on the extended family group and possessed higher material aspirations than those Aborigines in the rural sample (pp. 86–102).

In this chapter, the available information on the socio-economic status of Aborigines in cities is gathered, with a concentration of attention upon Sydney, Brisbane and Adelaide, where a number of studies have recently been conducted under the auspices of the Social Science Research Council and the Commission of Inquiry into Poverty.

Demographic and migratory patterns

In Table 35, the 1971 census estimates of the Aboriginal population in the major urban centres of Australia are presented. It will be seen from these figures that some 16,456 Aborigines or 15.48 per cent of the

Table 35. *The Aboriginal population of major urban areas, 1971*

Major urban area	Aboriginal population	Total population	Proportion of Aborigines to total population (per cent)
Sydney Statistical Division	5,479	2,807,828	0.20
Melbourne Statistical Division	2,923	2,503,450	0.12
Brisbane Statistical Division	2,766	867,784	0.32
Perth Statistical Division	2,672	703,199	0.38
Adelaide Statistical Division	1,800	842,693	0.21
Wollongong Statistical District	278	199,048	0.14
Hobart Statistical Division	215	153,216	0.14
Newcastle Statistical District	196	351,537	0.06
Canberra Statistical Division	82	158,880	0.05
Geelong Statistical District	45	122,087	0.04
Total	16,456	8,709,722	0.19

Source: Australian Bureau of Statistics (1973, 1975a).

Aboriginal population enumerated in the 1971 census lived in major urban areas in that year. In no city did Aborigines represent more than 1 per cent of the total population, with Perth (0.38 per cent) having the largest proportion of Aborigines to total population. Overall, Aborigines represented some 0.19 per cent of Australia's population in major urban centres.

However, the accuracy of these 1971 population estimates has been questioned in a number of recent studies. For example, Scott (1973a, p. 4) found 3,000 more Aborigines in the Sydney metropolitan area in 1972 than enumerated in the 1971 census. However, as the National Population Inquiry (1975, p. 502) has noted, this may mean not only that some Aborigines were omitted from the 1971 count, but also that others may not have identified as Aborigines. On the other hand, J. W. Brown *et al.* (1974, p. 13) estimated that 2,651 Aborigines and Islanders resided in Brisbane in 1973, as against 2,901 enumerated in the 1971 census. Despite these questions over the accuracy of the census, it seems best to accept the 1971 census figures as being the most reliable.

Reports on the age structure of the Aboriginal major urban population vary. Gale (1972,p. 142) suggested that the Aboriginal population structure in cities would more closely resemble white standards, for a variety of reasons. Firstly, she noted that a high proportion of Aborigines in the city remain single. Secondly, inter-racial marriages in the city are more common. And thirdly, there is a greater knowledge of contraception and socio-economic pressure to limit family size. She found (p.142) that urbanisation had a strong influence on the Aboriginal demographic structure, with 44.2 per cent of the Adelaide Aboriginal population being under 15 years of age (in 1966) as against 48.6 per cent in rural South Australia. Scott (1973a, p. 3) similarly found that 43 per cent of the Sydney Aboriginal population was under 15 years of age, and this is well below the New South Wales rural figures presented in the previous chapter. However, two more recent studies contradict these findings. J. W. Brown *et al.* (1974, p. 13) found that of a sample of 406 Aborigines and Islanders in Brisbane, 58 per cent were children, and Gale and Binnion (1975, p. 10) found that of a sample of 411 Aborigines in Adelaide, 45 per cent were under 10 years of age. There seems to be little conclusive evidence, as yet, that Aboriginal urbanisation has resulted in a demographic transition.

The rate of urbanisation of the Aboriginal population is also difficult to calculate, owing to the divergence of definition of 'Aboriginal' in the 1966 and 1971 censuses. Even if accurate and comparable population estimates were available, it would be difficult to determine to what extent urbanisation is due to actual migration, and to what extent it is due to people already in urban areas changing their racial identification (National Population Inquiry, 1975, p. 496). The only method available to gauge the rate of urbanisation seems to be to examine the case studies of Sydney, Adelaide and Brisbane that have asked those in sample groups what their place of origin was.

Gale (1972, p. 72) has shown that from 1950 up to 1966 the major cause of Aboriginal population growth in Adelaide has been migration, predominantly from rural parts of South Australia. She noted (p. 74) that in 1965, four-fifths of the urban (Aboriginal) population increase in Adelaide was accounted for by rural migrants. Between 1957 and 1966 (p. 94), the proportion of South Australia's Aboriginal population residing in Adelaide increased from 6.25 per cent to 25 per cent (although this does not take into account racial immigration). Of 1,700 Aborigines contacted by Gale's survey in Adelaide in 1966, 90 per cent were born elsewhere (p. 86).

Beasley (1970) in her survey of 100 Aboriginal households in Sydney (703 people) found that over 50 per cent were migrants (p. 150). Scott (1973) in their Sydney survey found that 81.7 per cent of respondents had grown up on a reserve, mission or on the fringe of a country town and that only 16 per cent of respondents were born in Sydney or had lived there all their lives (p. 4.8). They reported (p. 3.18) that 60 per cent of household heads and spouses had lived in Sydney for less than ten years, 39 per cent less than five years, and 21 per cent less than two years. Approximately 66 per cent of the sample had migrated to Sydney from New South Wales country areas.

The situation in Brisbane appears similar. J. M. Smith and Biddle (1975) found that, of a sample of 2,103 Aborigines in Brisbane in 1965, 81 per cent of adults had migrated to Brisbane, but that over 50 per cent had been in Brisbane for more than ten years (pp. 52–3). Most of the migrants had come from small towns and rural areas in Queensland. J. W. Brown *et al.* (1974, p. 19) almost duplicated this result in their 1973 survey, finding that only 17 per cent of Aboriginal respondents claimed Brisbane as their childhood home. The bulk of the Brisbane Aboriginal population came from country (47 per cent), government reserves (18 per cent) and provincial towns (17 per cent). However, they did note (p. 19) that of those under 20 years of age, almost 40 per cent had grown up in Brisbane. All these findings correspond with those of the National Population Inquiry (1975) which found (pp. 500–1) that, while there may have been a great deal of rural/urban drift between 1966 and 1971, there was little inter-State movement of Aborigines.

What are the reasons given by Aborigines for migrating to cities? Beasley (1970, pp. 151–2) found that the major reasons stated by Aborigines for coming to Sydney were to find employment and to provide opportunities for children. Illness was also a major explanation given for coming to the city. Beasley noted that it was mainly young adults who came to the city in search of work. Similarly, Scott (1973a, p. 3.20) observed that it was mainly young Aborigines who were migrating to the city and that the three most frequent reasons given for migration were: (1) employment, (2) better general opportunities, both for migrants and their children, and (3) improved housing and more money. Gale (1972, pp. 86–8) examined why Aborigines migrated to Adelaide in 1966. She found that a surprisingly large proportion (40 per cent) of total migrants in her sample moved involuntarily. Thirteen per cent were children brought to the city for placement in foster homes and 8 per cent were committed children, whom the government has the authority to remove forcibly from parents declared unable to provide satisfactory guardianship. A second major group of people who came to the city involuntarily did so for medical reasons, and comprised some 12 per cent of migrants in the sample. The remaining involuntary migrants had been sent to Adelaide as criminal offenders – and, after serving their sentence, chose to remain in the city. Of voluntary migrants, 30 per cent came for education, 13 per cent for no particular reason and 1.6 per cent as sportsmen. The only conclusion that can, it seems, be drawn from these figures is that in New South Wales socio-economic factors may have been of more importance in the decision to migrate than in South Australia, where kinship ties and involuntary factors were often determining causal influences.

Health

Here, various aspects of both physical and mental health are examined in an attempt to describe the overall health status of Aborigines residing in the major urban areas of Australia. The most aggregative statistic available is the infant mortality rate (per thousand live births). The only estimates of this are for Sydney and Perth. In Sydney, Scott (1973a, p. 8.11) estimated that the infant mortality rate was 36.0 and in Perth the rate for 1971 (Department of Aboriginal Affairs, 1977a, p. 20) was 27.0. These figures, while still above the average Australian rate, represent a vast improvement on the situation for Aborigines in other parts of Australia. Scott (1973a, p. 8.11) suggested that the rate may not be significantly greater than in comparable (socio-economic) European groups.

The health problems that Aborigines suffer in the city appear to be similar in type to those experienced elsewhere. Gale (1972, p. 192) noted that children in Adelaide are hospitalised most frequently owing to respiratory infections, pneumonia, gastro-enteritis and ear infections. As noted before, overcrowding, undernutrition and poor hygiene are contributory factors to these conditions. The Aboriginal and Islander Community Health Service (AICHS) of Brisbane, started in 1973, reported (Workshop on Aboriginal Medical Services, 1975, p. 59) that the major problems of patients were skin conditions (44.4 per cent of patients), respiratory tract infections (30.8 per cent) and gastrointestinal tract conditions (16.0 per cent). In the same report (p. 62), the Aboriginal Medical Service of Redfern, Sydney, reported that respiratory infections (diagnosed in 52 per cent of patients), skin conditions (34 per cent), ear infections (30 per cent) and gastro-intestinal problems (14 per cent) were the major complaints of patients.

Lickiss (1970, 1971a,b,c,) conducted a study in 1968 which concentrated on the health status of 120 Aboriginal children in Sydney. She found a high rate of child morbidity. Of 69 children aged five or more in her sample, 23 (33 per cent) had been in hospital at least three times in the first five years of life. Twelve (17 per cent) had been in hospital at least 5 times in that period (Lickiss, 1970, p. 996). Of 112 children for whom information was adequate she reported (p. 996) that 32 (29 per cent) had been admitted to hospital for respiratory infection and 24 (21 per cent) for gastro-intestinal symptoms.

However, it has been suggested (Scott, 1973a, p. 8.11) that Lickiss' sample may have been biased towards families that had greater health problems. This assertion seems to be borne out by data presented by the Sydney Aboriginal Medical Service (Workshop on Aboriginal Medical Services, 1975, p. 63). They found that in 1974 only 3.3 per cent of children examined were below the 10th percentile for height and 2.2 per cent for weight. This contrasts markedly with Lickiss' (1970, p. 997) results, which found that 48 per cent of children in the sample were below the 10th percentile for height and 46 per cent for weight.

It appears that by and large, urban Aborigines are healthier than rural Aborigines (Gale, 1972, p. 203). However, this does not mean that Aborigines in cities are as healthy as their white counterparts. A major factor responsible for their improved health status must be the availability of community-based medical services and out-patient clinics in the cities – there is the Aboriginal Health Unit in Adelaide, the Aboriginal Medical Service in Perth, the Victorian Aboriginal Health Service in Melbourne and the services available in Sydney and Brisbane. These health services are staffed almost completely by

Aborigines and this seems to alleviate many of the cross-cultural tensions that Aborigines experience when seeking medical attention at white institutions. In general it appears that Aborigines in the cities avail themselves more readily of medical services. J. W. Brown *et al.* (1974, p. 70) reported that 75 per cent of respondents in the Brisbane survey had consulted a doctor within a year prior to their survey and 90 per cent had done so within three years. However, preventative dental consultation still appears a problem; only 33 per cent of respondents having consulted a dentist in the year prior to the survey, and 53 per cent having not seen a dentist for three years or more. This explains to some extent the chronic dental caries reported by Scott (1973a, p. 81).

Few studies have examined the psychosocial health status of Aborigines or what Lickiss (1970, p. 999) has termed psychological morbidity. As noted in Chapter 5, Gault (1968) and Gault *et al.* (1970) revealed extremely poor psychsocial health status for adolescent Aborigines in Victoria. (Included in their samples were Melbourne Aborigines.) Lickiss (1970, p. 995) comments on the seriousness of childhood delinquency among Aboriginal children in Sydney and suggested (p. 999) 'that in the next decade childhood psychological discomfort manifested and aggravated by educational difficulties and antisocial behaviour may emerge as the most serious problem concerning the total well-being of the Sydney Aboriginal children'.

There are, it seems, no studies of the psychosocial health status of urban Aboriginal adults. However, Lickiss (1971b, pp. 221–2) did suggest that Aborigines in Sydney experienced alienation and a tendency to anomie which may be more marked than in their white neighbours of similar socio-economic status. It seems extremely difficult to establish whether psychosocial stress in the city is merely a feature of the 'culture of poverty' (Lewis, 1966) or whether it is accentuated by Aboriginality. Certainly problem drinking among Aborigines is evidenced in the city, as elsewhere in Australia. Lickiss (1971b, p. 216) noted that in her Sydney study, almost 30 per cent of fathers were problem drinkers, and that in four households (out of twenty-two) excessive drinking had disrupted socio-economic function to a severe degree. She also noted that problem drinking occurred among Aboriginal women in Sydney (p. 216). Others have commented on the incidence of alcoholism among Sydney Aborigines (for example, Scott, 1973, p. 8.13). A crude analysis of the medical conditions treated at the Aboriginal and Islander Community Health Service in Brisbane (Workshop on Aboriginal Medical Services, 1975, p. 59) revealed that

13.2 per cent of patients (over a six-month period) were treated for psychiatric conditions. In Sydney, the Aboriginal Medical Service (p. 62) noted that psychosocial difficulties, evidenced in 16 per cent of adult patients, was the third most common broad diagnostic problem.

The poor statistical material in this section makes it difficult to be conclusive on the health status of urban Aborigines. It seems that the physical health status of urban Aborigines is superior to non-urban Aborigines. A recently completed study by Dobbin (1977) which compared the health status of two samples of Aboriginal children in Victoria (one drawn from the Melbourne Metropolitan area and the other from a rural area of Victoria) bears out this impression.

Housing

There are many aspects that need to be examined if an accurate analysis of the housing status of urban Aborigines is to be presented. As noted, many urban Aborigines are recent arrivals in the major urban areas of Australia, and tend to come from rural areas. Not surprisingly, when Aborigines first arrive in cities, they seek temporary accommodation with relatives who may have moved to the city at an earlier date. Gale (1972, p. 74) commented on this 'chain migration' syndrome and its similarity to the migration pattern of Southern Europeans who come to Australia. As suggested in Chapter 5, vestiges of the traditional social structure remain intact today even with detribalised communities in settled Australia, the most important being the extended kinship system. Often the presence of relatives in the city may directly or indirectly influence the decision to migrate. The extended family unit may remain intact for some time after moving to the city. After a time, with integration, this type of family unit would tend to disintegrate as Aborigines adopt the nuclear family model of other Australians.

In Table 36, the average sizes of Aboriginal households in Sydney, Adelaide and Brisbane are presented. As can be seen, in Sydney the average size of households has decreased rapidly since the late 1960s. In Adelaide and Brisbane, average household size is well below that recorded in the previous chapter for the non-major urban areas of settled Australia. These figures indicate that the average Aboriginal household is still larger than the Australian average (which is approximately 3 persons per household). This situation may be explained by the household composition.

Beasley (1970, p. 171) found 132 nuclear family units in her 100 household sample in Sydney – that is, an average of 1.32 nuclear family per dwelling. She found that 51 per cent of households were of a single nuclear nature, 23 per cent were single nuclear plus supernumeraries

Table 36. *Some estimates of household size in major Australian cities*

City	Year	Persons per household
Sydney	1966	7.03
Sydney	1968	8.60
Sydney	1972	4.84
Adelaide	1973	6.40[a]
Brisbane	1973	5.54[b]

[a] This figure includes non-Aborigines living in Aboriginal households. The Aborigines-only figure is 5.9.
[b] Including Torres Strait Islanders.
Sources: Beasley (1970); J. W. Brown *et al.* (1974); Gale and Binnion (1975); Lickiss (1971a); Scott (1973).

and 25 per cent were multiple unit households (extended). Scott (1973a, p. 6.27) found that 44.8 per cent of the households in their sample were nuclear, 9.8 per cent were fractured households, 13.6 per cent were nuclear extended, and 5.5 per cent were fractured extended. J. W. Brown *et al.* (1974, p. 41) found that in Brisbane, 78 per cent of households contained one nuclear family, sometimes with additional individuals present, 12 per cent contained at least two nuclear families, 5 per cent contained less than a nuclear family and 5 per cent contained a group of individuals. These figures support the suggestion that even in the cities, vestiges of traditional Aboriginal kinship may remain.

However, the question arises as to whether Aborigines live in large households voluntarily or owing to economic necessity (that is, owing to a housing shortage or high costs). This question may be answered by examining the extent of overcrowding experienced by urban Aborigines. Beasley (1970, p. 158) found a degree of overcrowding in her Sydney sample, with accommodation pressure being 2.6 persons per bedroom (1.25 persons per room). She suggested (p. 162) that economic factors, such as high rents, perpetuate the larger size of households. Lickiss (1971b, p. 204) found in her Sydney survey that mean accommodation pressure for her 22 household sample was 2.56 persons per room. Gale (1972, p. 131) reported an accommodation pressure index of 1.8 persons per room in Adelaide Aboriginal households, as against a South Australia average of 0.6 persons per room. Scott (1973a, p. 6.39) in their sample calculated the accommodation pressure index to be 1.25 (the same as Beasley's). However, the averaging process often hides extremes. Scott noted (p. 6.41) that 23 per cent of households were overcrowded with accommodation pressure of 1.6–2.5 persons per room (excluding bathroom and toilet). Extreme overcrowding occurred in 5 per cent of households with the accommodation pressure index being greater than 2.5. They compared these figures with the average for the major urban areas of New South Wales, which was 0.66. In Brisbane, J. W. Brown *et al.* (1974, p. 41) found that large family units did not have correspondingly large houses; households with more than eight persons averaged an accommodation pressure index of about 2, while those with four people or less averaged fewer than one person per room used for sleeping of living. In Adelaide, Gale and Binnion (1975, p. 37) suggested that overcrowding in Aboriginal households had been reduced, with the accommodation pressure index in their sample being 1.1. The accommodation pressure indexes strongly suggest that urban Aborigines do experience a housing status inferior to that of the average European Australian. Even if Aborigines choose to live in large households, there is no reason to believe that they have a preference for overcrowded homes. Again, it must be pointed out that on a spatial basis, the housing status of Aborigines in major urban areas is superior to that of other Aborigines.

Next, the quality of the environment in which Aboriginal houses are located, and the quality of the houses themselves, are examined. It seems that recent Aboriginal arrivals in the cities are accommodated in the poorer sections of the city, predominantly the inner city or central business district while established assimilated families live in the suburbs. Scott (1973a, p. 3) noted that 43 per cent of their Sydney sample lived in the inner city (Redfern, Chippendale and St Peter's), 30.5 per cent lived in the western suburbs in Housing Commission estates (Green Valley and Mount Druitt), and 22 per cent lived in suburbs surrounding the inner city area. They did note (p. 3.21) that since 1966 there has been a significant move from the inner city to the outer metropolitan areas of Sydney, with the proportion in the outer suburbs increasing from 25 per cent to 30.5 per cent. Gale and Binnion (1975, p. 4) noted that while there are no Aboriginal ghettos in Adelaide, areas of high Aboriginal density tended to be in poorer sections of town like the inner suburbs around the central business district, and Port Adelaide. J. M. Smith and Biddle (1975, pp. 69–70) report that Aboriginal housing in Brisbane was not segregated, and was spread throughout the city. The indications here are that in the larger cities, like Sydney, certain suburbs (Redfern) may have higher concentrations of Aborigines than are evident in the smaller cities, like Adelaide. To the extent that Aborigines do congregate in the poorer sections of cities, this could be due to their low income status (see below) and because kin are already established in these regions.

The actual quality of the houses in which Aborigines are accommodated, also appears low by general Australian standards. This is best illustrated by Scott (1973a, pp. 6.30–1). They found that 13 per cent of the Aboriginal households in their Sydney survey (1972), shared a kitchen as against 1.53 per cent of all major urban households in New South Wales (1971); and that 22 per cent shared a bathroom as against 2.22 per cent for all major urban households in New South Wales. Furthermore, 27 per cent of Aboriginal households had no hot running water in their bathroom. Subjectively, they assessed at least 10 per cent of the houses they visited to be in poor physical condition (p.10). J. M. Smith and Biddle (1975, p. 70) found that in Brisbane 80 per cent of Aboriginal houses were of adequate quality, but 19 per cent were grossly inadequate. In Adelaide, Gale and Binnion (1975, p. 37) subjectively judged 74 per cent of Aboriginal homes in their sample to be in good condition, 14 per cent to be in medium condition, and 12 per cent to be in poor condition. This situation is not surprising given the extent to which Aborigines reside in the inner city where older, more run-down housing is generally located. Given some fixed rent constraint, it seems that Aborigines sometimes (that is when private sector housing is available to them) have the option of renting a tidy but small conventional house and living in extremely crowded conditions, or a larger more dilapidated house. The extent to which they take the latter course of action is indicated by the above statistics.

The extent of Aboriginal home ownership is also an important indicator of housing status, especially in a country where close to 70 per cent of metropolitan dwellers are home owners (ABS, 1977a, p. 2). Estimates of urban Aboriginal home ownership are presented in Table 37.

Table 37. *Aboriginal home ownership in some major urban areas*

City	Year	Percent of housing that is owner-occupied
Sydney	1966	24
Sydney	1972	8
Brisbane	1965	20
Brisbane	1973	8
Adelaide	1966	11
Adelaide	1973	10

Sources: Beasley (1970); J. W. Brown *et al.* (1974); Gale (1972); Gale and Binnion (1975); Scott (1973a); J. M. Smith and Biddle (1975).

Two features of this table are significant. One is the low degree of Aboriginal home ownership. The second, is the apparent decline in home ownership in all three cities from the mid-1960s to the early 1970s. This can be explained either by sample bias, or because a recent influx of poorer Aboriginal migrants has resulted in a decline in the proportion of Aboriginal home owners. The balance of Aboriginal householders rent either privately or publicly, the proportion in each city varying considerably. Scott (1973a, p. 10) reported that in Sydney 22 per cent of housing is rented from the State Housing Commission or some other government body. J. W. Brown *et al.* (1974, p. 42) suggested that the corresponding figure for Brisbane is 12 per cent, and Gale and Binnion (1975, p. 35) indicated that in Adelaide, the government is the landlord for almost 70 per cent of households. It appears that the South Australian Housing Trust has been more active in housing Aborigines than similar bodies in other States. The significance of public housing will be discussed further under the heading of income status, for it is generally provided at reduced rental for people in various categories of need, and may be instrumental in raising the level of living of poor Aboriginal families.

A feature of urban living which is noteworthy is the high propensity for Aborigines to move within cities. Lickiss (1971b, p. 205) noted that, in her sample of 120 Aboriginal children in Sydney, 54 per cent had more than one place of residence over a nine-month observation period. Of 90 children aged three years or more, 39 per cent had more than two places of residence over a three-year period. As mentioned above, Scott (1973a, p. 3.26) also noted a substantial residential mobility among Sydney Aborigines. J. M. Smith and Biddle (1975, p. 53) likewise observed a high degree of intra-city mobility in Brisbane. Twenty per cent of the families in their sample moved during their study period (1965) and 35 per cent of household heads had lived less than one year at their present address. J. W. Brown *et al.* (1974, p. 21) reported that in their survey, 61 per cent of Aborigines and Islanders had been at the same address for at least one year; 23 per cent had moved once, 8 per cent twice, and 8 per cent three times or more.

The reasons for this high residential mobility vary. The type of mobility described by Scott (1973a, p. 3.21) suggested that migrants were merely moving from the inner city as they became established in the city and as their socio-economic status improved. This type of mobility is evidenced amongst most migrants who accept cheap accommodation on arrival to a city, but only on a temporary basis. Similarly, mobility owing to the availability of more suitable accommodation must be viewed in a positive light. However, Lickiss (1971b, p. 205) suggested a number of more negative precipitators of residential mobility. These include difficulties with landlords, domestic crises and difficulties with community welfare, health or legal agencies (movement as an evasive action). She also noted (1971a, p. 36) a case of a household moving on the basis of neighbourhood social pressure.

The final question in this section is whether Aborigines in the large cities experience discrimination in housing to the extent described in Chapter 5. Both J. M. Smith and Biddle (1975, pp. 69–70) and Lickiss (1971a, p. 77) found evidence of discrimination against Aborigines. Only J. W. Brown *et al.* (1974, p. 43) and Bochner (1972) have examined the extent of discrimination in the housing field. All respondents in J. W. Brown *et al.*'s Brisbane survey were asked to describe any problems experienced in finding accommodation. Sixty per cent stated that they had personally experienced no problems, while 20 per cent claimed that colour was their main problem in finding accommodation; they had either been rejected by landlords or claimed that rent was higher for them than for white Australians. When respondents were asked what they felt were the main problems facing Aboriginal and

Islanders in finding accommodation, 34 per cent claimed that discrimination was the main problem. Bochner (1972, pp. 335–7) conducted a survey by placing two advertisements in the 'Wanted to rent' classification of a Sydney newspaper. One advertisement was attributed to a young Aboriginal couple, while the other did not specifically state the couple's race. He found that fewer flats were offered to the couple identified as being of Aboriginal descent. The evidence here, scant as it is, suggests that Aborigines experience some discrimination in housing in the major urban areas of Australia.

Education

The educational status of urban Aborigines is obviously an important determinant both of their level of living and economic status in the metropolitan milieu. For as J. M. Smith and Biddle (1975, p. 71) stress, formal education is of special importance for a minority in an industrialised society. Without literacy and comprehension of the workings of social institutions, people have problems in coping with such fundamental aspects of living as jobs, child rearing, product consumption, health maintenance, home management and civic participation. And as Scott (1973a, p. 5.2) noted, 'It is plausible to expect that education would be the spear-head for Aboriginal advancement. It should offer economic mobility and the increase of job opportunities; it should increase the self-reliance of the community.'

It seems that the educational status of urban Aborigines is relatively low. Gale (1972, pp. 246–9) found that in an Adelaide sample in 1966 only 30 per cent of Aborigines of 15 years of age and over had continued their education beyond primary school. Only 5 per cent of Aboriginal adults (20 years of age and over) sampled had completed the intermediate level of secondary school which was the minimum pass standard required for entry into semi-skilled or skilled jobs.

In Brisbane, J. M. Smith and Biddle (1975, p. 84) reported that in 1965 Aborigines in their sample averaged a remarkably low 6.1 years at school, and left school at an average age of 13.6 years. Twenty-five per cent left school before the legal leaving age (which was 14 at that time). They also noted that as Aboriginal children grew older, they fell further behind whites at school; 45 per cent of children, 10 years or older, were at least one grade behind at school. The reasons for this situation (pp. 77–8) seem similar to those elsewhere in settled Australian, and include: (1) the poor health status of students, (2) a lack of parental models to imitate, (3) a lack of ability of schools to modify their teaching for Aborigines who, even in the urban context, are more community than individually oriented and (4) a growing awareness by students, as they approach puberty, of their Aboriginal identity and discrimination against them. J. M. Smith and Biddle (p. 83) did find a positive correlation between length of stay in Brisbane and probability of completing primary education. They also found that occupational skill was a direct function of level of education, as was the occurrence of higher prestige jobs.

J. W. Brown *et al.* (1974, pp. 31–3) found in their Brisbane survey in 1973 that 5 per cent of Aborigines had no formal schooling or left school before the age of nine; nearly 60 per cent had left school by age fifteen, and only 3 per cent of Aboriginal students stayed at school past the age of seventeen. The level of education attained was also low. In their sample (here including Torres Strait Islanders), 24 per cent had not completed primary school, 36 per cent had completed primary school but no more, 26 per cent had some secondary schooling, 10 per cent had finished grade 10 (4th form) and only 1 per cent finished grade 12 (6th form). They suggested that the low grade-for-age level they observed could be due either to Aborigines starting school later than whites, or because they had to repeat certain grades to achieve the prescribed standard. In Sydney, Scott (1973a, pp. 5.1–3) noted that 45 per cent of men and 48 per cent of women in their sample had some secondary education; 12 per cent and 18 per cent respectively had higher secondary (past 2nd form) education, and only 7 per cent and 9 per cent passed School Certificate (4th form).

Kendall (1976), in a report to the Aboriginal Consultative Group conducted a survey late in 1975 that included a sample of urban Aborigines in Perth, Adelaide, Sydney and Melbourne. He reported (p. 29) that 68 per cent of this sample spent less than 10 years at school, and only 6 per cent had 12 years or more schooling. Thirty-one per cent of the major urban sample had obtained School Certificate (p. 73) which was an improvement on the 17.24 per cent in a sample from settled (non-metropolitan) Australia, and 2.27 per cent for a remote sample (from Yuendumu settlement). The major reasons Kendall reports for Aborigines leaving school (p. 30) are to seek employment owing to a feeling of alienation and owing to family commitments. He found a positive and significant correlation (p. 41) between gaining a certificate at school and being employed.

The above statistics leave little doubt that the educational status

Aborigines acquire from schooling is low compared with the standard achieved by European Australians (see Chapter 1). But there is some evidence of improvement because of growing educational opportunities, especially for young Aborigines. For example, the ABSEG scheme is extensively used by Aborigines residing in major urban areas. At 30 June 1976, 2,434 Aborigines in Sydney, Melbourne, Perth, Adelaide and Brisbane received ABSEG scheme grants (DAA, 1976b, p. 32), which represented 27 per cent of the total grants in those five States.

As noted in Chapter 5, opportunities for post-school study have also increased with the introduction of the ASGS scheme and the NEAT scheme for mature students. The extent to which urban Aborigines take advantage of these schemes is not clear, owing to a shortage of quantitative studies. J. W. Brown *et al.* (1974, p. 35) noted that only 16 per cent of their Brisbane sample had any further education or training since leaving school. Some Aboriginal migrants who had come from reserves had been trained for specific jobs, but did not have any formal qualification which was recognised in the city.

Kendall (1976) in his survey of Technical and Further Education (TAFE) institutions throughout Australia, found (p. 25) that the enrolment of Aborigines (and Torres Strait Islanders) in major urban areas was disproportionate to the percentage of each State's population except in Western Australia (where they represented 7.2 per cent of TAFE Aboriginal enrolment) and South Australia (18.8 per cent). In New South Wales, 61.9 per cent of total TAFE Aboriginal enrolment was from major urban areas, in Victoria 63.3 per cent and in Queensland 55.4 per cent. This situation could be due to the greater availability of TAFE institutions in metropolitan areas. Kendall also reported (p. 23) that Aborigines in major urban areas enrol for higher qualifications. In 1975, they represented 62.5 per cent of students enrolled for diploma courses, 85.7 per cent of those enrolled for a certificate, 71.5 per cent of those participating in apprenticeship courses, 45.7 per cent of those in pre-employment courses and only 7.2 per cent of those in 'other' courses. In his sample survey of 98 urban Aborigines, Kendall reported that 51 per cent have participated in formal post-school education, and 39.2 per cent (of these) had obtained some qualification from this study. He found a close correlation between participating in post-school education and obtaining employment.

It seems that the post-school educational standard of Aborigines in the metropolitan sector is higher than that of Aborigines elsewhere.

This is due partly to a greater knowledge of available courses (Kendall, p. 33 reports that over 80 per cent of Aborigines in his urban sample knew of special courses for Aborigines). As the DAA (1977c) report on vocational training pointed out, most of the institutions that offer special vocational and pre-vocational courses for Aborigines are located in State capitals (p. 2). Hence, urban Aborigines have greater opportunity for training than those living in rural or remote regions. It is also probable that, living in large cities, the majority of employment opportunities for Aborigines would be in the secondary and tertiary sectors and that there may be a greater necessity for further education to obtain secure employment.

Employment

The employment status of urban Aborigines is an integral component of their economic status. It is also of extreme importance for another reason: Aborigines, as noted above, have often migrated to the city for better employment prospects. Therefore, the extent to which they can find employment is an important determinant of the extent to which Aborigines (a migrating racial minority) can improve their relative economic standing compared with other Australians in urban areas.

In Brisbane in 1965, the level of Aboriginal unemployment stood at 7.5 per cent – which at that time was almost six times the rate for the total Brisbane work force. Lickiss (1971b, p. 207) reported that in Sydney in 1968, unemployment for Aborigines was rare, provided labouring work was acceptable. By 1972, the situation appeared to have changed somewhat. Scott (1973a, p. 7.2) estimated that 18.9 per cent of the Sydney Aboriginal work force was unemployed, and 7.24 per cent was casually employed. They noted that unemployment was higher in the inner city (21.7 per cent) than in the outer metropolitan areas and that youth unemployment was particularly high, with 31 per cent of the 15–19 age group being unemployed. A comparison (p. 7.12) with a sample of whites of a similar socio-economic status (living at the Housing Commission estate at Mount Druitt) revealed a disparity in unemployment rates, with the latter experiencing a rate of 3–4 per cent.

The employment situation for urban Aborigines appeared to have deteriorated somewhat by the early 1970s. In Brisbane, J. W. Brown *et al.* (1974, p. 50) reported that in the week prior to their survey, 45 per cent of the adult Aborigines in their sample were working – 79 per cent of men and 20 per cent of women. However, as work force participation rates were not reported, the rate of unemployment cannot be calculated. Somewhat surprisingly, J. W. Brown *et al.* found (p. 51) that people whose childhood home was in Brisbane had a lower propensity to work – with only 23 per cent working as against 40–50 per cent for migrants. (They also reported (pp. 50–1) that the percentage of people working was highest among those under 20. This assertion appears dubious and shows that unless calculations of the work force participation rate are made, ambiguous statements about the state of employment may arise.)

Gale and Binnion (1975, p. 40) in a fashion similar to J. W. Brown *et al.* found that only 48 out of 157 Aboriginal adults in their Adelaide sample were working – that is a 'crude' employment rate of only 30 per cent. Of 37 white adults living in Aboriginal households (and hence supposedly of a similar socio-economic status), 23 (62 per cent) were employed. They reported (p. 41) a marked tendency for young people (under 21 years of age) and people over 50 years of age to experience higher levels of unemployment. Unemployment (p. 42) was also significantly higher among people with no dependants.

Kendall (1976, p. 36) found that of his urban sample in 1975, 41.6 per cent were not employed (again, this is a crude measure of unemployment). This figure compared favourably with the crude unemployment rate for a rural sample in settled Australia (73.46 per cent) and a tribal sample at Yuendumu (59.09 per cent), but was higher than the rate of a sample from Darwin (23.25 per cent).

Recent figures (April 1977) on the number of Aborigines registered for employment with the Commonwealth Employment Service (CES) are available, and are presented in Table 38. The value of these figures is limited for two reasons. Firstly, the size of the Aboriginal labour force in metropolitan areas (as well as for the whole of Australia) is unknown and hence the unemployment rate cannot be determined. Secondly, as noted in earlier chapters, Aborigines do not register for employment to the same extent as non-Aborigines (DAA, 1976e, p. 9). However, one can assume that greater accessibility to the Department of Employment and Industrial Relations in cities would result in a higher proportion of metropolitan unemployed registering for employment.

Table 38 does demonstrate the extent of youth unemployment, with 61 per cent of total registrants in metropolitan areas being youths or school leavers. The indications are that the employment status of urban Aborigines is low.

As regards the occupational status of those that are employed, Beasley (1970, p. 178) recorded that Sydney Aboriginal males were

Table 38. *Aborigines registered for employment at 1 April 1977*

Metropolitan area of:	Adults	School-leavers	Other youth	Total	per cent of total[a]
New South Wales	421	25	231	677	22.2
Victoria	69	2	49	120	22.6
Queensland	220	17	133	370	10.23
South Australia	176	15	78	269	38.37
Western Australia	334	32	156	522	17.24
Tasmania	10	3	4	17	31.48
Total: all states	1,230	94	651	1,975	16.07

[a] Per cent of total number of Aborigines in Australia registered for employment with the Commonwealth Employment Service.
Source: Department of Employment and Industrial Relations (1977).

generally in unskilled jobs of an industrial nature, such as factory work or general labouring. The majority of females were employed in factories or in full- or part-time domestic work. J. M. Smith and Biddle (1975, p. 90) found that Aborigines occupied jobs with the lowest occupational ranking, with 68 per cent of adults having no occupational skill, 24 per cent being semi-skilled, and only 6 per cent being skilled (p. 98). Sixty per cent of Aborigines were employed in personal, domestic and other service and as unskilled labour – three times the proportion for non-Aborigines (p. 90). Scott (1973a, p. 7.13) found that 63.2 per cent of their 'in-depth interview' sample held unskilled jobs. They suggested that overall the level of skill required for jobs held by Aborigines was low, even relative to comparable socio-economic groups. Finally J. W. Brown *et al.* (1974, p. 51) found in their Brisbane study that 59 per cent of those employed held unskilled jobs, 20 per cent held semi-skilled jobs, and 22 per cent held skilled, professional or semi-professional occupations.

It seems that Aborigines in the large cities experience a disadvantaged employment position, as elsewhere in Australia, and that a need still remains to integrate them into the open labour market. The reasons for their low employment and occupational status are many (and include poor health and housing discussed above) but only two features are mentioned here: low educational status, and direct prejudice against Aborigines. Low educational status restricts access by Aborigines to the labour market. As Beaumont (1974, pp. 165–6) noted, in a simple 'queue' model of the labour market, where workers are ranked on a preferred scale according to the relation between potential productivity and wage rates, Aborigines are placed at the rear of the queue. This means that Aboriginal employees in major urban areas are particularly vulnerable to economic recessions, and retain the 'last hired/first fired' employment characteristic, noted in the previous chapter. Data contained in Kendall's study (1976) reinforce this assertion; a statistically significant relationship existed between being employed and obtaining a school certificate, doing post-school study and having done on-the-job training. In his 1975 survey, Kendall asked his urban sample the nature of their present employment, and found only one unskilled worker out of 52 employed persons. When respondents were asked their previous jobs, 58 (out of 87) replied unskilled work. This implies that many of those who had previously held unskilled work had been laid off, although there was some evidence of upward job mobility especially into semi-professional occupations.

Prejudice can further restrict the opportunities of Aborigines in the labour market. As Beaumont states (1974, p. 167) 'The operation of the labour market is far from perfect and custom, convention and prejudice can restrict the degree to which minorities such as Aborigines can encroach into the market. These social pressures act to reduce the employer's inclination to employ more Aboriginal labour independently of any objective efficiency considerations and the result is an artificially-depressed demand for their labour.' In terms of the queue model mentioned above, discrimination against Aborigines would place them even further back in the queue.

Only two studies have systematically examined this issue. The more thorough was conducted by Gale and Lewis (1966) in Adelaide in 1966. Their results were ambiguous. They found (p. 115) that 14 per cent of employers would not employ Aborigines, purely on the basis of negative stereotyping – the most common being that Aborigines were unreliable and 'went walkabout'. However, another 14 per cent (p. 188) stated that they would like to employ Aborigines if only some would apply. Of the employers in their survey currently employing Aborigines, nearly 90 per cent of those who commented felt that Aborigines were as satisfactory as any other group of employees.

In Brisbane in 1973, J. W. Brown *et al.* (1974, p. 52) asked respondents the main problems they had encountered in finding jobs. Seventy per cent reported no problems; 13 per cent said colour was their main problem and 4 per cent lack of qualifications. When respondents were asked to describe the main problems facing Aborigines (and Islanders) generally, 13 per cent said none; 24 per cent said colour was the main problem; 16 per cent said lack of qualifications; and 15 per cent said that a minority of Aborigines who were lazy or unreliable gave everyone a bad name.

Racial discrimination does not seem as severe a problem for Aborigines in the large cities as in the smaller country towns of settled Australia, yet the negative stereotype that Aborigines 'go walkabout' appears indeed to die hard. To examine the question of Aboriginal job mobility is not easy, given their high rate of migration into cities in recent times. Most questions on job mobility ask respondents the length to time they have held their present job; with recent arrivals in the sample such a question inadvertently introduces bias. In Gale and Lewis's study (1966) about 43 per cent of Aboriginal employees had held their present job for over one year (p. 116). Several large-scale employers stated that Aboriginal staff turnover was really no greater than for other employees doing the same work. Scott (1973a, p. 7.19) in their Sydney survey, found that 50 per cent of respondents held the same job for over two years, and that 68 per cent were in one job for at least twelve months. They suggest that the job mobility rate for Aborigines was no higher than for the population as a whole. In Brisbane, J. W. Brown *et al.* (1974, p. 51) found that 56 per cent of their sample who were employed held the same job for over one year, and that 27 per cent held the same job for three years or more. There seems to be little factual evidence to support the allegation that Aboriginal labour is unreliable.

In general it appears that the low employment status of urban Aborigines is due primarily to two factors – the low educational and skill status of the Aboriginal work force, and to employer prejudice. Aborigines, because of their relatively low level of acquired skills, are particularly susceptible to demand-deficient unemployment, such as is being experienced in 1977.

Finally, mention may be made of the extent of government efforts to integrate Aborigines into the labour market. In general, all the schemes discussed in the previous chapter are available to urban Aborigines. The exceptions are schemes, such as the public sector Special Works Projects (SWP), that are concentrated in areas (particularly rural areas of settled Australia) where Aboriginal unemployment is at higher levels than in the metropolis. However, urban Aborigines do have the advantage in other schemes - such as private sector SWP and NEAT, owing to their location in the cities.

Overall, it appears that by general Australian standards, urban Aborigines do experience low employment status. But this situation is rather disguised by two features: firstly, there is the relative superiority of their position in comparison with other Aborigines in Australia; and secondly, and perhaps of greater importance, urban Aborigines are more closely integrated into the larger society. Hence, they do not form 'distinct' communities where unemployment is particularly 'visible'. In the next section, the income status of Aborigines in the cities will be examined, and this may further elucidate their poor employment status.

Table 39. *Per capita disposable income of Aborigines in Sydney*

Year	Per capita disposable income per annum ($)	Australia-wide disposable income per capita ($)	Aboriginal as percentage of Australian disposable income (per cent)
1966–7	563	1,316	43
1968–9	486	1,472	33
1972–3	760	2,138	36

Sources: Australian Bureau of Statistics (1977c); Beasley (1970); Lickiss (1971b); Scott (1973a).

Poverty

As noted in earlier chapters, the incidence of poverty is not purely a function of employment and occupational status, but also of the dependency ratio. Studies of poverty among Aborigines in the cities are of two types. On the one hand there are the earlier studies of Beasley (1970), Lickiss (1971a) and Scott (1973a) that estimated the incomes of Aborigines as one of a number of socio-economic variables. The other type of study has been for the Commission of Inquiry into Poverty, and its major objective has been to discuss 'primary poverty' or poverty due to inadequate income.

The income estimates of the earlier studies are presented in Table 39. These figures indicate that the per capita income of urban Aborigines was well below that of other Australians. However, they are in general higher than the estimates made for Aborigines residing in other parts of both settled and remote Australia (see Chapters 2 and 5 in particular).

The Commission of Inquiry into Poverty research reports examined the income status of Aborigines in Adelaide, Brisbane and Perth during 1973 and 1974. Instead of per capita or household income, the concept of an 'income unit' was used by the Commission (1975, p. 12).[1] The idea of the income unit was to measure the income available to a family group. Members of a household who were independent (e.g. independent children living at home) were regarded as an income unit, as was the standard family (consisting of a man, wife and dependent children). In Table 40 a comparison is made between Aboriginal and all Australian income levels, in relation to a 'poverty line' calculated by the Commission.

Table 40 indicates that between 55 and 76 per cent of Aboriginal income units are in poverty. This is $2\frac{1}{2}$ to $3\frac{1}{2}$ times the proportion for the whole of Australia.

What are the features that may cause this degree of poverty? The first is employment and occupational status. For the earlier estimates, both Beasley (1970, p. 178) and Lickiss (1971b, p. 207) commented on the low occupational status of the Aboriginal work force, and it was this, not the employment status of urban Aborigines, that affected income levels in the late 1960s. (Lickiss (1971b, p. 207) noted that employment for Aborigines was available and also reported (p. 206) that only 27 per cent of the households in her Sydney sample in 1968

---

[1] The precise definition of the income unit is as follows: (1) An adult income unit head, spouse (if head is married) and dependent children for whom the head or spouse is responsible; a dependent child is defined as a person not married and either less than 15, or 15–20 and still engaged in full-time secondary education; an adult is a person 20 and over, or a person 15–20 who is at present married (or is responsible for a dependent child). Or (2) An independent juvenile who is a person 15–20 not engaged in full-time schooling, not at present married and not responsible for a dependent child. (Commission of Inquiry into Poverty (1975, p. 12).)

derived more than 30 per cent of their income from non-employment sources.) Scott (1973a, p. 7.15) provided figures that substantiate the assertion that low occupational status will result in low wage rates which will cause low income status. In 1972 they found that the

Table 40. *Weekly income of income units in relation to 'poverty line'*

Survey	Less than poverty line (very poor) (per cent)	100–120 per cent of poverty line (rather poor) (per cent)	Total poor (per cent)
Australian population			
National Income Survey	12.5	8.1	20.6
Aborigines			
Brisbane, May 1973	48.0	7.0	55.0
Adelaide, late 1973	22.3	33.1	55.4
Adelaide, late 1974	32.5	22.5	55.0
Perth, late 1974	58.3	18.3	76.7

Sources: J. W. Brown *et al.* (1974); Commission of Inquiry into Poverty (1975); Gale and Binnion (1975); Killington (1977).

average weekly take-home pay of Aborigines in Sydney was $69.22, as compared with the average wage for the population as a whole of $99.20. (Skilled workers averaged $77.67 per week and unskilled workers averaged $63.93.)

J. W. Brown *et al.* (1974) in their Brisbane survey examined household as well as individual and income-unit income. They found (p. 61) that, of households with no workers, 94 per cent were below or marginally above the poverty line (100–120 per cent of poverty line), compared with 63 per cent of those with one worker and 35 per cent of those with two or more workers (these figures are of income after housing costs). In their analysis of individual incomes they found that 70 per cent came from employers, 25 per cent came from government and 5 per cent came from other sources. They did note however (p. 58), that Aborigines were not receiving all the government benefits to which they were entitled and this may have further depressed income levels. While 7 per cent of their sample was eligible for unemployment benefits, only 1 per cent received them, and similarly while 4 per cent of their sample was eligible for an old age pension only 1 per cent received it.

In Table 41, the relation between occupation status and poverty in the sample studied by J. W. Brown *et al.* (p. 64) is presented. The relationship between occupational and income status is self-evident. Like Scott, J. W. Brown *et al.* compared the mean income (from em-

Table 41. *Income of income units in relation to occupation of head of income unit, Brisbane, 1973*

Occupation of income-unit head	Per cent below poverty line (0–100 per cent of line)	Per cent of income units in group
Professional	—	–
Semi-professional	23	6
Clerical, sales	9	5
Skilled	0	5
Semi-skilled	7	14
Unskilled	50	32
Not working	73	38

Source: J. W. Brown *et al.* (1974).

ployers) of Aborigines with comparable socio-economic groups – in their case, Torres Strait Islanders and white spouses. They reported (p. 57) a mean weekly income for Aborigines of $55.75, of $67.03 for Islanders and of $77.84 for white spouses.

Gale and Binnion (1975, p. 42) found a similar situation in Adelaide. Twenty-one per cent of income units with an employed head were in poverty (that is, below or marginally above the poverty line) as against 75 per cent of income units with an unemployed income unit head. Employment status appears to have affected the income status of units. They found (p. 40) that non-employment income (government benefits) was directly supporting 54 per cent of the 142 income units in their sample.

Killington (1977, p. 9) found that while in Perth 100 per cent of unemployed income units were in poverty (again defined as 0–120 per cent of the poverty line) in Adelaide only 25 per cent of unemployed were in poverty. However, when he examined unemployed income units with large families, 100 per cent were in poverty in both cities in 1974.

Killington (1977, p. 8) analysed the main source of income for his

Perth and Adelaide samples – dividing the samples into households with male and with female heads. (In Perth 76 per cent of households had male heads, and in Adelaide only 49 per cent of households had male heads.) He reported that in Perth, employment income was the major source of income in 54 per cent of households with male heads and in Adelaide, 56 per cent. In only 7 per cent of Perth and 5 per cent of Adelaide households with female heads was employment the major source of income. The low significance of employment income sources reflects the low employment status of urban Aborigines.

What of the effect of the dependency ratio on income status, for it is generally assumed that the number of dependants and high dependency ratios have resulted in low per capita incomes for Aborigines? J. W. Brown *et al.* (1974, p. 26) showed that income units without children tend to be better off than those with children. Thirty-seven per cent of income units with one adult and no children have income below 120 per cent of the poverty line, and 12 per cent of income units with two adults are in poverty. On the other hand, 89 per cent of income units with one adult and children (single parents) are in poverty, and of income units with two adults and children, 70 per cent are poor. They found that the presence or absence of children had a more marked effect on income than the number of children.

Gale and Binnion (1975, pp. 34–5) found that the number of dependent children in any household was not a critical factor in the poverty level of the household. They reported some relationship between the number of dependent children and the poverty level of income units; those with no children appeared to be better off than those with children, and those with several children appeared to be poorer than those with a few. However, these differences were not statistically significant. Gale and Binnion suggest (p. 33) that it is the number of income units in a household and not the size of the household or the dependency ratio which determines the level of income. Generally speaking, it appears that the greater the number of income units the better off is the household. This finding is reinforced in that more households with a single income unit are below the poverty line than households with multiple income units (p. 28) – there appears to be an economic justification for large Aboriginal households in the urban environment.

One feature which may cause a lower income status for Aborigines is the high occurrence of households with female heads. As noted above, Killington reported that 24 per cent of the Perth households and 51 per cent of the Adelaide households in his sample were matrifocal. Gale and Binnion (1975, p. 31) reported that 32 per cent of their sample of Adelaide households were headed by single parent (almost inevitably a female). In Killington's study (1977, p. 9) in Perth 95 per cent of fatherless families were in poverty (defined again as 0–120 per cent of the poverty line) as against 76.7 per cent of the total Aboriginal sample, and in Adelaide 67.7 per cent of fatherless families were in poverty as against 55.0 per cent for all Aboriginal families. It appears that this demographic variation has a greater consequence for Perth than Adelaide Aborigines. This is borne out by Gale and Binnion (1975, p. 31) who found that while 62 per cent of single parent family units were in poverty, the difference with married family units (53 per cent in poverty) and de facto family units (42 per cent in poverty) was statistically too small to matter.

In summary, therefore, urban Aborigines appear to experience a far lower income status than Australians in general. The main reason for this is probably low employment (and occupational) status. There is also some association between poverty and the dependency ratio; and between poverty and single adult (generally fatherless) households. One factor that appears to ameliorate the extent of poverty among urban Aborigines is their large, composite households – a vestige of their traditional culture which is either formed or held together by economic necessity.

Expenditure

The final aspect of the economic status of urban Aborigines to be examined is their expenditure patterns. Unfortunately very little work has been done in this area, and only housing expenditure has been comprehensively investigated.

Likiss (1971b, p. 207) noted in her study that rent for Aboriginal houses in Sydney was an important expense and that it sometimes involved over one-third of household income. She also observed that spending on alcoholic beverages sometimes influenced the financial situation of households. Scott (1973a, p. 6.43) noted that rent payments made up an average 25 per cent of the weekly income of their sample. However, people who occupied public (Housing Commission homes) only spent on average 19 per cent of income on rent (p. 6.44). This implies that expenditure on housing for these people was subsidised to some extent (by lower rent).

In the research reports for the Commission of Inquiry into Poverty income levels were calculated both before and after housing costs. In Brisbane, J. W. Brown *et al.* (1974, p. 42) reported that housing costs constituted a severe problem for Aborigines (and Islanders). Before housing costs, 55 per cent of households (*not* income units) were below the poverty line or marginally above it; after housing this figure increased to 59 per cent. Overall they noted (p. 60) that 55 per cent of households were in the same (income) category after housing as before; 31 per cent moved down one category after housing and 14 per cent moved up one category. This finding is quite surprising, for the Commission of Inquiry into Poverty (1975, p. 15) found that the proportion of adult income units (annual income basis) in poverty in Australia decreased from 17.9 per cent to 9.7 per cent after housing costs had been taken into account. The implication here is that, given their low income status, Aborigines are not benefiting sufficiently from public housing (in fact only 12 per cent of Brisbane Aboriginal households were in rented Housing Commission houses), or the rents and bonds they were paying were excessive in comparison to what other Australians (on similar incomes) would pay. The practice of charging Aborigines high rent is discussed in J. W. Brown *et al.* (1974, p. 42).

In Adelaide, where 69 per cent of households were renting from a government agency, Gale and Binnion (1975) reported a different situation. Whereas before housing costs were considered, 53 per cent of Aboriginal households were in poverty (0–120 per cent of the poverty line), after rent this proportion decreased to 41 per cent (p. 36). This implies that the calculations used by the Commission of Inquiry into Poverty (1975, p. 12) to determine rent deductions were based on rents higher than those paid by most Adelaide Aborigines. After housing costs, 86 per cent of households were better off. Gale and Binnion (p. 36) suggest that the (South Australian) Housing Trust is clearly significant in helping the poor and marginally poor. A comparison of average weekly rents paid exemplifies this: in 1973 the average rent for a Housing Commission home was $6.87 in contrast to $12.37 for a private home (p. 35). Hence it can be seen that public housing in Adelaide acts like income-in-kind for urban Aborigines.

Killington (1977, p. 9) showed a similar drop in poverty in his Perth and Adelaide samples when housing expenditure was taken into account. In Perth, the number of income units in poverty dropped from 76.6 per cent of the sample to 69.2 per cent, and in Adelaide from 55 per cent to 53.7 per cent. Of greater significance was the move of income units out of extreme poverty (0–100 per cent of poverty line) owing to the beneficial effect of subsidised rental. In Perth the proportion of income units below poverty line (in extreme poverty) fell from 58.3 per cent to 42.5 per cent, and in Adelaide from 32.5 per cent to 26.2 per cent.

It is evident that while spending on accommodation for urban Aborigines is a major expenditure, the overall consequences on income status depend on the extent of availability of government housing. In Perth and Adelaide, subsidised housing appears to improve the income status of urban Aborigines significantly; however, in Brisbane, where most housing available is in the private sector (and where prejudice appears to exist in terms of higher rent for Aborigines), housing expenditure appears to increase the incidence of poverty among Aborigines.

Only one of the research reports, that of J. W. Brown *et al.* (1974), examined other aspects of expenditure patterns of urban Aborigines – and even this study confined itself to some aspects of contract expenditure. They found (p. 65) that 37 per cent of respondents in their sample survey in Brisbane had some items on hire purchase – with television sets, furniture, and motor vehicles being the major items. Payments were highest on vehicles, ranging from $5 to $20 per week. Of income units, 51 per cent had some hire purchase commitment; 17 per cent had less than $5 per week; 13 per cent had $5 to $10; and 13 per cent had $10 to $15. Generally, J. W. Brown *et al.* (p. 65) found that a larger percentage of income units with high incomes had undertaken hire purchase and that their payments were higher than those with low incomes.

J. W. Brown *et al.* also found that a relatively low percentage of Brisbane Aborigines were contributing to house insurance (5 per cent of respondents); vehicle insurance (3 per cent); superannuation (3 per cent); medical benefits (8 per cent); or life insurance (12 per cent). Only 18 per cent of the total sample claimed union membership. These statistics further illustrate the low economic status of urban Aborigines. For as Rowley (1971a, p. 345) has noted 'It is probably a truism that those who need insurance policies are the least likely to have them, and the Aboriginal worker illustrates the cycle of poverty in this respect.'

Conclusion

An important question arising from the material in this chapter is whether there are, in general and on balance, likely to be economic advantages for Aborigines who migrate to the cities? The evidence presented relies primarily on surveys undertaken in Sydney, Adelaide and Brisbane. Overall, the socio-economic status of urban Aborigines seems to be substantially better than that of Aborigines elsewhere in Australia. On all the counts mentioned – health, housing, education, employment and income – urban Aborigines seemed more favourably placed than those elsewhere. Even the extent of discrimination and prejudice against Aborigines (affecting their socio-economic standing) seemed less marked in the cities. However, the apparently better conditions for Aborigines in the large cities compared with other regions do not imply an absence of inter-city differences, for Aboriginal communities in the cities (as elsewhere) have experienced different histories and different policies, depending on the State in which they are located.

The socio-economic conditions among urban Aborigines which this chapter has described, using Western-oriented indicators, seem substantially better than those obtaining among detribalised Aboriginal communities in other parts of settled Australia. But there are two strong provisos on any optimism about the comparatively better socio-economic standards possessed by urban Aborigines. Firstly, while urban Aborigines may be better off than rural Aborigines, their standard of living is extremely depressed relative to that of the majority in Australian society. In particular the recession experienced by Australia in the 1970s has brought more pronounced consequences for urban Aborigines (especially in terms of employment and income status) than for the general population. Secondly, it must be reiterated that it is in general Aborigines from 'settled' Australia who have formed the bulk of Aboriginal migrants to the cities. A similar urbanisation by more traditionally-oriented Aborigines from remote Australia might not have a similar result, since the latter group would be required to undergo a far greater social and economic transformation in adjusting to the city than the former. Consequently, while their continued urban residence, and apparent disinclination to migrate back to rural areas implies that, for urbanised Aborigines, the economic benefits of urbanisation outweigh the costs, the cost–benefit balance need not be the same for tribalised Aborigines.

7
Some economic issues

If an aboriginal in the seventeenth century had been captured as a
curiosity and taken in a Dutch ship to Europe, and if he had
travelled all the way from Scotland to the Caucases and seen how
the average European struggled to make a living, he might have
said to himself that he had now seen the third world and all its
poverty and hardship.
G. Blainey, *Triumph of the Nomads*

The popular belief that unemployment is due to the absence of
development, is clearly without foundation. On the contrary,
development is itself in a sense the primary cause of (measured)
unemployment, since it is development which opens up the gap
between modern and traditional earnings, converts disguised into
open unemployment, and accelerates population growth.
W. A. Lewis, *Development Planning*

This chapter aims to highlight some of the economic issues raised in
previous parts of the book. In discussing the implications of the
economic status of Aborigines, a qualification made in the preface
bears repeating, namely the value-laden assumption that economic
growth and development may be desirable, or at least worth discussing. Some authors, especially in affluent societies, have condemned an
'obsession' with economic growth because of its aesthetic and ecological implications. On the other hand, as W. A. Lewis (1955,
pp. 420–1) has argued, 'the advantage of economic growth is . . . that it
increases the range of economic choice . . . the case for economic
growth is that it gives man greater control over his environment, and
thereby increases his freedom'. In the context of Aboriginal Australia,
the question of the benefits of economic growth, compared with its
costs, especially in the form of social disruption, are of special impor-
174

tance. In discussing the possibility of effecting economic improvements in Aboriginal living conditions, it is not presumed that all the people concerned would necessarily opt for economic changes, however beneficial materially, if the price for these was to be high in terms of social dismemberment or ecological disfiguration.

Moreover, the attempts to attain economic improvements face the suggestion that poverty seems sometimes to create insuperable obstacles to its conquest. 'Vicious circles' of poverty have been described: for example, low income levels are said to make saving impossible and thus to prevent the accumulation of capital necessary for an increase in income. While Bauer (1971, Chapter 1) has argued that the thesis is demonstrably invalid, it is also true, as previous chapters have indicated, that a great number of factors contribute to poverty, and that it often appears, at least superficially, as though these causes interact so as to prevent their cure.

Population

Two features of the Aboriginal population are of special importance in their effect on present and future living standards: the relatively high rate of growth of the population, and the relatively high dependency ratio, compared with the total Australian population. While allowance needs to be made for the haziness of statistics, it seems clear that (1) the rate of growth of the Aboriginal population is about double that of the natural rate of growth of the total Australian population, and (2) the Aboriginal population is composed far more heavily of young people than is the total Australian population (in 1971, 46.4 per cent of the Aboriginal population was under 15 years of age, compared with 28.8 per cent of the total population of Australia).

High population growth rates and high dependency ratios also characterise many developing countries. But Australia is a rich country in which Aborigines represent less than one per cent of the total population and in which – with a natural overall average population growth rate of only around one per cent in the 1970s – considerable efforts have been made to increase the general population through immigration. And, consequently, neo-Malthusian fears about the inability of long-run consumption to rise above a bare minimum subsistence level are scarcely as apposite in Australia in general as in most developing countries. Nonetheless, where the natural economic resources of Aborigines in remote Australia are concerned, rapid population growth does present a problem. Moreover, the causes of rapid population growth among Aborigines bear comparison with the experience in developing countries. In many of these countries, the 'demographic transition' is the name given to the shift from stable population with high infant mortality and general death rates to one of rather lower death rates. Even a constant birth rate, with a declining death rate, has been sufficient to account for population growth as high as 3 per cent per year experienced in some developing countries.

Unfortunately, because of the paucity of information on Aboriginal population growth rates as described in Chapter 1, it is not possible to trace the changes down the years, let alone to ascribe any increases which might have occurred to those (or other) features which seem evident in developing countries, such as improved health services and the eradication of certain diseases. But the extreme youthfulness of the Aboriginal compared with the general population is akin to the comparisons that may be made between developing and more economically developed countries.[1] The effects of the comparatively higher ratio of young people in Aboriginal society and developing countries (compared with the total Australian population and with more economically developing countries, respectively) can readily be seen. As Kindelberger and Herrick (1977, p. 242) have said: 'Each person in the working ages in poor countries must support a greater number of persons in the dependent ages. From the standpoint of human welfare, the situation is even more pressing. Each worker must support more dependents, and since workers in poor countries have lower productivity than workers in rich ones, even less is available for dependents than is shown by an international comparison of the dependency ratios.' This comment seems to apply equally to the dependency ratios among Aborigines compared with those of the general Australian population. When it is recalled that Aborigines are not a homogeneous group, this comment becomes especially important for those segments of the Aboriginal population outside the cities which have not yet begun moving towards smaller family sizes.

Health

Health conditions among Aborigines are closely related to population and demographic questions, and indeed to all aspects of economic

[1] For example, as calculated by Bogue (in Kindleberger and Herrick, 1977, p. 241), Latin America, Africa and Asia had some 110 people under 20 for

improvement. Previous chapters have described the relatively poor health standards and services for Aborigines, and have noted that the general incidence of infant mortality and morbidity rates among them are far higher than for the overall population. And it is not difficult to see the debilitating effects which ill health, some of it stemming from malnutrition, has on economic activity. As in most developing countries, poor health conditions are intimately linked with almost every aspect of Aboriginal life. Because improved health has an important and independent value for individuals, the availability of health facilities is an important item in the standard of living of Aborigines. But at the same time, the availability of almost every other item of consumption, including foodstuffs, housing, clothing, sanitation and formal education, is relevant to health conditions. Improved health conditions should increase labour input and efficiency, and are obviously a determinant of mortality and therefore of population growth rates.

Because of the interrelationship between all of the features involved in health problems (the health deficiencies themselves, environmental and wage and income conditions, and preventative actions) the effect of any one health policy measure depends on all other measures and is by itself somewhat indeterminate. As Myrdal (1968, p. 1618) has observed, 'it is impossible to impute to any single (health) measure or set of measures a definite return in terms of improved health conditions . . . there is only the frailest basis of knowledge about the factors involved and their causal inter-relationships.' It seems, consequently, that working towards better health conditions requires a broad approach including a number of mutually supporting measures: there are clearly health aspects in efforts to improve productivity, general living standards and formal educational facilities. Even where, therefore, as a matter of practical responsibility, a narrower field is defined as 'health policy', a wide perspective must be maintained. In particular, as argued by Tatz (1966, p.56) 'ignorance as a factor in health can be said to be a two-sided thing . . . education programmes for health personnel in the customs and lore of the (Aboriginal) people they are attending are still in their infancy.' In recent years, a number of special services designed to improve Aboriginal health have been created, including Aboriginal Health Centres and travelling trachoma clinics. The difficulty in expecting a rapid result from additional health atten-

every 100 people in the ages from 20 to 64. In Europe, those under 20 were slightly more than half as numerous.

tion is, however, that poor health is only one aspect of poor living conditions, and is inextricably related to other features.

Housing

As with health, the poor housing conditions for Aborigines noted in previous chapters are at once a symptom and a cause of poverty. Overcrowding in the cities, urban and rural communities has implications for health and education. Prejudice against Aborigines seeking homes for rental inhibits improving the standard of accommodation, while in the remote areas (for example, government settlements and missions) the quality and availability of Aboriginal housing is sorely wanting. As remarked in Chapter 2, this deficiency has been compounded by a failure in the remote areas to cater for the traditional family and cultural needs of the Aboriginal people.

An encouraging development in efforts to improve Aboriginal housing conditions has been the growth of Housing Societies, funded by the DAA. However, serious backlogs still exist in meeting the demand for houses, and it is to be hoped that considerably more attention will be given by government in assisting the people concerned to obtain improved housing accommodation.

Education

Expenditures on education are in a sense permissive, since they create opportunities for output growth without being its sufficient condition. Their direct output is also not easy to measure, and their effects are diffuse and spread over a long period. Moreover, the consequences of increased education expenditure are often correlated with other causes of higher productivity from which they are not easily separable. In the light of this indeterminacy, what can be said of the features and conditions of formal education given to Aboriginal communities in Australia, as described in previous chapters? It may be recalled that the figures presented in Chapter 1 showed the very small proportion of Aboriginal children who attended formal (Western-style) school compared with the general population (in 1971 some 24.7 per cent of Aborigines had never attended school compared with 0.8 per cent of the general population). The figures also indicated the important consequences of this, especially the constraints which it placed on the type of occupations for which Aborigines became eligible. For example, in Chapter 2 the comment of the Senate Standing Committee (1975, p. 48) was noted that many school buildings for Aborigines in remote areas would be regarded as totally unacceptable for whites.

But if it is easy to point to the unequal formal amenities for education provided for Aborigines compared with those for the general population, it is difficult to say what form improvement should or might take. In view of the self-determination philosophy, it would no doubt be presumptuous to propose an educational programme of one form or another. It might even be unwise to adopt the maxim which seems in many developing countries to motivate planners, namely 'when in doubt, educate'. For even if economists appear convinced that returns to education are high, they are much less sure about how to measure these returns in comparison with others from different kinds of investment, and to determine 'cut-off points'. And some would prefer to limit the planning of education to making sure that the skill requirements of the labour market are met.

Many questions remain to be considered by those assessing education policy for Aborigines. For example, should educational resources be concentrated so as to provide a general education for adults and children alike in basic 'reading, writing and arithmetic'? Should resources be employed so as to seek to carry a relatively small number of pupils as far as possible, that is to university level? Or should resources be directed towards technical training to equip people for the job market? Should teaching be in the vernacular? Again, should training which is general or specific (as distinguished by Becker (1975, Chapter 2)) be favoured? (General training can be provided by a variety of employers and public expenditures and subsidies might well best be made to assist it.) Perhaps the role of the government should be to offer the widest possible range of alternative forms of education for communities to choose from, in their own ways. Clearly, this is a field in which great care and study is essential, particularly in view of the parent–school hostility which has developed in some communities, as discussed in earlier chapters. But while differing opinions no doubt proliferate in the answers to the questions raised above, there is a healthy willingness in recent government initiatives and in the policies of educational institutions to experiment with various approaches to assist formal education for Aborigines. For example, as mentioned in previous chapters, there are special provisions for assistance for individuals through Aboriginal study group schemes, NEAT, ETSA, and so on. And in some colleges, special courses are being developed to cater for particular difficulties that Aborigines may experience.

One special aspect of formal education is whether or not it increases 'need achievement'. Hagen (1975, p. 288) has pointed out that 'there is little support in modern psychology for the notion that entrepreneurial attitudes can be taught by formal instruction'. As to pre-schooling experience Hagen has himself (1975, p. 283) advanced a broad cultural argument concerning the origins of innovative entrepreneurship in 'traditional' societies. This asserts that 'the personality typical in traditional societies, the hierarchical and authoritarian social systems of those societies, and traditional economic conditions interlock to create a system in quasi-stable equilibrium . . . initiative by the child brings not reward but rebuke or restraint. The child learns to avoid anxiety by not using his initiative. Rather, he waits for directions.'

In the 'traditional' Aboriginal social system individual status appears to be ascribed rather than earned, with a philosophy of the 'community first' which seems to place a constraint upon individuality. And in previous chapters attention has been drawn to the apparent clash between the values indoctrinated by home and by school in Aboriginal communities. However, value judgements would be involved in suggesting that one system needed to be diluted to serve the goals of another. And the concluding words of this section are therefore best left to Rowley (1971a, pp. 351-2):

> In the last two decades, large administrative structures and works
> programs have been devoted (to the cause of changing Aborigines
> through education). Money and services have been wasted
> through the innocence of politicians and public servants about the
> nature of social change, through simple faith that it can be
> directed by an educational program . . . But exhortation, 'social
> engineering' or education do not produce social changes in any
> pre-determined direction . . . No imposed system of education or
> administration will produce predictable attitudes and goals. . .
> Essentially . . . the problem is one of how to maintain, within
> Australian society as a whole, areas of security within which
> Aboriginal groups can make their own adaptations to the hard
> facts which face them.

Employment

Previous chapters have described the diverse employment conditions and income sources of Aborigines, and have documented as far as

seems possible the incomes obtained from employment and the relatively inferior occupational ranking of the jobs available to Aborigines
in the market or money economy. In particular, the extreme importance of the employment status of urban Aborigines was noted in
Chapter 6: Aborigines have in many instances migrated to the cities in
search of better employment prospects.

Away from the cities, a topic of economic interest is whether, in
remote Australia, the well worn literature on the backward-bending
supply curve of labour is of any relevance.[1] More than forty years ago
Robbins (1930, p. 36) converted the backward-bending supply curve
for labour into a demand curve for income in terms of effort. Viewed as
a trade-off between leisure and income, where leisure is an object of
choice, a backward-bending supply curve does not imply limited
wants or uneconomic behaviour: when wages rise and effort is with-
drawn, additional leisure is the 'commodity' sought. This trade-off has
been extensively dabbled with. For those who may find its application
in the context of the supply of Aboriginal labour in remote Australia of
interest, Appendix II has been included. This appendix offers a dia-
grammatic leisure–income indifference curve presentation to illustrate
possible outcomes and issues in remote Australia, where more traditional (pre-contact) Aboriginal value systems remain partly intact, and
where status is not so closely correlated with income (or consumption)
as in the general Australian society. In particular this kinship system
involves a great deal of reciprocity between certain categories of
relatives, a form of behaviour that may serve as a disincentive to work
effort. The implications of the 'model' in Appendix II are that, if there is
indeed a disincentive to effort, either through traditional reciprocity
patterns among some Aborigines or through a 'target worker' effect,
then the standard working hours (per day or weeks per year) may not
appeal equally to all Aborigines compared with the general Australian
society. And there is indeed some empirical basis for the assumption.
But although exceptions can be thought of (for example BHP's subsidi-

---

[1] In poorer or 'developing' countries or communities, low-income workers
whose supply curves for labour are backward-bending are sometimes
referred to as 'target workers' with wants assumed to be limited. The
classic example is a person who migrates to the city in order to earn
sufficient money to attain a 'target' purchase. For a strictly target worker
the length of time spent in the city will vary inversely with the wage rate.
But, as Berg (1961, pp. 468–92) has shown, although individual supply
curves may be backward-bending, the total supply of labour to
wage-paying jobs may be positive.

ary GEMCo on Groote Eylandt, and some employers in the pastoral industry), employers have not always been readily prepared to alter the general standard or number of hours per week or even days per year that their Aboriginal employees are permitted to work, if they wish to be employed. Clearly, one answer is for employers of those people who prefer to work fewer hours or days than the general Australian norm to provide more flexible work arrangements. And this is indeed being done with Community Development Employment Projects, an innovation of the DAA. Under this scheme, lump sum grants are being made to Aboriginal Councils on remote communities, and wages will be paid from this grant. A settlement or mission which chooses to participate in this scheme will do so on the understanding that, by participation, the right to unemployment benefits will be sacrificed. Under this scheme, Aborigines who are represented in the Appendix II format would be able to achieve their 'first-best' work-leisure trade-off. However, a danger of the scheme is that, if funding is not adequate, Aborigines who might wish to work the 'standard' week may be unable to do so. Moreover, 'income preferrers' who may be willing to work beyond the standard number of hours (at a penalty wage rate higher than the award) may be disadvantaged.

The shift of people from a 'traditional' society to a factory or regulated employment system is not easy. In the literature, the elusive characteristics of the industrial labour force necessary for the 'smooth flow of development' have been emphasised. Kerr *et al.* (1962) have divided the process into recruitment, commitment, advancement and maintenance. Of special interest in relation to Aboriginal employment outside the 'traditional' economy are 'commitment' and 'advancement'. The former means the process by which workers become permanently attached to industrial employment as a way of life, whereas the latter implies the acquisition of skills, work habits and incentives for production wage or 'money economy' employment. Where there is little commitment to regularised Western-style employment for cash, absenteeism becomes a problem especially if there is a high turnover through the presence of target workers, as previously defined. But while it is difficult to generalise, previous chapters have suggested that, especially in major urban centres in Australia, it is not true to say that absenteeism (or alleged tendencies to 'go walkabout') are special problems among Aboriginal employees.

Another issue of interest under the heading of employment is the role of trade unions. In general, in developing countries, it seems that the proportion of the labour force belonging to unions is much lower than in economically more advanced ones. This is partly because of the differing composition of the economies concerned: industrial sectors in developing countries are generally, almost by definition, smaller as a proportion of total employment and activity compared with developed countries; and union organisation in the (often self-employed) agrarian, artisan and petty services sectors in developing countries is not, in general, strong. In developing countries (for example see Davies, 1966, Chapter 4) unions are often exclusively urban.

In the Australian context, the consequences of a dualistic social and economic structure are apparent in the impact of unionism on Aboriginal labour organisation. There are instances (for example, in Western Australia as described by Rowley (1971a, p. 254)) of 'walk-offs' from pastoral properties. But perhaps the major influence of unionism on Aboriginal labour has been through the transmission of wage 'disputes' to the arbitration system for settlement. In particular, the events described in Chapter 3 and the inclusion of Aborigines in the Cattle Station Industry (Northern Territory) Award, are of importance. This inclusion followed the successful application by the North Australia Workers Union for the application of the award to Aborigines, on the argument of 'equal pay for work of equal value'. Its implications for employment, also discussed in Chapter 3, are much the same as those which scatter the considerations discussed in a lengthy literature on the impact of minimum wages in developing countries. Do minimum wages merely create uncompetitive industries? Do they result only in unemployment, by raising labour costs unduly? Do they in fact assist low-paid workers, or do they simply raise wages generally? Do they improve productivity by increasing nutritional standards? And is a rise in minimum wages a good way to try and alleviate poverty, or should this be attempted by other means? In the pastoral industry, discussed in Chapter 3, it is not clear how far the impact of minimum wages has contributed to declining numbers of Aborigines employed, since a variety of other forces have been at work as well. Clearly, this is an issue which merits continuing examination.

The possible consequence of minimum wages for employment is related to another point: that raised by the quote from W. A. Lewis at the head of this chapter. Development *may* well be the primary cause of measured unemployment; but the situation that has to be faced is one of accelerated population growth and of a gap between 'modern' and 'traditional' earnings, of open rather than disguised unemployment.

In seeking to improve employment possibilities, on-the-job-training (which consists of gaining skills in the work situation) is of special interest. This form of training is usually thought of as being pursued through formalised apprenticeship programmes. But in some developing economies, less highly structured ways of spreading new industrial work skills prevail. This philosophy, sometimes propounded by the International Labour Office, is summed up in the expression 'learning something by doing something'. In this view, skill is best and most easily gained by exposure to a work situation over a number of years. This concept seems of special importance in the context of the employment patterns among Aborigines which previous chapters have described. In particular, it was noted in Chapter 5 that the hallmark of the employment status of Aborigines in the private sector in settled areas was a lack of job security and work skills; a low propensity to join trade unions; and a difficulty in relating to assistance agencies. Moreover, an additional employment disadvantage facing Aborigines is prejudice and discrimination. As noted in Chapter 5, the major way in which discrimination affects Aborigines is that, when they apply for advertised vacancies, they are told that these have been filled.

To counter this depressing picture, it is encouraging to note that the Commonwealth government has been discriminating positively in favour of Aborigines since 1969 (as described in Chapter 5). This was initially through the ETSA and SWP schemes and now within NEAT. As also mentioned in Chapter 5, there are in addition study and secondary grant schemes for Aborigines. While many aspects of the schemes are difficult to implement, and require careful surveillance of their consequences and impacts, it is at least hopeful that initiatives by government are being taken.

Mining: the centre and the periphery

In Chapter 2 it was noted that a new category of employment for Aboriginal people living on missions and settlements has been in the mining ventures which some large Australian or multinational mining concerns have begun in adjacent areas. A small number of extremely remote missions and settlements have come into sudden prolonged contact with the Western world through the discoveries of mineral resources on or near Aboriginal reserves. The major discoveries to date have been bauxite at Gove in the Arnhem Land and at Weipa in the far north of Queensland, and manganese at Grotte Eylandt off the

Arnhem Land coast. Large extractive plants have been established by Nabalco, Comalco and GEMCo respectively. But while the employment policies of the various companies have been rather mixed, and while the conditions provided for and the impact on Aboriginal communities has varied, the greatest effect seems yet to come. And it seems likely to be felt through the possible mining of a mineral over which there is currently (1977) great contention – uranium.

Some 800 Aborigines living in the Alligator Rivers region of the Northern Territory were the subject of concern of the discussion of the Second Report of the (Fox) Ranger Uranium Environmental Inquiry (1977). This report went to great lengths (in Chapters 4, 13, 14 and 15) to examine the rights of the Aborigines in the region and the consequences for them if uranium were to be mined there. Already, the relatively remote groups of people concerned had been affected by recent development of pastoral properties. But the proposed exploitation of uranium deposits raised many more questions: the Inquiry proposed a national park, controls for an envisaged tourist industry, and a system of royalty payments for members of Aboriginal groups with land right claims in the region. (The Inquiry spent a great deal of its second report on the issue of land rights.) Clearly, the sudden arrival of such an important (and profitable) industry in the vicinity of a group of previously remote people and especially the payment of substantial royalties per head, would produce completely new circumstances, akin to those confronted by the people of Nauru, whose island is used for phosphate mining, or indeed of those of Kuwait, whose oil revenue gives them a new and dramatically high living standard.

The impact of mining such as proposed by the Fox Report (whose recommendations seem still in the long-term balance) would clearly stand in danger of structurally altering the income status and life-style of a small group of Aboriginal people. Other similar projects in areas populated by Aborigines would do the same. But this is obviously a far cry from speaking of 'reverberative impacts' or 'leading sectors' for the 'Aboriginal economy' at large, along the lines of the development literature. While, therefore, general consequences may flow for all members of the Aboriginal community from central government decision and actions, mining ventures – past and future – seem likely to influence directly only some members of the Aboriginal population. Moreover money channelled into the Aboriginal Benefits Trust Fund (now called the Aboriginal Benefits Trust Account) from mining ventures is usually directed only partly to the groups in whose land the mines are situated.

It will be interesting to see whether, in the course of time, mining developments can do anything to counteract the cumulative processes toward regional inequality which Myrdal (1957, Chapter 3) has described. As Myrdal has written (p. 27): 'It is easy to see how expansion in one locality has "backwash effects" in other localities. More specifically the movements of labour, capital goods and services do not by themselves counteract the natural tendency to regional inequality. By themselves, migration, capital movements and trade are rather the media through which the cumulative process evolves – upwards in the lucky regions and downwards in the unlucky ones. In general, if they have positive results for the former, their effects on the latter are negative.' And (p. 26) 'if things were left to market forces unhampered by any policy interferences, industrial production, commerce, banking, insurance, shipping and indeed, almost all those economic activities which in a developing economy tend to give a bigger than average return . . . would cluster in certain localities and regions, leaving the rest of the country more or less in a backwater'.

These ideas (which Myrdal extended to inter-country relationships and which have been developed by others, for example Brookfield (1975)) are of some relevance to the material described in previous chapters, and to the expansion of mining in remote Australia. It will be recalled that housing, sewerage, health, water, roads, electricity, shopping, schooling and almost any form of private or public 'facility' is of a generally lower standard (compared with white Australia) in the areas in which the majority of Aborigines (as a predominantly rural group) live. This must surely be due, at least in part, to the 'cumulative causation' processes of regional inequality which Myrdal and others have described. It is not difficult to see how developments are interlinked. For example, the decision to locate an industry in a particular community may give a spur to its general development. Opportunities of employment and higher incomes are provided for those unemployed. Local business can grow as the demand for products and services increases. Labour, capital and enterprise are attracted from outside. Markets widen, as does the general increase of incomes and demand. Rising profits increase savings, investment acts cumulatively to push up demand once more, as well as the level of profits. In Myrdal's words (1957, p. 25) 'the expansion process creates external economies favourable for sustaining its continuation'.

But this cumulative causation in Australia's economic expansion has so far largely been removed from remote Australia. The process described by Myrdal is clearly not predominantly a part of the scene on government settlements and missions, pastoral stations, and decentralised communities. And in seeking to explain why this is so, another part of the literature on developing economies may be helpful namely that concerned with metropolitan – colonial or industrialised – non-industrialised country relationships. In this literature (for example Myint, 1964) various supply and demand 'leakages' are said to have occurred in the trading and general economic relationships between countries, which have served to limit the impact of an initial bout or impetus of economic activity. For example, it has been pointed out that savings leakages occur, in that companies and their employees remit earnings and profits to their 'home' country; that the local (colonial) economy suffers from a supply deficiency in being unable to cater for the demands of expanding industry; and that, when investment in the colonial economy occurs in response to increased demand for its products, this is often in capital widening rather than more reverberative capital deepening ways.

If the traditional Aboriginal economy (that in remote Australia) is viewed as a colonial dependency of the new technology introduced by latter-day Australians, there are some links between the above explanations and the way in which even those developments which have occurred have failed to spark off processes of cumulative expansion. The new mining towns in remote Australia, for example, have become enclaves in the world of traditional Aboriginal life. They may have provided, as mentioned, some new avenues of employment for Aboriginal labour and a new, closer market for artefact production. But the savings and investment of the companies and their employees have largely been directed to the acquisition and development of resources and technology as part of a society far wider than the neighbouring Aboriginal clans. Materials for house building, industrial and railway construction have had to come from afar; consumption goods, such as food, have largely been 'imported' from areas distant from the immediate environs of the mining concerns; and even the major export – labour – which the Aboriginal 'economy' could provide has not been fully used, nor has it always been accorded the proper training facilities which would have reaped higher rewards for its providers.

But it would be wrong to conclude that it is the forces of the market – of cumulative causation or of the interlinkage which maximises the economic aftermath of an initial economic impact – that has been at the heart of the inequalities which this book describes. Government attitudes and policies, and in particular the acceptance of double standards for people of different skin pigmentations, are also part of the explanation. Indeed it is especially ironical that Australia, a country with notions of equal treatment between the States embedded in its constitution and general economic and federal–state relationships, should have countenanced such disparities in the public and other facilities provided to its Aboriginal inhabitants.

The role of government

The most important government initiative in recent years in regard to policy towards Aborigines in the economy was the Constitution Alteration (Aboriginals) Act of 1967, which was unanimously approved by both Houses of Parliament, and which was subsequently acceded to by 89 per cent of voters in the May 1967 referendum on the issue. Some years later, in 1973, the then Prime Minister, Gough Whitlam, referred to this overwhelming referendum vote in a statement to Federal and State ministers at a meeting of the Australian Aboriginal Affairs Council, at which State ministers received a formal offer from the Federal government to take over their activities in Aboriginal policy and planning. All States except Queensland have accepted the offer and there is now, through the Federal Department of Aboriginal Affairs, a central authority for the administration of policy.

With centralisation has come a flurry of activity, as mentioned in previous chapters: a programme of acquiring properties on behalf of Aboriginal communities has been undertaken; an Aboriginal Land Fund Commission, with majority Aboriginal membership, has been established; the (Woodward) Commission on Land Rights reported in 1974 and its recommendations were accepted by the Whitlam government (these recommendations included full Aboriginal ownership of all existing reserves in the Northern Territory and certain other lands and the establishment of a Land Commission to enquire into claims outside the reserves); also in 1974, two new funds (the Aboriginal Enterprises Fund and the Aboriginal Housing and Personal Loans Fund) were created to provide loans for Aborigines; and in 1975, legislation was enacted to safeguard Aboriginal land tenure. A National Aboriginal Consultative Committee was also established to provide formal machinery for Aborigines to be consulted by the Minister on policy matters.

In the centralisation of policy and the initiatives on land rights, capital availability, and so on, a new government role in influencing attitudes to economic development and growth in Aboriginal communities is clearly in evidence. These initiatives have seemed designed not merely to protect the communities from land incursion but also to provide avenues for self-help under the policy of self-determination (as defined earlier). Clearly, as the literature on economic development shows, economic 'progress' depends substantially upon the extent to which the community has attitudes favourable to growth. Attitudes to work, thrift, family size, inequalities of income, caste, social mobility, new techniques, and so on are all, as W. A. Lewis has mentioned (1955, p. 37), of importance, and governments can influence each: 'It is true that [governments] are circumscribed by public opinion; they cannot go too far in advance of public opinion, or lag too far behind it. But it is also true that they help to determine public opinion . . . In this context, government is exercising the function of leadership.'

Earlier chapters have described some of the particular aspects and consequences of Federal government leadership in relation to various Aboriginal communities. Among these have been a variety of employment projects; encouragement given to the decentralised communities; and the purchase of pastoral properties for Aborigines. These changes involve a variety of assumptions. Firstly, they assume that change, if it is to occur, must take place within the context of self-determination. Secondly, they aim to provide the facilities for new economic activities. Thirdly, they do not suppose that economic development necessarily involves urbanisation and industrialisation. And fourthly, they have not included nationalisation of local means of production (for example, the pastoral stations on which Aboriginal employment, as described in Chapter 3, has been recently declining).

Clearly, in the three aspects of the possible role of government to which special attention is drawn (influence on attitudes, economic institutions and income distribution) the Labor administration between 1972 and 1975 began some substantial programmes. By its assertion of special concern for the economic plight of Aborigines; by its attempts to provide them with security of land tenure; by its efforts to substantially increase the flow of funds to Aboriginal communities, and the means for their disbursement under financial institutions in which the people themselves have a say; and by its assumption of central control from the States over Aboriginal policy; by all these actions, and others, the Whitlam administration gave a lift and a lead to the chances of economic improvement among Aborigines.

In this respect, it is perhaps useful to mention the public expenditure on social services for Aborigines (and Torres Strait Islanders) as a proportion of total public expenditure in Australia on social services over the last couple of decades. There was a dramatic increase, in both absolute and relative terms, when the Labor government came to power in 1972. According to figures from the Melbourne Institute of Applied Economic and Social Research data bank, in money and proportionate terms expenditure on Aborigines (and TSIs) was relatively static over the eleven years to 1965. It then began rising gradually, but took off from 1971–2: in the period 1972–3 the amount of money expended on Aborigines (and TSIs) nearly quadrupled, while as a proportion of total expenditure, it increased by nearly twofold.

One special problem here is the delivery cost of assistance. In this respect, an important report was published in June 1976: the Report on the Delivery of Services by the Department of Aboriginal Affairs (Hay, 1976). This Report assessed the capability of the Department of Aboriginal Affairs to fulfil its responsibility for the 'development and administration of national policies for the advancement and welfare of the Aboriginal people'. As the report (p. 4) commented 'From its creation in 1972 the Department . . . had to put into effect massive Ministerial initiatives in such areas as housing, local government and legal aid. As examples, *all* Aboriginal families were to be properly housed by 1982, and Aboriginals were entitled to free legal advice and representation in *all* courts. These initiatives involved large scale financial grants. The Department was not equipped to administer grants of this size. The pressure for urgent return forced itself to organise itself on the run.'

Another issue is whether government may assist by encouraging trade rather than aid. Trade is said to imply self-help, to offer advantages proportionate to effort, and to call for competitive standards of efficiency, technical progress, and capacity for adaptation. Aid, on the other hand, can be instrumental either in complementing the benefits derived from trade or, on the contrary, in discouraging such efforts owing to its availability irrespective of performance. This issue is of relevance to the decentralised communities. And many of the projects and devices undertaken by the DAA may well fall into the useful category of aid or assistance in order to complement the growth of trade.

There is little which provides a measuring rod against which the advisability of these actions can be weighed. But it can at least be said with W. A. Lewis (1955, p. 377) that, in exercising leadership, the government shares a function 'with many others in the community – with the priests, with newspaper editors, with trade union leaders, with teachers, and with all others whose opinions carry some weight. In stable communities government interferes in very few matters: it is content to leave it to the priests to pronounce on the birth rate, or to scientists to pronounce on artificial fertilisers, but in communities which are undergoing a rapid transition there is hardly anything that the government can afford to ignore.' In this apparent need to intervene, however, the uncertainty of opinion as to the likely economic consequences of given acts of government intervention should act as an inhibitor; and it is in this respect comforting that current intervention is in the framework of self-determination. However, self-determination seems of less relevance in settled than in remote Australia. In particular the Aboriginal population in the major urban centres is probably more akin (in its relation to possible government intervention) to other less privileged urbanised groups than to those Aboriginal communities among whom self-determination is being adopted in remote Australia.

Land

Land ownership is for the majority of Aborigines an issue of the greatest importance. In its second report, the Aboriginal Land Rights Commission (1974, p. 9) commented that 'at the beginning of the year 1778 the whole of Australia was occupied by the Aboriginal people of this country. It was divided between groups in a way which was understood and respected by all. Over the last 186 years, white settlers and their descendants have gradually taken over the occupation of most of the fertile or otherwise useful parts of the country. In doing so, they have shown scant regard for any rights in the land, legal or moral, of the Aboriginal people.'

As mentioned in Chapter 4, in seeking to describe the 'traditional' relationship of Aboriginal people to the land, there is some difficulty. Firstly, there is the problem of knowing whether Aboriginal ideas and arrangements are fully captured by available English language usage. Some of these ideas have been eloquently discussed by Stanner (1968). Indeed, it seems that some Aboriginal concepts of 'land ownership' do not have a parallel in European law. Among these, as noted by the first report of the Aboriginal Land Rights Commission (1973, p. 5), the most important and widespread of the rights in land which lie outside European arrangements is the managerial interests of a nephew in the country of his maternal uncle: 'Everywhere the religious rites owned by a clan were the "title deeds" to the land and could only be celebrated by clan members. Such rites, however, could not be held without the assistance of the managers whose essential task it was to prepare the ritual paraphenalia, decorate the celebrants and conduct the rite. The agreement of managers had to be secured for the exploitation of specialised local resources such as ochre and flint deposits and for visits by the clan owners to their sacred sites.'

Another difficulty in understanding the 'traditional' relationship between Aborigines and the land is that social organisation differs from one area to another. Nonetheless, the first report of the Aboriginal Land Rights Commission (1973, pp. 4–10) did seek briefly to explain the link between clans and the land.

Membership of a clan is retained for all time, including after physical death; and the link between a person's spirit and the land is regarded as timeless. A land-owning clan is simply a group of people sharing links with the same land, but these links are spiritual and an intricate part of religious belief, which views land as given to them, or claimed by ancestors on their behalf, in the Dreamtime. Stories, songs and ceremonies bind spirit ancestors with particular places, and sacredness is strengthened by the importance of a place in legend. Legends are frequently linked with natural resources and, because of either legend or resources, some portions of the land are more important than others. But, even if boundaries are blurred, all country is of importance and is identified with some clan or grouping. And, as the Aboriginal Land Rights Commission (first report, 1973, p. 7) remarked 'the spiritual connection between a clan and its land involves both rights and duties. The rights are to the unrestricted use of its natural products; the duties are of a ceremonial kind – to tend the land by the performance of ritual dances, songs, and ceremonies at the proper times and places.'

From the economic point of view, it is clear that the rights of Aboriginal people to land ownership or title is of crucial importance.[1] Chapter 4, dealing with decentralised communities, has noted the

[1] This is much the same issue in developing countries. For example see Dorner (1972), Meier (1970, Chapter 7) and Myrdal (1968, Chapter 26).

detrimental effect of the removal of Aboriginal people from the land to which they held strong spiritual ties, and the impact, in sedentary settlements, of life among a conglomeration of clan groups with various geographical origins, differing dialects, and other points of dissimilarity. The centralised communities, established for administrative ease and economy, have damaged the traditional Aboriginal social structure through the creation of new inter-clan or group tensions. On the other hand, it was noted that on decentralised communities (although there was a danger of the marginal productivity of labour becoming zero or negative) there was a new incentive and independence which even extended its effects to physical and mental health improvements.

It is not claimed, of course, that the tensions and incohesions of life in centralised communities are an insuperable barrier to community or individual effort. Indeed, the literature on economic development has in some instances (for example Hagen, 1975, Chapter 11) pointed to the emergence of innovative, growth producing activity as a consequence of changing patterns of social relationships. But the pattern of life on the centralised communities, as described in Chapters 2 and 3, displays a sufficient aura of dependency, listiessness and lack of motivation to enable one, intuitively, to describe it as in need of some regenerative impulse if economic improvements, at the initiative of the people themselves, are to occur. And, in view of the intense concern for land rights evinced on frequent occasions by a wide array of spokesmen on behalf of the Aboriginal people, it is not an unreasonable further step, from the economists's viewpoint, to say that this regenerative impulse may well come only from restitution of Aboriginal land rights. This is particularly so in view of the conjunction of calls for land rights and the policies of self-determination to which we have previously referred.

In what have these calls consisted, and what progress has been made towards the achievement of recognition of land rights for Aborigines? As noted by the Senate Select Committee (1976, p. 246) attempts by Aborigines to regain land through legal channels have so far been fruitless. The best known case was heard in 1971 and concerned the Nabalco company. The central legal questions were those of 'proprietary rights' and the application of the doctrine of communal 'native' title, that is, did rights under native law or custom persist under common law until or unless they were validly terminated? The court ruled, however, that the doctrine of communal 'native' title had never formed part of Australia's common law, and that land settlement had proceeded without any provision for the recognition of the doctrine. Despite this rebuff from the court, however, demands by and on behalf of Aboriginal people have been persistently made. For example, a fairly comprehensive list of demands has been made by the Federal Council for the Advancement of Aborigines and Torres Strait Islanders. This includes Aboriginal ownership of existing reserves; recognition of Aboriginal ownership of traditional tribal land at present owned and leased by the Crown; Aboriginal consent for, and benefit from, mining and other development on all Aboriginal land; and the establishment of an Aboriginal Land Claims Court and a Lands Trust Fund.

In recent years, there has been a considerable response to this form of demands. The (Woodward) Aboriginal Land Rights Commission which was appointed in 1973 to report on 'the appropriate means to recognise and establish the traditional rights and interests of the Aborigines in relation to land, and to satisfy in other ways the reasonable aspirations of the Aborigines to [land rights]'. A large number of conclusions emerged from the enquiry, of which the following are but some (taken from the second report of the Aboriginal Land Rights Commission, 1974, pp. 8–10): '(1) Cash compensation in the pockets of this generation of Aborigines is no answer to the legitimate land claims of a people with a distinct past who want to maintain their separate identity in the future; (2) there is little point in recognising Aboriginal claims to land unless the Aboriginal people concerned are also provided with the necessary funds to make use of that land in any sensible way which they wish; and (3) it is important that Aboriginal communities should have as much autonomy as possible in running their own affairs.' In order to give effect to these proposals, it was proposed (1) that freehold title to Aboriginal reserve land should be owned by Aborigines, and the title held by an Aboriginal corporation called a Land Trust; (2) that Regional Land Councils should be incorporated to direct the Land Trusts and to carry out general administration; (3) that an Aboriginal Lands Commission should be established to enquire into traditional Aboriginal claims to pastoral lease lands, register these claims and make recommendations about them. Some pastoral leases should be purchased as tribal lands or as economic ventures (or both), and a fund established to purchase these lands. Finally, (4) it was recommended that minerals and petroleum on Aboriginal lands should remain the property of the Crown; that Aborigines should have the right to prevent exploration on their traditional lands; and that

:his right should be overridden only if the national interest required
t.

The major recommendations of the Woodward Commission have
℩een enacted by the Aboriginal Land Rights (Northern Territory) Act
1976. (Agreement had already been reached, in 1975, with all the
℩tates, except Queensland, in order to co-ordinate the implementation
℩f the Woodward recommendations with the policies then being pur-
℩ued in the States.) However, there remains the question of cash
compensation. The (Woodward) Aboriginal Land Rights Commission
(second report, 1974, p. 9) suggested that 'the only appropriate direct
recompense for those who have lost their traditional lands is other
land'. But other commentators, for example, the Senate Select Committee (1976, p. 256), have been concerned that 'there may be many
Aborigines, especially those living in cities, who will not benefit at all
from the granting of areas of land. They, too, should have the right to
choose their own styles of living. In order to exercise this right effec-
tively, they may require material assistance.' This is an important
issue, to which we return later.

Despite the stated enthusiasm of both major political parties in
Australia for land rights justice for Aborigines, and the acceptance of
the Woodward Report, progress in the acquisition of land has been
slow. The Aboriginal Land Fund Commission, which began opera-
tions in May 1975, had (by June 1976) acquired or funded the acquisition of a total of only sixteen properties. The Commission was allocated
$2.018 million for expenditure in 1975/76. However, in the latter part of
the year, $1 million of this amount was frozen until July 1976 as part of
general economy measures, resulting in the deferral of the acquisition
of some properties. Up to the middle of 1976, the Commission had
purchased some 3 million hectares of land, to which must be added
nearly 2 million hectares purchased prior to the Commission's establishment. Adding these figures to those for the extent of Aboriginal
reserves (54.6 million hectares) it seems that the 'Aboriginal' share of
Australia's total area of land (767.4 million hectares) is about 7.8 per
cent. (Much of this land is, however, in the less fertile and more remote
regions of Australia.)

In summary, therefore, it can be seen that there have been moves to
secure land rights for Aborigines, and (so far limited) financial
resources to acquire properties on their behalf. What can economists
say of this in their assessment of the relationship between the land and
the potential for economic development and growth among

Aborigines? It probably bears repeating that restitution of access and claims to land in a society in which there are such intimate links between the land and the people may well serve to buoy up efforts at economic improvement from within the community. But the positive economic impact which may well ensue through a new independence among those groups of Aborigines who will have their own land should not be overestimated. As mentioned in Chapter 4 (on decentralised communities) the potential for economic independence or viability is not certain or assured in all or even many of the communities. While a land rights policy is, therefore, enshrined in the law, and while acquisitions are proceeding slowly, there is no room for complacence, either that the 'land problem' is on the way to being solved for or by Aborigines, or that, even if a much more rapid rate of land acquisition were to ensue, this would greatly assist all other aspects of the many facets of economic standards and conditions among Aborigines. In particular, attention must be drawn to the perennial problem of the relationship between the economic development of the land while many of the more innovative individuals are leaving the land for life in the cities.

Further research

Previous paragraphs have pointed to a large number of areas in which research seems to be called for. Special research needs to include the following:

(1) *The need for better information*. Time and again in this work, it has been necessary to call attention to the lack of adequate information on the various aspects upon which a full assessment of the socio-economic status of Australia's Aboriginal population depends. It would be of assistance in further research if more detailed and comprehensive information on the housing, education, employment, income and other aspects of the economic life of Aborigines were available.

(2) *Implication of age-structure*. In Chapter 1, the relative youth of Aboriginal compared with other Australian families was noted. The higher dependant-age ratio for Aboriginal families was observed. It would be useful to have a study of the social policy implications of this demographic characteristic. Does it warrant any special measures not now being undertaken?

(3) *Education and training.* An overall review of education programmes as they affect Aborigines (especially in remote Australia) would be of assistance. How effective are the various systems of special grants? Is the training offered by NEAT suitable? Are the different styles of education and training appropriate?

(4) *Housing.* A study of the progress of State and Commonwealth assistance in providing housing for Aborigines (its efficacy and impact, and the means for any possible improvements) would be helpful.

(5) *Employment.* A survey seems necessary of the employment patterns among Aborigines, and the way in which various private and public sector employers are offering jobs and training. In particular, a wide ranging review of the extent to which prejudice or impatience by employers is hampering the growth of Aboriginal employment would be interesting. A study of these features on a national basis might well serve to focus attention on the shape of the policies of companies and governments.

(6) *Pastoral industry employment.* A special review of the employment of Aborigines in the pastoral industry, especially following the decline in numbers employed in recent years, seems specially desirable. A study of the progress of property purchases for Aboriginal control, and means to further expedite this trend would also be of interest. Perhaps even more important, the question of the economic operation and viability of the properties purchased needs to be carefully surveyed.

(7) *The economic future of decentralised communities.* An examination of the economic prospects of the decentralised communities, and of ways to assist them, should aid be requested, would possibly produce some helpful suggestions. In particular, the ways and means of aiding decentralised communities, especially through extension services, needs examination. The institutions for offering advice are concentrated in Australia's overseas aid effort – their direction to local problems needs research attention. As noted by the Second Workshop on the Nutrition of Aborigines in Relation to the Eco-System of Central Australia (Alice Springs, October 1977) 'there is an urgent need to develop and co-ordinate extension work and training programmes within Aboriginal communities, in the technical aspects of land use, water use, crop production, nutrition, building, transport and communication.'

(8) *Problems of migration and integration.* An overview of the problems of migration and integration of Aborigines in major urban areas could

well highlight ways in which this process might facilitate the passage of those who choose or are forced to make it.

(9) *Fringe dwellers in rural towns*. A survey of the special economic problems, including unemployment, of those Aborigines living on the fringes of white society in smaller towns might provide suggestions for helpful policies towards them.

(10) *The interconnections of the causes of poverty*. A study of the various ways in which the cycle of poverty among Aborigines operates, in more detail than suggested in the present work, and undertaken by an inter-disciplinary team, might well call to Australia's further attention the pressing socio-economic problems and deprivation of its Aboriginal citizens.

APPENDIX I
Aborigines in the rural sector: dimensions of economic development

	Pre-contact (pre-1788)	Post-contact A (1788 to 1967)	Post-contact B (post 1967)
PART I: RESOURCE ENDOWMENT			
Land:			
Area under societies control	Exceeds subsistence needs	Not sufficient to meet subsistence needs (alienated)	Increasing availability but not sufficient for needs (land rights)
Labour:			
Working population	Not fully employed in subsistence	Definitely underemployed	Definitely under- and unemployed (50 per cent at least)
Capital:			
Metal tools and equipment	Absent	Not readily available (scarcity of funds)	Becoming more available (capital funds)
Technology and skills	At unsophisticated level	At relatively unsophisticated level	Education raising skill level (ABSEG Scheme, ASGS, NEAT, etc.)
PART II: TRADITIONAL SOCIAL SYSTEM			
Economic:			
Productive unit:	Small and socially integrated	Heterogenous group (large number of clans congregated)	Heterogenous group – some reversion to small integrated group
Entrepreneurship:	Stress on conformity	Lacking in managerial skills	Education opportunities raising entrepreneurial level
Specialisation:	Little division of labour by specialisation	Lack of skills	Education raising skill level (from low base)
Exchanges:	Reciprocity/barter/ redistribution	Reciprocity/money exchange limited	Reciprocity/monetary
Consumption:	Absorbing total production	Greater than total production	Greater than total production (dependent economies)
Savings and investment:	Absent	Short time horizon: saving for consumption goods	Short time horizon: more consumer durable investment e.g. motor vehicles

199

	Pre-contact (pre 1788)	Post-contact A (1788–1967)	Post-contact B (post 1967)
Social:			
Organisation:	Hierarchical	Disintegrating	Disintegrating/some renewal of traditional ways (decentralisation)
Status:	Ascribed and based on non economic factors	Achieved/ascribed	Achieved still not based on economic factors
Land tenure:	Vague group tenure	Insecure and non-existent	Land rights securing tenure in some instances
Inheritance pattern:	Destroy property in some cases	Destroy property/ maintain property	Maintain property/little traditional destruction
Reciprocity:	Group members acting as constraint on ambitious men	Group members acting as less of an inhibiting factor	Group members acting as less of a constraint/outside influence stronger
Leisure:	Valued highly	Valued highly	Valued highly
Time horizon:	Extremely short-term	Fairly short-term	Fairly short-term
Prestige criterion:	High reciprocity level/ consumption conspicuous	High reciprocity level/ consumption conspicuous	High reciprocity/ consumption conspicuous
Religious beliefs:	Encourage periodic lavish expenditure	Encourage saving (Christianity) versus lavish expenditure (traditional)	Encourage saving (Christianity)
Political:			
Leadership:	Based on individual qualities; age; loosely defined	Based on individual quality/communications possibilities/literacy/ etc.	Some confusion/ability to communicate with whites/ traditional also
Clans:	No competition	Little competition	Little (inter-clan) competition

PART III: EXTERNAL CONTACT

Colonisation:	None	Unmitigated exploitation	Reduced exploitation
Technology:	Limited	Limited (education)	Increasing as result of capital funds
Cash crops (barter crops):	Few (trade with Macassans)	Few with limited outlets (foodstuffs)	Few with limited but increasing outlets (artefacts)
Marketing:	None – ritual exchanges only	Some large-scale organisation	Some large-scale organisation
Shop goods:	None	Limited range	Increasing range
Transport facilities:	Limited	Few good road/rail link-ages with market	Improving linkage with market

Source: Based on a summary table in Epstein and Penny (1973, pp. 248–51).

APPENDIX II

The work effort of Aborigines in remote Australia

In Chapter 2, reference was made to the work patterns of Aborigines in remote Australia, which may vary somewhat from the norms of the general Australian society. This observation was based on the assumption that in remote Australia the traditional (pre-contact) Aboriginal value system remains intact to varying extents. Hence status may not be attached to high levels of income (and consumption) to the same extent as in the general society, and the traditional kinship system may result in a great deal of intra-clan reciprocity and redistribution (usually between kin). In this appendix an attempt is made to assess how these factors may modify a basic work-effort model.

The model presented in Figure 1 is based on the work of Moses (1962). Income is measured along the vertical axis and work and leisure along the horizontal. At position 0, leisure is at a maximum and zero work effort is expended, while at position Z''' work effort is at a physical maximum. BAL is a hypothetical labour offer curve (that may or may not bend back at high levels of income) and U^1 to U^4 are indifference curves depicting different levels of utility: the higher the indifference curve the greater is utility. 0Z'' represents a 'standard' or 'acceptable' quantity of labour in European Australian terms. (It can represent either a 40-hour week or a 48-week working year.) Finally, the slope of the line 0Y''' represents the award wage rate.

To simplify the analysis three assumptions are made. Firstly, it is assumed that tax considerations do not complicate the analysis; hence 0Y''' can depict a 'net' wage rate or alternatively the tax rate may be proportional. Secondly, the assumption is made that labour is not offered if total income can be maximised by not working. Hence in

201

Figure 1, the labour offer curve originates at point B, and not at point 0, if minimum non-employment income is depicted by the line Y*Y*. If minimum (non-employment) income dropped to Y**Y** point E would represent the origin of the labour offer curve. The final assump-

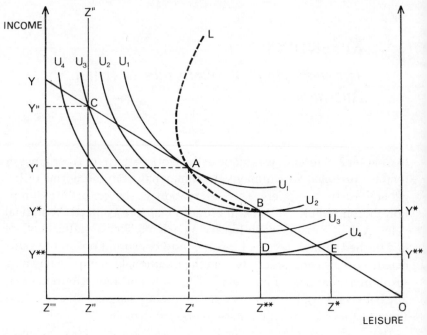

Figure 1

tion is that employment and non-employment incomes are mutually exclusive. If one earns employment income, then non-employment income is zero, and vice versa. It would be safe to assume that non-employment income takes the form of unemployment benefits. Linked to this assumption is the proviso that while traditional redistribution and reciprocity may occur if a person is not employed, it would not occur or would not affect his work effort level, if he were employed.

In Figure 1, position A represents the point of highest utility at the current wage rate. At this point the labour offer curve cuts the wage rate line; thus work is desired but not for the standard week or year. Aborigines demonstrating such an offer (or labour supply) curve could be termed leisure preferrers (Moses, 1962, p. 322). Y' represents the optimal level of income at the current wage rate, with 0Z' labour being expended.

Position B represents a lower point of utility and is associated with a level of income Y*Y*. This level of non-employment income is positive owing to transfer payments from government (that is unemployment benefits) and to redistribution from employed to unemployed. Hence Aborigines can achieve this cash income level with zero work effort. (It could be assumed that at some communities cash income here could be supplemented by non-cash (subsistence) income, as time would be available for the pursuit of traditional economic activity such as hunting and gathering.)

At position C, Aborigines are required to work the standard period. The important point here is that utility declines to U^3 which is below U^2, the level of utility enjoyed with zero work effort. The positive utility derived from the increase in income (from Y* to Y") is outweighed by the disutility of working the standard time (loss of leisure time 0Z"). This implies the derivation of a relatively small amount of utility from marginal income than from leisure (perhaps owing to the lack of availability of a wide range of goods and services at government settlements and missions or to a lack of status-attachment to high levels of income. This form of situation has been much discussed in the development literature. See, for example, Fisk, 1962). It should be noted that both positions B and C are disequilibrium positions as the indifference curves intersect (rather than being tangential to the wage rate line. (Point C can never be an equilibrium in the example (Figure 1) as the labour offer curve does not intersect Z"Z".)

The implications of this 'model' are as follows: assuming that a positive non-employment level of income exists, Aborigines may not be willing to participate in the labour market at the European Australian standard (number of hours, or weeks). Where employment opportunities do exist for Aborigines in remote Australia, employers have shown a reluctance to alter this standard – except perhaps in the pastoral industry where Aboriginal participation has fluctuated with the seasonal demands of the industry.

If Aborigines are to be encouraged to participate in a European-style labour market there are two possibilities. Firstly, the payment of unemployment benefits to Aborigines could be halted. This would result in a drop in income (say to Y**Y**, which is still positive owing to redistribution) and a drop in utility to U^4; making U^3, associated with working the standard time preferable. Such a policy however would not be acceptable for it involves discrimination against Aborigines in the payment of unemployment benefits. The second alternative would be to introduce flexible work arrangements to Aboriginal communities in remote Australia. This is in fact what is being done by the Community Development Employment Project (CDEP) Scheme – a new initiative of the DAA (DAA, 1977d). Under this scheme, lump sum grants are made to Aboriginal Councils on remote communities and wages are paid at the award rate from this grant. The residents of a community that participates in this scheme automatically lose the right to unemployment benefits. Under this scheme, Aborigines who wish to work less than the standard week or year should be able to achieve their 'first-best' work–leisure trade-off. Others, who may wish to work the standard week should theoretically also be able to do so. However, discussions with DAA personnel in Canberra indicate that funding for the CDEP scheme is not adequate. Hence some Aborigines who wish to work the standard week are not able to do so.

APPENDIX III
Food expenditure patterns in remote Australia

In Table 42, the proportion of food expenditure devoted to each of eleven categories of foodstuffs is presented for Yuendumu (1970), Kowanyama (1972) and for the urban Australian households with household income less than or equal to $80 per week in 1974–5 (the lowest category in the ABS Household Expenditure Survey 1977A).

Table 42 indicates that Aboriginal food expenditure is heavily concentrated on meats, cereals and cereal products and sugars. Expenditure on quality foodstuffs, predominantly dairy products and fruit and vegetables, is proportionally lower than that of European Australians.

In Table 43 income elasticities of demand for a number of commodities procured at Kowanyama and Edward River have been calculated. The figures presented are only estimates. The formula used for their derivation was:

$$Ey = \frac{\text{percentage change in quantity demanded}}{\text{percentage change in income}}$$

However it should be noted that at Kowanyama data were based on two budget studies one year apart, and at Edward River on studies two years apart. The income elasticity of demand estimates may have been affected by changed availability of certain goods over time – the most striking example being the availability of alcoholic beverages at Kowanyama after the opening of the 'wet' canteen.

The figures in Table 43 indicate little. As expected the income elasticity of demand for alcohol is high, but this is probably because demand had been suppressed. Most goods exhibit an income elasticity of demand between 0 and 1 which indicates that they are normal goods, with a demand tending towards saturation (as income rises). The

Table 42. *Expenditure on certain categories of foodstuffs (as percentage of total food expenditure)*

Category	Yuendumu (1970)	Kowanyama (1972)	Australia (1974–5)
1. Meat	33.9	31.7	27.9
2. Cereal and cereal products	18.9	16.0	8.3
3. Sugars	12.2	10.6	2.2
4. Fruit and vegetables	11.6	13.2	16.7
5. Beverages (non-alcoholic)	9.4	6.7	5.2
6. Milk and milk products	4.7	10.8	13.7
7. Cakes	4.1	0.9	4.9
8. Fish	2.2	– [a]	2.1
9. Sweets	0.7	1.7	2.3
10. Oils and fats	– [b]	4.8	2.4
11. Miscellaneous	2.2	3.5	15.6[c]

[a] Included with meat.
[b] Included with Miscellaneous.
[c] Includes dining out.
Sources: Australian Bureau of Statistics (1972a); Middleton and Francis (1976); Queensland Institute of Medical Research (1973).

Table 43. *Estimated income elasticities of demand for various foodstuffs at Kowanyama and Edward River*

Commodity group	Kowanyama (Ey)	Edward River (Ey)
1. Beverages (including alcohol)	+34.8	+14.2
2. Cereal foods	+ 0.3	+ 0.0
3. Eggs	+ 1.0	+ 5.1
4. Fats and oils	+ 0.7	– 0.1
5. Fish and meat	+ 0.7	– 0.2
6. Dairy food	+ 0.2	+ 0.5
7. Sugars	– 0.2	+ 0.2
8. Fruit and vegetables	+ 2.9	+ 0.0

Sources: Queensland Institute of Medical Research (1972, 1973, 1974, 1975).

exceptions are (1) fats and oils and fish and meat at Edward River which give the impression of being 'inferior' goods (but this could be as a result of a supply constraint); (2) eggs (at both communities); and (3) fruit and vegetables at Kowanyama, which have an income elasticity of demand greater than unity, implying a high demand for these goods. The basic problem with these estimates of income elasticity of demand is that they are for broad categories and may hide preferences or dislikes for individual goods.

The data in Tables 42 and 43 support the findings in Chapter 2 that food expenditure among Aborigines tends to be concentrated on low quality foods and that nutritional education and/or subsidisation of healthy foods may be necessary before expenditure patterns are changed. Increased income alone seems unlikely to achieve this.

APPENDIX IV
Decentralised communities: a model

The production function of the traditional (pre-contact) household could be represented simply by the equation: $Q = f(\bar{K}, \bar{L}, N)$,

where Q is subsistence output (a range of foods, housing and clothing)

$\bar{K}$ is technology and capital (assumed fixed)

$\bar{L}$ is land assumed constant (but fairly substantial in area) and

N is labour input.

This simple production function implies that output is some function of labour input. In Figure 2 the production function is represented by the curve 0A, with labour input measured on the horizontal axis and subsistence output on the vertical axis.

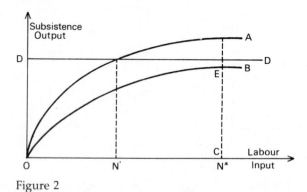

Figure 2

Following Fisk (1962, pp. 462–78), it could be assumed that as clans were nomadic, and subsistence output was either perishable or immobile (for example housing), there was a demand ceiling for this output represented by the horizontal line DD. During normal times, it appears that the needs dictated by this ceiling could be met by expending DN' labour input, leaving N'–N* labour time available for other uses, predominantly leisure activities. During abnormal years, the production function may drop to 0B (for example owing to floods or droughts) meaning that with maximum labour utilisation (N*) only CE subsistence output could be produced. There would be a production shortfall of DE, which would mean either starvation for some clan members, or a need to forage on territories normally associated with other clans.

The situation today is quite different. The nature of subsistence activity and the expectations from this activity have changed quite markedly. This is a result of the migration of Aborigines, in post-contact times, to centralised government settlements and missions and their experience with European (market) goods. This has resulted in the development of a preference for some goods unobtainable by traditional means of production. In today's circumstances a production shortfall will not have the ramifactions of pre-contact times, as Aborigines can turn to the market to supply their basic needs. Hence the 'model' must be changed.

In Figure 3, 0A, DD and 0N' have the same meaning as in Figure 2. 0C represents a new production function, resulting from the utilisation

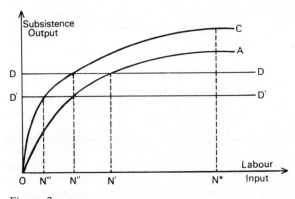

Figure 3

of Western technological innovations (for example, vehicles, rifles, nylon fishing nets, steel axes, and so on) and new (previously unknown) production techniques (for example, horticulture). Hunting and gathering activities could these days be called 'neo-traditional'. However, the experience of a European way of life (even if at an extremely low status level) has resulted in different expectations.

The true demand ceiling for all goods would now be well outside the possibilities of the traditional (modified) production function. Assuming that the substitution of European goods for traditional output results in the demand ceiling now dropping (to D'D') there would be a greater labour surplus equivalent to N'''–N*, now available for cash income earning activities, necessary for the procurement of European goods.

One further prospect may be examined. In pre-contact times Aboriginal clans were nomadic. This meant that the environment that supplied their subsistence needs was, in normal times, never overtaxed. There is also reason to believe that, owing to population controls, the population was fairly stable. There is evidence that the decentralised communities developing today will tend to be far more permanent in order to maintain communications with resource centres. There is thus a real possibility that the marginal productivity of labour will tend to zero (or even become negative) either owing to rapid population growth, resource depletion (especially where the environment is fragile) or a combination of both factors.

In Figure 4, 0A is the production function of Figures 2 and 3. If we assume labour input is some function of a community's population,

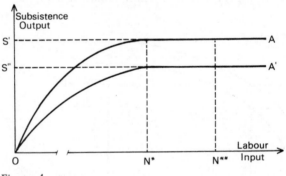

Figure 4

then as population grows from N* to N** zero marginal returns to the variable factor (labour) may set in and total product may reach a saturation point. If resources are depleted without population growth, then the production function may shift down from 0A to 0A' over time and output with N* labour input would fall from S' to S''.

Bibliography

Aboriginal Affairs Planning Authority and Aboriginal Land Trust, Western
Australia (1976): *Annual Report 30th June 1976*. Perth: Government Printer of
Western Australia.

Aboriginal Land Fund Commission (1977): *Second Annual Report and Financial
Statements for the period 1st July 1975 to 30th June 1976*. Canberra: Australian
Government Publishing Service.

Aboriginal Land Rights Commission (1973): *First Report, July 1973*. Parliamentary
Paper no. 138 of 1973. Canberra: Australian Government Publishing Service.

– (1974): *Second Report, April 1974*. Parliamentary Paper no. 69 of 1974. Canberra:
Australian Government Publishing Service.

Anderson, P. J. (1976): Report on Research into Aboriginal Income Distribution and
Expenditure Patterns at Yuendumu, Northern Territory. Unpublished report for
the Australian Institute of Aboriginal Studies.

Austin, J. R. and Murray, G. (1974): Aborigines in Seasonal Industry. Unpublished
research paper presented at seminar on 'Aborigines and the Law', Centre for
Research into Aboriginal Affairs, Monash University, Melbourne.

Australian Bureau of Statistics (1973): *The Aboriginal Population, 1971 Census of
Population of Housing*. Bulletin no. 9, Ref. no. 2.91. Canberra: ABS.

– (1975a): *Pocket Compendium of Australian Statistics*. Ref. no. 1.2. Canberra: ABS.

– (1975b): *Official Yearbook of Australia no. 60, 1974*. Canberra: ABS

– (1976a): *Social Indicators no. 1*. Ref. no. 13.16. Canberra: ABS.

– (1976b): *Australian National Accounts: National Income and Expenditure 1974–5*. Ref.
no. 7.1. Canberra: ABS.

– (1977a): *Household Expenditure Survey, 1974–5: Expenditure Classified by Income of
Household*. Ref. no. 17.22. Canberra: ABS.

– (1977b): *Employment and Unemployment Bulletin*. Ref. no. 6.4. Canberra: ABS.

– (1977c): *Australian National Accounts: National Income and Expenditure 1975–6*. Ref.
no. 7.1. Canberra: ABS.

Barwick, D. E. (1963): A Little More Than Kin: Regional Affiliation and Group
Identity among Aboriginal Migrants in Melbourne. Unpublished Ph.D. Thesis,
Australian National University, Canberra.

Bauer, P. T. (1971): *Dissent on Development*. London: Weidenfeld and Nicolson.

Beasley, P. (1970): The Aboriginal Household in Sydney. In *Attitudes and Social*

211

Conditions, eds. R. Taft, J. L. M. Dawson and P. Beasley, Aborigines in Australian Society no. 2. Canberra: Australian National University Press.

Beaumont, P. B. (1974): The Disadvantaged Labour Market Position of Australian Aborigines. *Pacific Viewpoint*, **15** (2), 165–70.

Becker, G. S. (1975): *Human Capital: A Theoretical and Empirical Analysis with special reference to Education*. National Bureau of Economic Research. New York: Columbia University Press.

Berg, E. J. (1961): Backward Sloping Labour Supply Functions in Dual Economies – The African Case. *Quarterly Journal of Economics*, **75** (3), 468–92.

Blainey, G. (1975): *Triumph of the Nomads — A History of Ancient Australia*. Melbourne: Macmillan.

Blaug, M. (ed.) (1968): *Economics of Education Vols. 1 and 2: Selected Readings*. Harmondsworth: Penguin.

Bochner, S. (1972): An Unobtrusive Approach to the Study of Housing Discrimination against Aborigines. *Australian Journal of Psychology*, **24** (3), 335–7.

Boeke, J. H. (1953): *Economics and Economic Policy in Dual Societies as exemplified by Indonesia*. New York: International Secretariat, Institute of Pacific Relations.

Brokensha, P. (1974): Report on Preliminary Field Work with Pitjantjatjara people, North West Reserve, South Australia, May–June 1974. Unpublished report for Australian Institute of Aboriginal Studies, Canberra.

– (1975): *The Pitjantjatjara and their Crafts*. The Aboriginal Arts Board. Sydney: Australia Council.

Brookfield, H. C. (1975): *Interdependent Development*. London: Methuen.

Broom, L. and Jones, F. L. (1973): *A Blanket a Year*, Aborigines in Australian Society no. 10. Canberra: Australian National University Press.

Brown, J. W., Hirschfeld, R. and Smith, D. (1974): *Aboriginals and Islanders in Brisbane*. Research report for the Commission of Inquiry into Poverty under the supervision of Professor Edna Chamberlain, Department of Social Work, University of Queensland. Canberra: Australian Government Publishing Service.

Brown, T. and Barret, M. J. (1971): Growth in Central Australian Aborigines: Stature. *Medical Journal of Australia*, **2**, 29–33.

Burnley, O. H. (ed.) (1974): *Urbanization in Australia – The Post-War Experience*. Cambridge University Press.

Caldwell, J. C. (1975): *The Demographic Report, The Torres Strait Islanders*, vol. 4. Department of Economics, Research School of Pacific Studies. Australian National University, Canberra.

Comalco Ltd (1976): *Aborigines and Islanders at Weipa – Notes on Background and Current Position*. Melbourne: Comalco Ltd.

Commission of Inquiry into Poverty (1974): *Rural Poverty in Northern New South Wales*. Research report by the Department of Sociology, University of New England. Canberra: Australian Government Publishing Service.

– (1975): *Poverty in Australia, First Main Report*, Commissioner R. F. Henderson. Canberra: Australian Government Publishing Service.

– (1976): *Social/Medical Aspects of Poverty in Australia, Third Main Report*, Commissioner G. S. Martin. Canberra: Australian Government Publishing Service.

– (1977): *Poverty and Education, Fifth Main Report*, Commissioner R. T. Fitzgerald. Canberra: Australian Government Publishing Service.

Commonwealth Bureau of Census and Statistics (1969): *Census of the Commonwealth of Australia, 30th June 1966, The Aboriginal Population of Australia: Summary of Characteristics*. Ref. no. 2.23. Canberra: Commonwealth Bureau of Census and Statistics.

Coombs, H. C. (1972a): The Employment Status of Aborigines. *Australian Economic Papers*, **11** (18), 8–18.
– (1972b): *The Future of the Australian Aboriginal*. The George Judah Cohen Memorial Lecture, University of Sydney.
– (1974): Decentralization Trends Among Aboriginal Communities. *Search*, **5**(4) 135–43.
– (1977): The Pitjantjatjara Aborigines: A Strategy for Survival. Unpublished monograph, Centre for Resource and Environmental Studies, Australian National University, Canberra.
Coombs, H. C. and Stanner, W. E. H. (1974): *Report on Visit to Yuendumu and Hooker Creek*. Council for Aboriginal Affairs Report. Canberra: Australian Government Publishing Service.
Copeman, R. Pashen, D. and Burger, G. (1975): The Health of the Aboriginal Children of Cunnamulla, Western Queensland. *Medical Journal of Australia*, **1** (special suppl.), 8–13.
Council for Aboriginal Affairs (1976): *Report on Arnhem Land*. Canberra: Australian Government Publishing Service.
Davies, I. (1966): *African Trade Unions*. Baltimore: Penguin.
Dawson, J. L. M. (1970): Aboriginal Attitudes Towards Education and Integration. In *Attitudes and Social Conditions*, eds. R. Taft, J. L. M. Dawson and P. Beasley, Aborigines in Australian Society no. 2. Canberra: Australian National University Press.
Department of Aboriginal Affairs (1975): *Annual Report 1972/73*, Northern Territory Division. Canberra: Australian Government Publishing Service.
– (1976a): *Statistical Section Newsletter no. 1*. (Roneo.) Canberra: DAA.
– (1976b): *Statistical Section Newsletter no. 2*. (Roneo.) Canberra: DAA.
– (1976c): *Special Work Projects, New South Wales*, Submission to the House of Representatives Standing Committee on Aboriginal Affairs. Canberra: DAA.
– (1976d): Special Work Projects Field Study – New South Wales North Coast Area. Unpublished report, DAA, Canberra.
– (1976e): Report of the Inter-departmental Working Party on Aboriginal Unemployment. Unpublished report, DAA, Canberra.
– (1976f): Analysis of Private Sector Special Work Projects Pilot Scheme. Unpublished report, DAA, Canberra.
– (1976g): *Department of Aboriginal Affairs Annual Report 1975–76*. Canberra: Australian Government Publishing Service.
– (1977a): *Statistical Section Newsletter no. 3*. (Roneo.) Canberra: DAA.
– (1977b): Social Accounting for Aboriginal Communities: The Cases of Willowra and Papunya. Unpublished monograph, Research Division, DAA, Canberra.
– (1977c): Vocational Training. Unpublished monograph, Research Division, DAA, Canberra.
– (1977d): Community Development Employment Projects (CDEP): Basic Outline and Guidelines. Unpublished report, DAA, Canberra.
– (1977e): Preliminary Report of Overview of Yirrkala and Groote Eylandt 13–27 June 1977. Unpublished report, Policy and Overview Division, DAA, Canberra.
– (1977f): Decentralization and the Outstation Movement – Background Paper. Unpublished report, Policy and Overview Division, DAA, Canberra.
– (1977g): *Statistical Section Newsletter no. 4*. (Roneo.) Canberra: DAA.
Department of Aboriginal and Islander Advancement, Queensland (1976): *Annual Report for the Year ending June 30, 1976*. Brisbane: Government Printer.

Department of Employment and Industrial Relations (1977): Submission requested by the House of Representatives Standing Committee on Aboriginal Affairs. Melbourne.

Department of Labour and Immigration (1975a): Submission to the House of Representatives Standing Committee on Aboriginal Affairs, 20 February 1975.

– (1975b): Submission to the House of Representatives Standing Committee on Aboriginal Affairs, 21 May 1975.

– (1975c): Supplementary Submission to the House of Representatives Standing Committee on Aboriginal Affairs, 23 July 1975.

Dobbin, M. D. H. (1977): The Health and Nutrition of Victorian Aboriginal Children. Unpublished Ph.D. thesis, Monash University, Melbourne.

Doobov, A. and Doobov, R. (1972): Queensland: Australia's Deep South. In *Racism: The Australian Experience, vol. 2, Black versus White*, ed. F. S. Stevens, pp. 159–70. Sydney: Australia and New Zealand Book Company.

Doolan, J. K. (1977): Walk-off (and later return) of various Aboriginal Groups from cattle stations: Victoria River District, Northern Territory. In *Aborigines and Change: Australia in the '70s*, ed. R. M. Berndt, Social Anthropology series no. 11, pp. 106–13. Canberra: Australian Institute of Aboriginal Studies.

Dorner, P. (1972): *Land Reform and Economic Development*. Harmondsworth: Penguin.

Drewnowski, J. (1972): Social Indicators and Welfare Measurement: Remarks on Methodology. *Journal of Development Studies*, 8 (3), 77–91.

Dugdale, A. E., Lesina, J., Lovell, S., Prestwood, U. and Lewis, A. N. (1975): Influence of Nutrition and Social Conditions on School Performance of Aboriginal Children. *Medical Journal of Australia*, 2 (special suppl.), 1–6.

Duncan, H. (1974): *Socio-economic Conditions in the Torres Straits: A Survey of four Reserve Islands, The Torres Straits Islanders*, vol. 1. Department of Economics, Research School of Pacific Studies, Australian National University, Canberra.

Edwards, J. (1977): Aborigines now have Land Rights – But no Schools. *The National Times*, 7–12 March 1977, 8–9.

Elkan, W. (1973): *An Introduction to Development Economics*. Harmondsworth: Penguin.

Elphinstone, J. J. (1971): The health of Australian Aborigines with no previous association with Europeans. *Medical Journal of Australia*, 2, 293–301.

Epstein, T. S. and Penny, D. H. (eds.) (1973): *Opportunity and Response: Case Studies in Economic Development*. London: Hurst.

Fink, R. A. (1957): The Caste Barrier – An Obstacle to the Assimilation of Part-Aborigines in North-West New South Wales. *Oceania*, 28(2), 100–10.

Fisk, E. K. (1962): Planning in a Primitive Economy – Special Problems of Papua New Guinea. *Economic Record*, 38(84), 462–78.

Franklin, A. E. (1976): *Black and White Australians – An Inter-racial History 1788–1975*. Melbourne: Heinemann Educational.

Furnival, J. S. (1939): *Netherlands India: A Study of Plural Economy*. Cambridge: Cambridge University Press.

Gale, F. (1964): *A Study of Assimilation – Part-Aborigines in South Australia*. Adelaide: Libraries Board of South Australia.

– (1972): *Urban Aborigines*, Aborigines in Australian Society no. 8. Canberra: Australian National University Press.

Gale, F. and Binnion, J. (1975): *Poverty Among Aboriginal Families in Adelaide*. Research Report for the Commission of Inquiry into Poverty. Canberra: Australian Government Publishing Service.

Gale, F. and Lewis, I. (1966): Aboriginal Employment in Adelaide. In *Aborigines in the Economy: Employment Wages and Training*, eds. I. G. Sharp and C. M. Tatz, pp. 109–19. Melbourne: Jacaranda Press.

Gault, E. I. (1968): Psychiatric and Behavioral Disturbances in Adolescent Aborigines in Victoria. *Australia and New Zealand Journal of Psychiatry*, **2**, 128–33.

Gault, E. I., Krupinski, J. and Stoller, A. (1970): Psychosocial Problems of Adolescent Aborigines in Victoria. *Australia and New Zealand Journal of Psychiatry*, **4**, 25–33.

Gibb Committee (1973): *The Situation of Aborigines on Pastoral Properties in the Northern Territory*, Report of Committee of Review, December 1971. Parliamentary Paper no. 62 of 1972. Canberra: Australian Government Publishing Service.

Gilbert, K. J. (1973): *Because a White Man'll Never Do It*. Sydney: Angus and Robertson.

Goffman, E. (1961): *Asylums: Essays on the Social Situation of Mental Patients and Other Patients*. Chicago: Pelican.

Gray, W. J. (1974): Decentralization Trends in Arnhem Land. Paper presented to the 1974 Australian Institute of Aboriginal Studies Conference, Canberra.

Gruen, F. H. (1966): Aborigines and the Northern Territory Cattle Industry – An Economist's View. In *Aborigines in the Economy: Employment, Wages and Training*, eds. I. G. Sharp and C. M. Tatz, pp. 197–216. Melbourne: Jacaranda Press.

Hagen, E. E. (1975): *The Economics of Development*. Illinois: Irwin.

Hamilton, A. (1971): Report on Economic Status, Population and Population Movement among the Aboriginal Community at Everard Park, South Australia for the year 1971. Unpublished paper for the Council for Aboriginal Affairs.

– (1972): Blacks and Whites: The Relationships of Change. *Arena*, **30**, 34–48.

Hay, D. O. (1976): *The Delivery of Services financed by the Department of Aboriginal Affairs*. Canberra: Australian Government Publishing Service.

Heppell, M. and Wigley, J. J. (1977): *Desert Homeland Centres – Their Physical Development*. Aboriginal and Torres Strait Islander Housing Panel, Occasional Paper no. 4. Canberra: Housing Panel.

Hetzel, B. S., Dobbin, M. Lippman, L. and Eggleston, E. (eds.) (1974): *Better Health for Aborigines*. Brisbane: University of Queensland Press.

Hetzel, B. S. and Frith, H. J. (eds.) (1977): *The Nutrition of Aborigines in Relation to the Ecosystem of Central Australia*, papers presented at a CSIRO symposium 23–6 October 1976, Canberra. Adelaide: CSIRO.

Higgins, B. H. (1968): *Economic Development: Principles, Problems and Policies*. London: Constable.

Hill, K. F. (1975): *A Study of Aboriginal Poverty in Two Country Towns*. Research report for the Commission of Inquiry into Poverty. Canberra: Australian Government Publishing Service.

Hirschman, A. O. (1958): *The Strategy of Economic Development*. New Haven: Yale University Press.

Hitchcock, N. E. and Gracey, M. (1975): Dietary Patterns in a Rural Aboriginal Town. *Food and Nutrition, Notes and Reviews*, **31**(3,4), 58–63 (Australian Government Publishing Service, Canberra).

Hitchcock, N. E. (1974): Dietary Patterns of Aborigines Living in a W. A. Country Community in South-West Australia. *Medical Journal of Australia*, **2** (special suppl.), 12–16.

House of Representatives Standing Committee on Aboriginal Affairs (1975): *Report on the Present Condition of the Yirrkala People*. Parliamentary Paper no. 227 of 1974. Canberra: Australian Government Publishing Service.

– (1976a): *Aboriginal Health in the South-West of Western Australia, Second Report*. Parliamentary Paper no. 296 of 1975. Canberra: Australian Government Publishing Service.

– (1976b): *Aboriginal Unemployment – Special Work Projects, Third Report*. Parliamentary Paper no. 295 of 1975. Canberra: Australian Government Publishing Service.

– (1977): *Alcohol Problems of Aboriginals, Interim report on Northern Territory Aspects.*
  Parliamentary Paper no. 242 of 1976. Canberra: Australian Government Publishing
  Service.
Johnson, H. G. (1964): Towards a Generalized Capital Accumulation Approach to
  Economic Development. In *Residual Factors in Economic Growth*, Paris, OECD,
  reprinted in *Economics of Education, vol. 1 : Selected Readings*, ed. M. Blaug, pp.
  13–34. Harmondsworth: Penguin.
Jones, F. L. (1973): Racial and Ethnic Minorities: The Case of Aboriginal Australians.
  Paper presented to the Conference of the International Union for the Scientific
  study of Population, Liège, Belgium.
Jose, D. G. and Welch, J. S. (1970): Growth retardation, anaemia and infection with
  malabsorption and infestation of the bowel. The syndrome of protein–calorie
  malnutrition in Australian Aboriginal Children. *Medical Journal of Australia*, **1**,
  349–56.
Jose, D. G., Self, M. H. R. and Stallman, N. D. (1969): A Survey of Children and
  Adolescents on Queensland Aboriginal Settlements. *Australian Paedriatric Journal*,
  5, 71–88.
Jose, D. G., Shelton, M., Belpin, R. and Hosking, C. S. (1975): Deficiency of
  Immunological and Phagocytic Functions in Aboriginal Children with
  Protein-Calorie Malnutrition. *Medical Journal of Australia*, **2**, 699–705.
Kamien, M. (1975a): The Doctor as an Agent of Change: An Action Oriented
  Epidemiological and Sociological Study of the Health of a Rural Aboriginal
  Community. Unpublished thesis, University of New South Wales, Sydney.
– (1975b): Cultural Chasm and Chaos in the Health Care Services to Aborigines in
  Rural New South Wales. *Medical Journal of Australia*, **2** (special suppl.), 6–11.
– (1975c): Attitudes to Family Planning in an Aboriginal Rural Community Before
  the Development of a Family Planning Service. *Medical Journal of Australia*, **1**
  (special suppl.), 19–21.
– (1975d): Family Planning in a Part-Aboriginal Community, 1970 to 1973. *Medical
  Journal of Australia*, **1** (special suppl.), 21–5.
– (1975e): Aborigines and Alcohol: Intake, Effects and Social Implications in a Rural
  Community in Western New South Wales. *Medical Journal of Australia*, **1**, 291–8.
– (1975f): Ear Disease and Hearing in Aboriginal and White Children in Two
  Schools in Rural New South Wales. *Medical Journal of Australia*, **1** (special suppl.),
  33–7.
Kamien, M., Woodhill, J. M., Nobile, S., Cameron, P. and Rosevear, P. (1975):
  Nutrition in the Australian Aborigines – Effects of the Fortification of White Flour.
  Australia and New Zealand Journal of Medicine, **5**, 123–33.
Kendall, L. (1976): TAFE for Aborigines. Unpublished report to the Aboriginal
  Consultative Group, The Commission on Technical and Further Education,
  Canberra.
Kerr, C., Dunlop, J. T., Harbinson, E. and Myer, C. A. (1962): *Industrialism and
  Industrial Man: The Problem of Labor and Management in Economic Growth.* London:
  Heinemann.
Killington, G. (1977): *Use of Health Services by Aboriginals.* Research report for the
  Commission of Inquiry into Poverty, Social/Medical Aspects. Canberra: Australian
  Government Publishing Service.
Kindleberger, C. P. and Herrick, B. (1977): *Economic Development*, 3rd edn. New
  York: McGraw-Hill.
Kirke, D. K. (1969): Growth Rates of Aboriginal Children in Central Australia.
  Medical Journal of Australia, **2**, 1005–9.
Kitaoji, Y. (1976): Family and Social Structure among Aborigines in Northern New

South Wales. Unpublished Ph.D. Thesis, Australian National University, Canberra.

Larsen, K., Dweyer, K. M., Hartwig, C., Whop, J. and Wyles, V. (1977): *Discrimination Against Aborigines and Islanders in North Queensland – The Case of Townsville*. Canberra: Australian Government Publishing Service.

Le Clair, E. E. and Schneider, H. K. (eds.) (1968): *Economic Anthropology: Readings in Theory and Analysis*. New York: Holt, Rinehart and Winston.

Lewis, O. (1966): The Culture of Poverty. *Scientific American*, **215**(4), 19–25.

Lewis, W. A. (1955): *The Theory of Economic Growth*. London: Allen and Unwin.

– (1966): *Development Planning*. London: Allen and Unwin.

Likiss, J. N. (1970): Health Problems of Sydney Aboriginal Children. *Medical Journal of Australia*, **2**, 995–1000.

– (1971a): The Aboriginal People of Sydney, With Special Reference to the Health of Their Children: A Study in Human Ecology. Unpublished M. D. thesis, University of Sydney, Sydney.

– (1971b): Aboriginal Children in Sydney: The Socio-Economic Environment. *Oceania*, **41**(3), 210–28.

– (1971c): Social Deviance in Aboriginal Boys. *Medical Journal of Australia*, **2**, 460–70.

Lippman, L. (1972a): Aboriginal–White Attitudes: A Syndrome of Race Prejudice. In *Racism: The Australian Experience, vol. 2, Black versus White*, eds. F. S. Stevens, pp. 25–34. Sydney: Australia and New Zealand Book Company.

– (1972b): Review of Schapper (1970) and Long (1970). *Oceania*, **42**, 245.

– (1973): *Words or Blows – Racial Attitudes in Australia*. Ringwood, Victoria: Penguin Books Australia.

Long, J. P. M. (1970): *Aboriginal Settlements – A Survey of Institutional Communities in Eastern Australia*, Aborigines in Australian Society no. 3. Canberra: Australian National University Press.

Maxwell, G. M. and Elliot, R B. (1969): Nutritional State of Australian Aboriginal Children. *American Journal of Clinical Nutrition*, **22**, 716–24.

Meehan, B. (1975): Shell Bend to Shell Midden. Unpublished Ph.D. thesis, Australian National University, Canberra.

– (1977): The Role of Seafood in the Economy of a Contemporary Aboriginal Society in Coastal Arnhem Land. Submission to the Joint Select Committee on Aboriginal Land Rights in the Northern Territory.

Meier, G. M. (1970): *Leading Issues in Economic Development: Studies in International Poverty*, 2nd edn. New York: Oxford University Press.

Metherell, T. A. (1975): Towards an Aboriginal Housing Strategy – Moree, N.S.W., 1974. Unpublished Master of Town and Country Planning thesis, University of Sydney.

Middleton, R. M. and Francis, S. H. (1976): *Yuendumu and its Children — Life and Health on an Aboriginal Community*. Canberra: Australian Government Publishing Service.

Mitchell, I. S. and Cawte, J. E. (1977): The Aboriginal Family Voluntary Resettlement Scheme: An Approach to Aboriginal Adaption. *Australia and New Zealand Journal of Psychiatry*, **11**, 29–35.

Monk, J. J. (1972): Socio-economic Characteristics of Six Aboriginal Communities in Australia: A Comparative Ecological Study. Unpublished Ph.D. thesis, University of Illinois, Urbana/Champaign.

– (1974): Australian Aboriginal Social and Economic Life: Some Community Differences and Their Causes. In *Cultural Discord in the Modern World: Geographical Themes*, eds. L. J. Evenden and F. F. Cunningham, pp. 157–74. Vancouver: Tantalus Research.

Moodie, P. M. (1972: The Health Disadvantages of Aborigines. In *Racism: The Australian Experience, vol. 2, Black versus White*, ed. F. S. Stevens, pp. 235–42. Sydney: Australia and New Zealand Book Company.

– (1973): *Aboriginal Health*, Aborigines in Australian Society no. 9. Canberra: Australian National University Press.

Morice, R. D. (1976): Women Dancing Dreaming: Psychosocial Benefits of the Aboriginal Outstation Movement. *Medical Journal of Australia*, **2**, 939–42.

Morphy, H. (1976): On the Possible Role of the Aboriginal Arts Council in the Marketing of Art from Yirrkala. Submission to the Senate Standing Committee on Education Science and the Arts.

Moses, L. N. (1962): Income, Leisure, and Wage Pressure. *Economical Journal*, **72**, 320–34.

Myint, H. (1964): *The Economics of Developing Countries*. London: Hutchinson.

Myrdal, K. G. (1957): *Economic Theory and Underdeveloped Regions*. London: Duckworth.

– (1968): *Asian Drama: An Inquiry into the Poverty of Nations*. Harmondsworth: Penguin.

National Population Inquiry (1975): *Population and Australia – A Demographic Analysis and Projection, First Report of the National Population Inquiry*. Parliamentary Paper no. 7 of 1975. Canberra: Australian Government Publishing Service.

Nettheim, G. (1973): *Outlawed: Queensland's Aborigines and Islanders and the Rule of Law*. Sydney: Australia and New Zealand Book Company.

O'Connell, J. F. (1977): Room to Move: Contemporary Alyawra Settlement Patterns and Their Implications for Aboriginal Housing Policy. Unpublished paper, Department of Prehistory, Research School of Pacific Studies, Australian National University, Canberra.

Perkins, C. N. (1975): *A Bastard Like Me*. Sydney: Ure Smith.

Peterson, N. (1977): Aboriginal Involvement with the Australian Economy in the Central Reserve During the Winter of 1970. In *Aborigines and Change: Australia in the '70s*, ed. R. M. Berndt, Social Anthropology series 11, pp. 136–45. Canberra: Australian Institute of Aboriginal Studies.

Pryor, R. J. (1974): The Aboriginal Population of North Queensland: A Demographic Profile. *Oceania*, **45**(1) 27–49.

Queensland Institute of Medical Research (1972): *Twenty-Seventh Annual Report for the '70s*, ed. R. M. Berndt, Social Anthropology series 11, pp. 136–45. Canberra:

– (1973): *Twenty-Eighth Annual Report for the year ended June 30, 1973*. Brisbane, Government Printer.

– (1974): *Twenty-Ninth Annual Report for the year ended June 30, 1974*. Brisbane: Government Printer.

– (1975): *Thirtieth Annual Report for the year ended June 30, 1975*. Brisbane: Government Printer.

Ranger Uranium Environmental Inquiry (1977): *Second Report*. Presiding Commissioner: R. W. Fox. Canberra: Australian Government Publishing Service.

Reay, M. and Sitlington, G. (1948): Class Status in a Mixed-Blood Community, Moree, N.S.W. *Oceania*, **18**,(3), 179–207.

Reynolds, H. (1972): *Aborigines and Settlers – The Australian Experience 1788–1939*. Melbourne: Cassell Australia.

Robbins, L. C. (1930): On the Elasticity of Demand for Income in Terms of Effort. *Economica*, **10**(30), 123–9.

Rogers, P. H. (1973): *The Industrialists and the Aborigines – A Study of Aboriginal Employment in the Australian Mining Industry*. Sydney: Angus and Robertson.

Rostow, W. W. (1960): *The Stages of Economic Growth: A Non-Communist Manifesto*. Cambridge: Cambridge University Press.

Rowley, C. D. (1970): *The Destruction of Aboriginal Society – Aboriginal Policy and Practice*, vol. 1, Aborigines in Australian Society no. 3. Canberra: Australian National University Press.

- (1971a): *Outcasts in White Australia – Aboriginal Policy and Practice*, vol. 2, Aborigines in Australian Society no. 6. Canberra: Australian National University Press.

- (1971b): *The Remote Aborigines, Aboriginal Policy and Practice*, vol. 3, Aborigines in Australian Society no. 7. Canberra: Australian National University Press.

Ryan, L. (1975): The Aborigines in Tasmania, 1800–1974 and Their Problems with Europeans. Unpublished Ph.D. thesis, Macquarie University, Sydney.

Sahlins, M. (1972): *Stone Age Economics*. Chicago: Aldine-Atherton.

Samuelson, P. A., Hancock, K. and Wallace, R. (1975): *Economics: An Introductory Analysis*, 2nd Australian edn. Sydney: McGraw-Hill.

Schapper, H. P. (1970): *Aboriginal Advancement to Integration – Conditions and Plans for Western Australia*, Aborigines in Australian Society no. 5. Canberra: Australian National University Press.

Scott, W. D. and Co Pty Ltd (1970): A Plan for a Pilot Project to Raise the Living Standards and Increase the Self-Sufficiency of Aborigines in South Australia. Unpublished report for the Aboriginal Land Trust of South Australia.

- (1971a): An Assessment of the needs and Opportunities for the Aborigines of the Kimberley. Unpublished report for the Minister of Community Welfare, Western Australia.

- (1971b): An Assessment of the Social and Economic Opportunities Open to the Aborigines of the North West Reserve Region. Unpublished report for the Minister of Aboriginal Affairs, South Australia.

- (1972): A Review of Aboriginal Welfare and Living Conditions on the South Coast of New South Wales. Unpublished report for the New South Wales Directorate of Aboriginal Welfare.

- (1973a): Problems and Needs of the Aborigines of Sydney. Unpublished report for the Minister for Youth and Community Services, New South Wales.

- (1973b): Housing Needs in the Australian Aboriginal and Torres Strait Island Population. Unpublished report for the Commonwealth Department of Aboriginal Affairs.

Senate Select Committee on Aborigines and Torres Strait Islanders (1976): *The Environmental Conditions of Aborigines and Torres Strait Islanders and the Preservation of Their Sacred Sites, Final Report*. Parliamentary Paper no. 199 of 1976. Canberra: Australian Government Publishing Service.

Senate Standing Committee on Social Environment (1975): *Report on the Environmental Conditions of Aborigines and Torres Strait Islanders and the Preservation of Their Sacred Sites, Second Progress Report*. Parliamentary Paper no. 59 of 1974. Canberra: Australian Government Publishing Service.

Sharp, I. G. and Tatz, C. M. (eds.) (1966): *Aborigines in the Economy: Employment, Wages and Training*. Melbourne: Jacaranda Press.

Smith, J. M. and Biddle, E. H. (1975): *Look Forward, Not Back – Aborigines in Metropolitan Brisbane*, Aborigines in Australian Society no. 12. Canberra: Australian National University Press.

Smith, L. R. (1975a): Availability of Aboriginal Health Statistics. Unpublished report to the Health of Aborigines (Standing) Committee of the National Health and Medical Research Council (National Population Inquiry, Canberra).

- (1975b): The Aboriginal Population of Australia. Unpublished Ph.D. thesis, University of New South Wales, Sydney.

Stanley, O. (1976): Aboriginal Communities on Cattle Stations in Central Australia. *Australian Economic Papers*, **15**(27), 158–70.

Stanner, W. E. H. (1968): *The 1968 Boyer Lectures – After the Dreaming*. Sydney: Australian Broadcasting Commission.

Stevens, F. S. (ed.) (1972): *Racism: The Australian Experience, vol. 2, Black versus White*. Sydney: Australia and New Zealand Book Company.

– (1974): *Aborigines in the Northern Territory Cattle Industry*, Aborigines in Australian Society no. 11. Canberra: Australian National University Press.

Stilwell, F. J. B. (1974): *Australian Urban and Regional Development*. Sydney: Australia and New Zealand Book Company.

Strang, E. J. (1970): Intermittent Chemotherapy in the Northern Territory of Australia. *Medical Journal of Australia*, 2, 948–50.

Stuart, J. E., Quayle, C. J., Lewis, A. N. and Harper, J. (1972); Health Hearing and Ear Disease in Aboriginal School Children. *Medical Journal of Australia*, 1, 855–9.

Taft, R., Dawson, J. L. M. and Beasley, P. (1970): *Attitudes and Social Conditions*, Aborigines in Australian Society no. 2. Canberra: Australian National University Press.

Tatz, C. M. (1966): The Relationship Between Aboriginal Health and Employment, Wages and Training. In *Aborigines in the Economy: Employment, Wages and Training*, eds. I. G. Sharp and C. M. Tatz,, pp. 197–216. Melbourne: Jacaranda Press.

Taylor, J. C. (1977): Some Consequences of Planned Social Change on an Aboriginal Community. In *Aborigines and Change: Australia in the '70s*, ed. R. M. Berndt, Social Anthropology series 11, pp. 147–58. Canberra: Australian Institute of Aboriginal Studies.

Taylor, T. G. (1947): *Australia – A study of Warm Environments and Their Effects on British Settlement*, 4th edn. London: Methuen.

Tonkinson, R. (1974): *The Jigalong Mob: Aboriginal Victors of the Desert Crusade*. Menlo Park, California: Cummings.

Treadgold, M. L. (1974): *The Economy of the Torres Strait Area: A Social Accounting Study, The Torres Straits Islanders, vol. 2*. Department of Economics, Research School of Pacific Studies, Australian National University, Canberra.

Turner, D. H. (1974): *Tradition and Transformation – A Study of Aborigines in the Groote Eylandt Area*, Australian Aboriginal Studies no. 53. Canberra: Australian Institute of Aboriginal Studies.

Watts, B. (1976): *Access to Education – An Evaluation of the Aboriginal Secondary Grants Scheme*. Commonwealth Department of Education. Canberra: Australian Government Publishing Service.

Wise, P. H., Edwards, F. M., Craig, R. J., Evans, B., Murchland, J. B. and Thomas, D. W. (1976): Diabetes and Associated Variables in the South Australian Aboriginal. *Australia and New Zealand Journal of Medicine*, 6, 191–6.

Workshop on Aboriginal Medical Services (1975): *Proceedings of Conference held at Albury, New South Wales, 5–7 July 1974*. Parliamentary Paper no. 249 of 1974. Canberra: Australian Government Publishing Service.

INDEX